Arts, Entrepreneurship, and Innovation

Joanna Woronkowicz
Editor

Arts, Entrepreneurship, and Innovation

Previously published in *Journal of Cultural Economics*
"Special Issue: Arts, Entrepreneurship, and Innovation"
Volume 45, Issue 4, 2021

Springer

Editor
Joanna Woronkowicz
Bloomington, IN, USA

ISBN 978-3-031-18194-8 ISBN 978-3-031-18195-5 (eBook)
https://doi.org/10.1007/978-3-031-18195-5

This Springer imprint is published by the registered company Springer Nature Switzerland AG
The registered company address is: Gewerbestrasse 11, 6330 Cham, Switzerland

Contents

Journal of Cultural Economics (2021) 45:519–526
https://doi.org/10.1007/s10824-021-09432-5

EDITORIAL

Arts, Entrepreneurship, and Innovation

Joanna Woronkowicz[1]

Published online: 15 October 2021

Abstract
There is growing interest in the relationships between the arts, entrepreneurship and innovation. Nevertheless, the concepts of arts, entrepreneurship, and innovation, and the overlaps between, lack specificity, especially in terms of how each supports the other. This article proposes a definition of art entrepreneurship both as a concept and a field of study. The definition proposed helped target articles to be included in the special issue that this article also describes, which focus on relationships between arts, entrepreneurship and innovation for workers, firms, and industry.

Keywords Arts entrepreneurship · Innovation · Cultural and creative industries · Crowdfunding · Arts incubators · Diversity

JEL Classification L26 · Z10

1 Introduction

There is growing interest in the relationships between the arts, entrepreneurship and innovation, in both the scholarly literature and in practice. In the latter, government and private enterprise invest in strengthening these relationships through programs that primarily emphasize arts workers' entrepreneurial behavior, and their innovative contributions to both artistic and non-artistic sectors. For example, policies aimed at stimulating production in the cultural and creative industries focus on supporting entrepreneurial workers in this sector. An array of local government agencies and private corporations now run artist-in-residence programs where the goal of the programs is to inject entrepreneurial thinking into decision-making (Antal, 2009; Antal & Strauß, 2013; Sherrod-Hale &Woronkowicz, 2020; Woronkowicz & Schert, 2020). The concept of "embeddedness"—where artists are recognized for their work contributions to non-artistic sectors—has taken hold globally, with

✉ Joanna Woronkowicz
jworonko@indiana.edu

1 O'Neill School of Public and Environmental Affairs, Indiana University, Bloomington, IN, USA

national governments demonstrating the prevalence of artists in non-artistic sectors (Australia Council for the Arts, 2017) and scholars following suit (Goldsmith & Bridgstock, 2015; Markusen, 2020).

These programs in both government and private enterprise largely rest on the assumption that artists and artistic work have entrepreneurial qualities that result in positive externalities, such as knowledge spillover (Audretsch & Keilbach, 2007). Program implementation, however, rarely integrates research that would buttress these assumptions, or theories of value creation in the cultural and creative industries, which can support practice. There is now a growing literature that encompasses how entrepreneurial activity in the cultural and creative industries translates to economic value (Chang et al., 2021; Ellmeier, 2003; Throsby, 2008). These theories rest on the assumption that there is a market for symbolic meaning tied to cultural and creative products that is unique to production in other sectors. While the process for creating meaning in the cultural and creative industries is becoming more clear through scholarship, the behavior of individuals and firms who engage in entrepreneurial activities is still rather fuzzy. This lack of clarity presents challenges for policymakers to apply theory on value creation in the CCI to practice. Therefore, the goal of this special issue was to highlight research that uncovers the activities of specific actors who are part of the entrepreneurial process in the cultural and creative industries, and the new forms they create.

This special issue is the third such issue out of the *Arts, Entrepreneurship, and Innovation (AEI) Lab*[1] that exclusively focuses on research that empirically investigates crossovers between arts, entrepreneurship and innovation—this one specifically by using the lens of cultural economics. In selecting the articles for this issue, it was my intention to choose ones that not only had clear implications for policy and practice, but that also contributed to theories of value creation in the cultural and creative industries. The result is a selection of seven articles that address relationships between arts, entrepreneurship and innovation for workers, firms, and industry that start to bring clarity to how value is created in the arts.

2 Toward a definition of arts entrepreneurship

The field of arts entrepreneurship is still relatively new and underdeveloped partly due to the fuzziness of concepts that support its existence. The terms "arts", "entrepreneurship", and "innovation" all have numerous definitions with most scholars and practitioners adopting or adapting one for their own particular purpose. Moreover, the overlap between the three terms lacks specificity, especially in terms of how one concept supports another. For example, arts entrepreneurs are sometimes defined as

[1] The *Arts, Entrepreneurship, and Innovation (AEI) Lab* conducts experimental and quasi-experimental research to better understand the role of arts and culture in innovation and entrepreneurship. It is a National Endowment for the Arts' Research Lab and is housed at the *Center for Cultural Affairs* at Indiana University. See culturalaffairs.indiana.edu for more information.

artists or arts firms who engage in entrepreneurial practices, or entrepreneurs who work in the arts (Woronkowicz, 2020).

Defining the field of arts entrepreneurship not only helped target articles to be included in this special issue, but it also starts to lay out a conceptual framework that can help with identifying the unique contributions that arts entrepreneurship makes to cultural economics and management. Without a conceptual framework, the field of arts entrepreneurship is merely a "hodgepodge" of research with a broad topical label (Shane & Venkataram, 2000).

In defining arts entrepreneurship, I focused on its three supporting concepts—the arts, entrepreneurship, and innovation. I took an expansive view of the arts by focusing on activities that take place by both workers and firms in the cultural and creative industries (CCI). UNESCO likely provides the broadest definition of the CCI: "Those sectors of organized activity that have as their main objective the production or reproduction, the promotion, distribution or commercialization of goods, services and activities of content derived from cultural, artistic or heritage origins." (UNESCO, 2009). The key point here being that UNESCO's definition not only includes activities taking place *in*, but also those activities that *support*, which could take place outside of the CCI. For example, an artist working outside of the CCI would still align with this definition since that person's work is ultimately supporting activity in the CCI. Other more specific definitions can be derived from elements of UNESCO's definition, including "those industries which have their origin in individual creativity, skill and talent which have a potential for job and wealth creation through the generation and exploitation of intellectual property" (i.e., creative industries) (DCMS, 2001), and the spillover effects to other parts of the economy (Hartley et al., 2012). (i.e., creative economies).

The term "entrepreneurship" is often confounded with the term "innovation". The former ultimately concerns leveraging opportunity and taking risk. Specifically, it involves discovering, evaluating, and exploiting opportunities (Venkataraman, 1997), which also requires a certain level of uncertainty, or risk. Leveraging opportunities is often in direct pursuit of bringing a new product, service, or operation to fruition (Eisenmann, 2013). Therefore, innovation can be a possible outcome of being entrepreneurial, but it is not a necessary condition of entrepreneurship. In other words, one need not be innovative in order to be entrepreneurial.

The term "innovation" has an array of definitions used in the literature. The Schumpeterian view of innovation concerns new combinations of knowledge, resources, equipment and other factors (Schumpeter, 1934 [1959]). Schumpeter's definition of innovation is predicated on production, and therefore commercial gain; however, other definitions of innovation do not use profit as a defining element. The concept of social innovation has a multiplicity of meanings, but in general relates to the improvement of living conditions for human beings (Pol & Ville, 2009). Moreover, social innovation helps broaden the economic focus of innovation, thereby accounting for the transition from an industrial- to a knowledge- and service-based society (Hochgerner, Franz, Howaldt, & Schindler, 2011). The point being that both concepts—business and social innovation—and the overall term "innovation" inherently involve, "the doing of new things or the doing of things that are already being done in a new way" (Schumpeter, 1947).

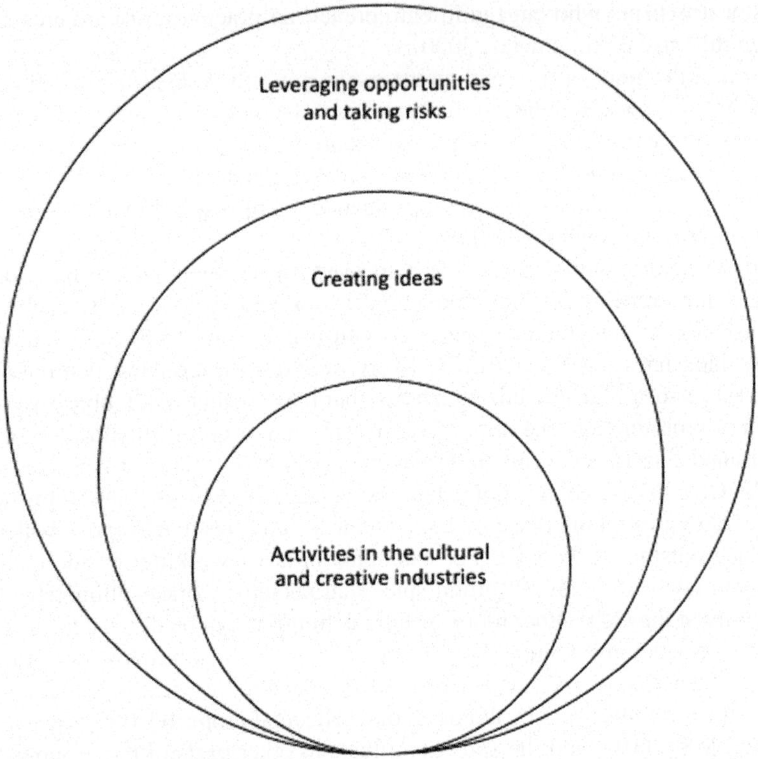

Fig. 1 The three layers of arts entrepreneurship

Building off of these definitions, I propose a working definition of arts entrepreneurship comprised of three layers, with each layer supporting the other, without necessarily being reciprocal: *Arts entrepreneurship is about leveraging opportunities and taking risks in the pursuit of new ideas that ultimately support activities in the cultural and creative industries.* As Fig. 1 makes clear, the major difference between the definition of arts entrepreneurship and general entrepreneurship is that engaging in activities in the cultural and creative industries is a necessary condition of being entrepreneurial and innovative, whereas in the definition of entrepreneurship, one can be entrepreneurial and innovative in different contexts (e.g., starting a business).

If we accept this definition of arts entrepreneurship, then we can extend upon it in order to define the field of arts entrepreneurship: *the field of arts entrepreneurship concerns itself with the study of the sources of opportunities and the processes of leveraging opportunities and taking risks for all of the actors involved in supporting the cultural and creative industries.* Therefore, in selecting the articles for this special issue, I focused on research that I believe contributes to a specific component of this definition—namely, workers and firms who use entrepreneurship and innovation to support activities in the cultural and creative industries.

3 The Articles

The special issue begins with an article that helps us understand who is an artist—a term that is as vague as art itself. Andrea Baldin and Trine Bille, in "Who is an artist? Heterogeneity and professionalism among visual artists," perform a statistical analysis of visual artists' income and working conditions using data on Danish artists. The results of the analysis show that not only is there great heterogeneity among the occupation, but also that there is a distinction between professional and amateur. The article is a valued contribution to a large body of literature on artists that fails to achieve a consensus on what defines an artistic profession. By understanding the profession, policymakers can better target programs directed at this particular segment of the labor market.

The special issue continues with two articles describing studies of arts entrepreneurial workers. In "What makes an artrepreneur? An exploratory study of artrepreneurial passion, personality and artistry", by Robert Hoffman, Bronwyn Coate, Swee Hoon Chuah, and Pia Arenius, the authors describe an experimental study they led that begins to disentangle the antecedents of entrepreneurial behavior of artists by examining the psychological and behavioral factors that motivate these workers to engage in entrepreneurial activities. Contrary to much of the literature on artist entrepreneurs, this preliminary study suggests that what motivates these workers is not much different than what we know for other types of entrepreneurs. Moreover, this study draws the important distinction between artists who work entrepreneurially, and those who do not, reminding us that the artist is not always synonymous with entrepreneur.

The second article on arts entrepreneurs is titled, "Flocking to the crowd: cultural entrepreneur mobility guided by homophily, market size, or amenities?" and is authored by Douglas Noonan, Shiri M. Breznitz, and Sana Maqbool. The article describes an analysis of crowdfunding data on projects in order to understand the migration patterns of arts entrepreneurs. While we might not expect there to be a great deal of migration among entrepreneurs who use digital platforms, this article finds that there is, and also that there are consistent patterns in migration among arts entrepreneurs that are tied to local market size and the presence of urban amenities. Using crowdfunding data, this study starts to uncover part of the mystery behind arts entrepreneurs—who often do not show up in traditional employment data because of their freelance nature—and their potential overlapping benefits to regional economies.

The next two articles in this special issue deal with entrepreneurial models for firms in the arts. In "Economies of scope in artists' incubator projects" by Amy Whitaker, the author introduces a novel framework for understanding cooperative strategies among arts organizations and then applies this framework to two cases of arts incubators. The framework centers around economies of scope, where organizations diversify their activities both operationally and financially.

The case studies exemplify the benefits of employing economies of scope for organizations, especially in terms of building organizational capacity and remaining flexible to changes in the market. As a collaborative governance model, this framework has particular relevance to a quickly growing landscape of freelancers and a fast-changing cultural and creative industry, all of which are constantly searching for new ways to create value.

The next article in this special issue looks at a model for international music publishing as a way to overcome challenges associated with copyright. In "Direct memberships in foreign copyright collecting societies as an entrepreneurial opportunity for music publishers—needs, challenges, opportunities and solutions," authors Stephan Klingner, Mihail Miller, Michael Becker, and Frank Schumacher describe the byzantine system of international music publishing, which often leads to challenges including payment delays, issues of transparency, and high transaction costs. The authors argue that many publishers have started to exploit an entrepreneurial opportunity made possible by trends in technology and internationalization, and are now becoming direct members of copyright collecting societies. Through interviews with publishers and analysis of CCS data, the authors identify key needs, challenges, opportunities and solutions related to the monetization of copyrights in this realm.

The last two articles in this special issue examine potentials for stimulating innovation in the cultural and creative industries (CCI). In "Do museums foster innovation through engagement with the cultural and creative industries?" authors Chiara Dalle Nogare and Monika Murzyn-Kupisz examine 261 Polish museums and their relationships with firms in the cultural and creative industries in order to assess whether these museums help grow the innovative potential of the greater CCI. While the authors do not find evidence that museums fuel innovation in the CCI, they do find evidence that knowledge spillover from museums have positive externalities in the local and national market, especially through museums' conservation and educational activities. The article highlights the need for CCI policy to directly specify levers for innovation and avoid over-generalizing when proposing increased collaboration among CCI firms.

The final article of this special issue, entitled, "Innovation and diversity in the digital cultural and creative industries," by Jen Snowball, Delon Tarentaal, and Jonathan Sapsed, examines the innovative potential of CCI firms in South Africa. Using survey data on CCI firms in Cape Town, the authors classify firms into groups based on the degree to which they combine digital technologies with creative design (i.e., fusion), and correlate this measure with firm growth, innovation, type of revenue source and business model. As an added layer to this study, the authors examine employer and employee demographics among CCI firms, and in gaming and animation firms specifically, in order to analyze the relationship between levels of diversity and inclusion and CCI innovation. The study concludes that fusion might lead to innovation, and that diversity also might support innovation in the CCI. More importantly, the authors argue for the CCI as an important component to consider in innovation policy in South Africa.

Funding Information that explains whether and by whom the research was supported.

Declarations

Conflicts of interest Include appropriate disclosures.

Availability of data and material Data transparency.

Code availability Software application or custom code.

References

Antal, A. B. (2009). *Transforming organisations with the arts: Research report*. TILLT Europe. https://www.wzb.eu/system/files/docs/dst/wipo/researchreport.pdf

Antal, A. B., Strauß, A. (2013). *Artistic interventions in organisations: Finding evidence of values-added*. Creative Clash. https://www.wzb.eu/system/files/docs/dst/wipo/effects_of_artistic_interventions_final_report.pdf

Audretsch, D. B., & Keilbach, M. (2007). The Theory of Knowledge Spillover Entrepreneurship. *Journal of Management Studies, 44*(7), 1242–1254. https://doi.org/10.1111/j.1467-6486.2007.00722.x

Australia Council for the Arts. (2017). *The national arts participation survey: state and territory results*. https://www.australiacouncil.gov.au/research/connecting-australians-states-territories/

Chang, Y. Y., Potts, J., & Shih, H. Y. (2021). The market for meaning: A new entrepreneurial approach to creative industries dynamics. *Journal of Cultural Economics*. https://doi.org/10.1007/s10824-021-09416-5

DCMS. (2001). *Creative Industries Mapping*. Department for Digital, Culture, Media & Sport. https://www.gov.uk/government/publications/creative-industries-mapping-documents-2001

Eisenmann, T. R. (2013). Entrepreneurship: A working definition. *Harvard Business Review*, 10. https://hbr.org/2013/01/what-is-entrepreneurship

Ellmeier, A. (2003). Cultural entrepreneurialism: On the changing relationship between the arts, culture and employment. *International Journal of Cultural Policy, 9*(1), 3–16. https://doi.org/10.1080/1028663032000069158a

Goldsmith, B., & Bridgstock, R. (2015). Embedded creative workers and creative work in education. *Journal of Education and Work, 28*(4), 369–387. https://doi.org/10.1080/13639080.2014.997684

Hartley, J., Potts, J., Cunningham, S. Flew, T., Keane, M., & Banks, J. (2012). *Key Concepts in Creative Industries*. Sage Publications. https://uk.sagepub.com/en-gb/eur/key-concepts-in-creative-industries/book236863#preview

Hochgerner, J., Franz, H.W., Howaldt, J. & Schindler, A. (2011). *Vienna Declaration*. http://www.eurosfaire.prd.fr/7pc/documents/1320944810_vienna_declaration_final_en.pdf.

Markusen, A. (2020). The embedded artist worker: shifting perspectives on artists in the labor force. In F. Martel and H. Wickert (Eds.), *Embedded artists* (pp. 94–113). Zürich University of Arts, Zürich. https://drive.switch.ch/index.php/s/f2pR7DSPxE9twsn

Pol, E., & Ville, S. (2009). Social innovation: Buzz word or enduring term? *The Journal of Socio-Economics, 38*(6), 878–885. https://doi.org/10.1016/j.socec.2009.02.011

Schumpeter, J. A. (1947). The Creative Response in Economic History. The Journal of Economic History, 7(2), 149–159. https://www.jstor.org/stable/2113338

Schumpeter, J. A. (1934). *The Theory of Economic Development: An Inquiry Into Profits, Capital, Credit, Interest, and the Business Cycle*. Cambridge, MA: Harvard University Press.

Shane, S. & Venkataraman, S. (2000). The Promise of Entrepreneurship as a Field of Research. *The Academy of Management Review, 25*(1), 217–226. https://www.jstor.org/stable/259271

Sherrod Hale, J., & Woronkowicz, J. (2020). Artists as public sector intrapreneurs: An experiment. *Small Business Economics*. https://doi.org/10.1007/s11187-020-00417-w

Throsby, D. (2008). The concentric circles model of the cultural industries. *Cultural Trends, 17*(3), 147–164. https://doi.org/10.1080/09548960802361951
UNESCO. (2009). The Cultural Economy. UNESCO Framework for Cultural Statistics. https://en.unesco.org/creativity/files/cultural-economy-unescos-framework-cultural-statistics
Venkataraman, S. (1997). The distinctive domain of entrepreneurship research: An editor's perspective. In J. Katz & R. Brockhaus (Eds.), *Advances in entrepreneurship, firm emergence, and growth* (Vol. 3, pp. 119–138). JAI Press.
Woronkowicz, J. (2020). The embedded artist worker: shifting perspectives on artists in the labor force. In F. Martel and H. Wickert (Eds.), *Embedded artists* (pp. 124–135). Zürich University of Arts, Zürich. https://drive.switch.ch/index.php/s/f2pR7DSPxE9twsn
Woronkowicz, J., & Schert, J. M. (2020). Artists in local government: local government artist-in-residence programs must include opportunities for public sector innovation. *Stanford Social Innovation Review*.

Journal of Cultural Economics (2021) 45:527–556
https://doi.org/10.1007/s10824-020-09400-5

ORIGINAL ARTICLE

Who is an artist? Heterogeneity and professionalism among visual artists

Andrea Baldin[1] · Trine Bille[1]

Received: 3 September 2019 / Accepted: 7 November 2020 / Published online: 12 January 2021

Abstract

The purpose of this article was twofold. Firstly, to investigate the heterogeneity among artists as an occupational category and secondly, to define arts as a profession and thereby to make a distinction between professional artists and amateurs. Artists' income and working conditions have been the subject of several studies, and many different sampling criteria have been used. Scholars have not yet achieved consensus on who should be included in the profession. In this article, we make an innovative contribution to this conversation. By applying a finite mixture model, which combines latent profile and latent class analysis, we have been able to identify different segments of artists in terms of professionalism. Each of these mutually exclusive classes is characterized by a particular income and working situation. We also include a membership function, estimated through a logistic regression, which allows prediction of the probability that an individual will belong to each class, given his/her socioeconomic characteristics. The subject of our study is Danish visual artists. The dataset consists of a combination of register data from Statistics Denmark and data collected from a questionnaire survey with 892 respondents. Based on the artists' civil registration numbers, the two sources have been merged into a unique dataset. Our finite mixture model shows the heterogeneity among artists. Combined with a theoretically definition of arts as a profession, our research propose a distinction between professional artists and amateurs that cuts across categories used in prior literature. The results can be beneficial to cultural policy.

Keywords Labor market · Visual artists · Finite mixture model

✉ Andrea Baldin
ab.mpp@cbs.dk

Trine Bille
tbi.mpp@cbs.dk

[1] Department of Management, Politics and Philosophy, Copenhagen Business School, Frederiksberg, Denmark

1 Introduction

The issue of who can be considered an artist, and of how to define the boundaries of the artists' professions, is a contentious matter, and scholars have not yet achieved consensus on who should be included in these professions. The problems relate to the fact that artists cannot be limited by a specific occupation or education given that the concept of artists is more broadly related with the quality of the art produced. The quality of the art is, however, in itself a fluent and undefined concept (see, e.g., Eliassen et al. 2018). While some theoreticians and artists, such as Joseph Beuys, consider every living person to be an artist, the theoretical discussion of the concept of artist relates mainly to the question of where the boundary between "professional artists" and "amateurs" should be drawn (Becker 1982). The same problems arise at the empirical level, given that there is no single criterion for defining an artist, unlike the case of, for instance, a lawyer, a doctor, or a teacher. Many artists have multiple jobs, more or less related to the arts (Menger 2006; Casacuberta and Gandelman 2012; Bille et al. 2017; Robinson and Montgomery 2000; Throsby 1994), and the quality of the artwork is difficult/impossible to conceptualize, let alone measure (Bille and Olsen 2018). For practical empirical research, however, a definition of the population of artists is necessary in order to undertake research into the economic and social living conditions of artists.

Artists' income and working conditions have been the subject of several research studies, e.g., Alper and Wassall (2006), Bille et al. (2018), Menger (1999, 2006), Heian et al. (2012) and Throsby and Petetskaya (2017). Previous research highlights the challenges of studying artists as a category of workers (Menger 2001 and Throsby 1992) and proposes various criteria to establish "who is an artist." Some empirical studies use membership of artists' associations as the main selection criteria (Throsby and Petetskaya 2017), sometimes combined with the receipt of national arts grants (Heian et al. 2012) and with an education in the arts (Bille et al. 2018), while other studies use occupation and income (Alper and Wassall 2006; Higgs et al. 2008). In other words, the studies use different criteria to define the group of artists they are including, and the results of these studies of artists' income will, of course, be dependent on the criteria used. The relatively inclusive demarcation criteria in most studies mean that a large and highly heterogeneous group of artists is often included: not only people with an ambition to work with or live from being an artist, but also people who have at some point worked as an artist, without necessarily considering arts practice to be the core of their employment.

The purpose of this article is to investigate the heterogeneity of artists as a population, and it aims at making a theoretically and empirically based distinction between professional artists and amateurs and thereby define arts as a profession We propose a new method of studying heterogeneity among artists, by defining a limited number of groups (classes) of artists with certain characteristics. These groups of artists, which vary in their degree of professionalism (defined by a multiple set of criteria), can be used for a more detailed study of the income conditions for different groups/classes of artists, as well as for making a distinction between professional artists and amateurs.

The study focuses on one group of artists, namely visual artists in Denmark. This population of artists is defined as those individuals who meet at least one of the following three criteria: a) membership of one of the two main artists' associations in Denmark, b) receipt of arts grants from the Danish Arts Foundation, and c) graduation from an arts academy. The dataset consists of a combination of microdata from the official tax, employment and educational registers in Statistics Denmark, and data collected in a survey submitted to the population of visual artists in Denmark. Using the artists' civil registration number, the two sources have been merged into a unique dataset at the level of the individual artist. Based on these data, a finite mixture model combining latent profile and latent class analysis has been conducted with the aim of identifying a set of discrete and mutually exclusive classes or categories of artists based on their response to a set of questions. The finite mixture model identifies different segments of artists (latent classes), each of which is characterized by a different pattern of answers that reveals a particular income and working condition. An extension of the finite mixture model includes a membership function, estimated through a logistic regression, which allows prediction of the probability that an individual will belong to each latent class, given his/her socioeconomic characteristics.

The article contributes to the literature on "artists" as a classification, and the conceptualization of the artistic labor force more broadly, by showing the heterogeneity among artists and proposing a definition of art as a profession, and thereby a distinction between professional artists and amateurs.

Our research contains important information for policy makers and artists' organizations in the formulation of artist policy. In the context of cultural policy or in the work of artists' unions to ensure better social security for their members, it is obviously essential to know the size and composition of the group of artists and how much they earn. A clear definition of artists profession and a more nuanced division into sub-groups will therefore provide crucial information for policy makers.

The structure of the article can be outlined as follows: Sect. 2 reviews the literature on defining the population of artists, Sect. 3 defines the concepts of a profession and professionalism and discusses the concept of professional artists, Sect. 4 describes the methodology, Sect. 5 describes the dataset and the variables used, Sects. 6 and 7 show the empirical results, and Sect. 8 provides the conclusions and policy implications of our research.

2 Literature review

The previous literature has proposed and applied various criteria to define the boundaries of the population of artists. Two different approaches stand out. One major part of the previous literature have used membership of artists' association or organization (sometimes supplement with a self-rapport statement of being active in the field), and the other major part have used occupation in the artistic field mainly drawing on official national statistics records. As we will argue in larger details in this section and in Sect. 3, none of these approaches are able to properly define the population of professional artists, as the criteria used will potentially leave out substantial parts of the population of artists or include people, who (for different reasons, see further below) cannot be considered as part of the artists' profession. If the population of artists is not defined correctly, this will, of course, create biases, when artists' income and working conditions are examined, and this will subsequently make it difficult for policy makers to conduct an evidence-based artists' policy and create efficient support schemes. In this section, we will show examples of the different approaches that have been applied.

Since 1983, Thorsby and co-authors have regularly conducted surveys with artists in Australia (Throsby and Petetskaya 2017). They use membership of a long list of artists' organizations as an *ex ante* criterion for being included in the survey, and a number of screening questions to establish whether he or she is professional and "currently practicing or training in the arts." In the screening questions, respondents were asked "if at some time during the past 3–5 years (depending on practice area), they had had a piece of writing published or performed; a work or works shown at a professional gallery, or work commissioned; had a composition professionally performed live, broadcast, recorded or filmed; had an engagement as a professional director or actor, or dancer or choreographer, with a professional company, had an engagement as a musician or singer in a professional venue, contributed to the development of a major community arts project, festival or event; had created a serious and substantial body of work as an artist in the last 5 years; or had full-time training or received a grant to work as an artist." (Throsby and Petetskaya 2017, p. 18). A similar type of survey has been conducted in Norway, where the population of artists was selected on the basis of membership of one or more of 33 artists' organizations, combined with data on recipients of national arts grants and those with their own registered business in the artistic field (Heian et al. 2012). As a screening criterion, respondents were asked if they had been actively working with their artistic occupation within the last five years, and it was up to the individual artist to determine whether this was the case. Criteria for inclusion are broad in both studies, with the result that artists who are less active, and do not necessarily consider their artistic practice to be at the heart of their employment, are also included.

Lena and Lindemann (2014) have used the US Strategic National Arts Alumni Project survey ($N = 13{,}581$), the largest survey undertaken of individuals who have pursued arts degrees in the US,A to explore who self-defines as a "professional artist." They have explored the professional artist as being the outcome of an identity process. They find some meaningful differences in artists who perceive themselves as "professional artists," various markers of cultural capital, and social integration within artistic communities.

Alper and Wassall (2006) have used US census data to study artists' occupations. The census requires respondents to choose a single occupation. This choice is based on time spent at work during a single reference week. This can of course create biases in the artists' population, as we know from prior research that many artists hold multiple jobs (Menger 2006).

Another branch of the literature (the creative industry approach) has studied the contribution of the creative industries to the general economy in terms of growth and employment. In these studies, the classification of creative worker (artist) is based on ICSO (job content) and NACE (industry) codes in the official national statistics records. A decision has to be taken as to which of the ICSO codes counts as creative, and similarly for the NACE codes. By doing this, it is possible to calculate the share of the economy that can be attributed to the creative economy. These mappings require subjective decisions as to whether or not an occupation or an industry is creative, with the added problem that many creative jobs are outside the creative industries, and there are many non-creative or humdrum jobs in the creative industries. Higgs et al. (2008) have proposed the model of a "Creative Trident" that differentiates between three employment "modes": (1) the specialist mode: workers within a creative occupation within a creative industry, (2) the support mode: workers in a non-creative profession within a creative industry, and (3) the embedded mode: workers in a creative occupation outside the creative industries.[1] This allows for calculation of the number of people employed in the creative industries and holding creative jobs, as well as their average incomes. The findings show that more people with a creative occupation are employed outside the creative industries than inside them. A similar approach has been applied in Bille (2012), but she has included a third dimension, namely an arts training. She finds little correlation between having an artistic education, having an artistic occupation, and working in the creative sector.

This review of the literature shows that many and various selection criteria have been used to select the population of artists to be studied, and it is evident that scholars have not yet achieved consensus on who should be included in the artists' profession and count as "professional artists." Furthermore, there is a lack of theoretical basis for defining who counts as an artist. In order to fill this gap and take the necessary next step of filling this gap, the next section will provide a theoretical bases defining the concepts of art as a profession and professional artists, drawing on the literature on professions (Wilensky 1964; Abbott 1988) as well as the literature on artists above and the different criteria proposed. Such an exercise is needed to properly define the profession and the population of artists, and to delineate different kind of artists (in terms of professionalism) from another. As elaborated on in the final discussion of this article, it is of immense importance for reaching unbiased results when it comes to artists' income and working conditions, and for developing policy and efficient funding schemes.

3 The concept of professional artists

In the everyday language, the word "professional" has two meanings. It can mean profession, as in main occupation, or it can be used to characterize work that meets the (high) professional standards within a particular profession. In most sectors, the word "professional" is used in the meaning of profession. In sports, you are considered a professional if you can earn all or part of your living through your participation in sports events, as opposed to amateurs, who do sports in their spare time. The professional normally meets the high professional standards of the chosen

[1] In Bakhshi et al. (2013), the model is further developed into what is called dynamic mapping.

profession, and therefore the two interpretations of the word coincide. In many occupations, a specialized education or training is a prerequisite for achieving high professional standards as well as for being accepted into profession. That is case for a doctor, a dentist, a schoolteacher, a lawyer, and for many other professions.

To make a distinction between professional versus amateur visual artist, it implies that we consider "visual artist" as a profession rather than an occupation. This distinction, as well as the process that that leads an occupation to become a profession, has been an object of debate in the sociological literature. In the functionalist approach, Wilensky (1964) identifies 5 phases that mark a profession in opposition to occupation: the emergence of a certain work activity as a full-time occupation; the establishment of schools for specialized training; the creation of professional associations; the legal protection of the monopoly of skills, and the adoption of a formal code of ethic. All these criteria can be met in the profession of visual arts, but as we will discuss below, should a visual artist necessarily comply all of them in order to be considered a member of this profession?

The functionalist approach has been criticized by later scholars. In particular, the seminal contribution to the theory of profession by Abbott (1988) does not agree with the notion of professionalization as a set of discrete phases, where each profession evolves independently of another. Instead, Abbott argues that professions are constantly in flux, competing each other for jurisdiction (i.e., by claiming expertise) over certain types of work, so that the boundaries of professions are continually negotiated and contested. In this setting, a key concept is the abstract knowledge, based on academic knowledge, whose application to particular cases is what define a profession. Then, the educational system through which individuals acquire this abstract knowledge—the arts academies in the visual art profession—becomes crucial.

The cultural economics literature review shows no conformity in the definition of artists profession and in turn "professional artists": Is a professional artist defined by "occupation" or in terms of "professional work" in the sense of meeting high professional standards? Furthermore, the two interpretations may not go hand-in-hand, as some artists might earn a decent living from their arts practice, but never receive a quality stamp from their peers. On the other hand, there can be artists who are widely recognized among their peers and art critics, but who are not able to earn a living from their arts practice.

The origins of the problems defining art as a profession are at least threefold. Firstly, the lack of objective criteria in defining quality in the arts, and thereby reaching definitions of professional standards; secondly, the characteristics of the labor market for artists that result in very few being able to live from their arts practice, and many artists therefore holding multiple jobs and "patchwork" careers (Abbing 2002; Mathieu 2012). And thirdly, the fact that many artist are self-taught and a formal education is not significant for a career in the arts (Towse 2006). This makes the definition of arts as a profession and the demarcation between professional and amateur artists extremely difficult, and perhaps therefore has the label "professional artist" become contaminated and sidestepped in many contexts.

In addition, assessment of who is an artist is not static, but dynamic. We all know the example of Van Gogh, who was not acknowledged as an artist in his own lifetime, neither in terms of his earnings nor in an artistic sense, but achieved posthumous recognition, and his paintings are now sold for staggering sums of money. However, in this article we will not include a dynamic and longer-term perspective, as we are only dealing with contemporary visual artists.

Frey and Pommerehne (1989) have suggested eight criteria that might be applied to determine who is an artist:

1. Professional qualifications (graduation from art school)
2. The amount of income derived from artistic activities
3. The amount of time spent on artistic activities
4. Membership of a professional artists' group or association
5. Recognition among other artists
6. Reputation as an artist among the general public
7. The quality of the artistic work produced (which means that artistic "quality" must be defined)
8. The subjective self-evaluation of being an artist

Of these eight criteria proposed by Frey and Pommerehne (1989), two relate to "occupation," namely income and hours worked, and five relate to being professional in the sense of meeting high professional standards and thereby to the quality of the artistic work (as assessed by peers, the general public, arts associations, or by the artist personally). Education relates to the human capital approach, and in most other sectors an education will lead to professionalism (Abbott 1988). In the following, we will further elaborate on these definitions of professionalism based on prior research and the literature review.

3.1 Meeting high professional standards

Membership of a professional artists' group or association, recognition among other artists, reputation as an artist among the general public, and the self-evaluation of being an artist, are all related to the quality of the artistic works produced in the sense of meeting high professional standards. The problem is that the quality of the art is a fluent and undefined concept (see, e.g., Eliassen et al. (2018)), and the understanding and perception of the quality will be dependent on the viewer, who can be a peer, the artist or the general public. It is a widely held view that only the art world itself (i.e., the arts experts/peers) can assess artistic quality.[2] This so-called Institutional Theory states that an object is art if acknowledged as such by the art world (Dickie 1974). One of the strengths of this theory is its capacity to accommodate the changes that characterize modern art. The theory can thus accommodate future concepts of art and thereby the dynamics of art. The Institutional Theory is reflected in the way in which arm's-length bodies such as Arts Foundations are organized: when

[2] Based on this view, the reputation of the artists among the general public cannot be seen as an indicator of high professional standards.

works of art are to be purchased and grants are to be awarded to artists, the quality of the art is evaluated by other artists and other representatives of the art world. In other words, the arm's-length principle draws on Institutional Theory. Likewise, membership of professional artists' groups or associations relates to the concept of quality, as most artists' associations have a set of criteria concerning the quality of the artists' work (as the artists having achieved a certain number of curated and peer-reviewed exhibitions). These criteria are defined by experts and peers, who decide if the artists applying for membership meet the required professional standards.

Therefore, membership of a professional artists' group or association and the receipt of recognized arts grants (such as grants from national arts foundations) can be used as proxies for meeting high professional standards and thereby for inclusion in the population of professional artists. How effective membership of professional arts associations is in terms of defining the population of artists will depend on the degree of organization among the artists, which will differ according to genres (e.g., musicians versus visual artists). Furthermore, it is well known that artists' associations differ widely in terms of their membership criteria and requirements when it comes to artistic qualifications and track record, some being highly elitist while others are broader and more inclusive with loose and wide-ranging admission criteria. This means that membership of these associations is not necessarily an ideal defining indicator—or to put it more precisely: as an *ex ante* criterion for delimit the population of artists it cannot stand alone. The same goes for recipients of national arts grants, because only a small proportion of artists get these grants (as they are limited in number).

3.2 Arts as an occupation

Artists who are able to live primarily from their artistic occupation and spend most of their working time on their artistic practice, must be considered members of the profession. As shown in the literature review, artists' working conditions in terms of hours worked and income from the arts are sometimes used as criteria for defining the population of artists, especially when US Census data are used (Alper and Wassall 2006) and in the creative industries' approach (Higgs et al. 2008; Cummingham and Potts 2015). The obvious problem is that this approach will exclude artists whose primary occupation is in a non-arts field. As many artists live on a broadly-composed income from many different types of jobs and employment (see, e.g., Menger 2006; Mathieu 2012, Alacovska and Bille 2020a, b), this definition would rule them out as potential members of the profession.

3.3 Arts education and human capital

Many studies have found little or no impact of a formal arts education on an artist's income (see, e.g., Throsby 1996; Bille and Jensen 2016). Based in human capital theory, Towse (2006) has discussed success and career in relation to artists, and why a formal education in the arts may not have as much impact (if any) on income and careers as a formal education has for other professions. In many other professions, a training in the subject is a condition for learning high professional standards as well as for working in the profession (Abbott 1988). In the arts, a formal training may not lead to "professionalism." Many artists are self-taught, and individual talent seems to be more important than a formal education (Alper and Wassall 2006; Throsby 1996) for a professional career in the arts. As an *ex ante* selection criterion for delimit the population of artists, the use of graduation from art school has serious drawbacks in terms of defining the population of artists, given that it will exclude all the artists who are self-taught, and furthermore, many art graduates do not work as artists. Therefore; a formal education in the arts not be used to define the population of professional artists, as prior literature clearly has demonstrated.

To sum up, we will not expect a formal education in the arts to be important for defining the artists profession, as is the case for many other professions (Abbott 1988). However, indicators for working in the profession (income and time spent) are required, along with indicators of meeting high professional standards (such as membership of artists' associations and receipt of important (national) arts grants). As professional artists do not comprise a uniform population, a combination of defining criteria is required. This has led us to take a new approach in our analysis of a very diverse group of artists in order to facilitate a better understanding of their income and working conditions, and thereby to differentiate between professionals and amateurs. To explain the heterogeneity, this article employs a finite mixture model, which is an innovative contribution to the literature.

4 Methodology: finite mixture model

A finite mixture model refers to a probabilistic model-based clustering approach, which aims to identify a set of discrete and mutually exclusive classes or profiles of individuals based on their patterns associated with different observed variables/indicators of interest. It is defined as a mixture modeling, in the sense that it is assumed the distribution of such variables can be expressed as a mixture of a finite number k of component distributions, where the number k (representing the number of latent classes) is unknown. Given this, individuals belonging to the same class are such that they exhibit a similar pattern across the observed set of variables, which are assumed to come from the same probability distributions. Thus, the goal of such analysis is to sort individuals into mutually exclusive clusters that maximize between-group variance and minimize within-group variance (Collins and Lanza 2010). From the data, each individual is probabilistically assigned into sub-populations by calculating his/her probabilities of being a member of each resulting profile.

According to the literature taxonomy, latent profile analysis uses continuous variables, which are assumed to be normally distributed within each profile; whereas when the observed variables are dichotomous or categorical, we talk about latent class analysis. However, recent developments allow for a combination of continuous and categorical variables (Berlin et al. 2014); we also combine both types of variables, using the generic term "finite mixture model" with regard to the model we employ.

In our case, each artist was asked to answer questions regarding the sources of their income and how this income relates to their work as an artist, if their private economy is dependent on other factors (partner's income or loan), how they divide their working-time between jobs more or less related to their art, if they perceive themselves to be a full/part-time artist, and if they have registered a company in their own name. Some of these questions provide a numerical (continuous) value, others are closed questions (see Table 1).

Let denote with $\boldsymbol{y}_i$. the vector of values on a set of J continuous and categorical variables (indicators) for individual i, so that y_{ij}. represents the value of a particular variable j; and with K the total number of classes. The basic model can be expressed as (Vermunt and Magidson 2002):

$$f(\boldsymbol{y}_i|\theta) = \sum_{k=1}^{K} \pi_k \prod_{j=1}^{J} f_k(y_{ij}|\theta_{jk}) \tag{1}$$

which is a finite mixture of K class-specific distribution functions f_k for the observed variables, with class-specific set of parameters θ_{jk} estimated by the model. π_k is the estimated probability to belong to class k o in other words, the proportion of the total population in each profile k. As each individual belong to one and only one class, we have $\sum_{k=1}^{K} \pi_k = 1$.

We specify the univariate distribution function for each y_{ij}: We choose normal and binomial distribution for continuous and dummy variables, respectively.

A development of our analysis considers the inclusion of a membership function, should sociodemographic data (otherwise called covariates) of the respondents be available (e.g., age, gender, etc.). The membership function allows for prediction of the probability for an individual to belong to each latent class, given the individual characteristics. Including covariates, Eq. (1) changes to the following form:

$$f(\boldsymbol{y}_i|\boldsymbol{x}_i, \theta) = \sum_{k=1}^{K} \pi_{k|x_i} \prod_{j=1}^{J} f_k(y_{ij}|\boldsymbol{x}_i, \theta_{jk}). \tag{2}$$

where $\boldsymbol{x}_i$. represents the set of the covariates, and $\pi_{k|x_i}$. is the probability of belonging to the latent class k, given the values of the covariates. The likelihood $\pi_{k|x}$ of the individual i belonging to class k can be inferred through a probabilistic assignment process called memrship function, which includes individual-specific variables. A multinomial logit specification is convenient form for the class membership model. Hence, the probability $\pi_{k|x_i}$. is given by:

$$\pi_{k|x_i} = \frac{\exp\left(\beta_k' \boldsymbol{x}_i\right)}{\sum_{k=1}^{K-1} \exp\left(\beta_{k'}' \boldsymbol{x}_i\right)}. \tag{3}$$

where $k = 1, ..., K - 1$. Including the covariates, an additional set of parameters β_k', that is the vector of parameters of the multinomial logit (one for each latent class), is estimated. Notice that for one latent class the parameters are normalized to 0 in order to secure identification of the model.

Table 1 Variables used in analysis

Variable	Description	Type	Source
Income	Annual total personal income before taxes (scaled by 10.000)	Continuous	Register data, Statistics Denmark
Pct. income art	Percentage of income from work as visual artist	Continuous	Survey
Pct. income-related job	Percentage of income from work in which the artist has used his/her skills from practice as visual artist (as an artistic consultant, teacher, lecturer, etc.)	Continuous	Survey
Pct. income government	Percentage of income from government subsidies (Danish students' Grants and Loans Scheme, sick leave benefits, unemployment benefits and cash benefits). Pensions are not included in this category	Continuous	Survey
Pct. income other	Percentage of other income, including income from jobs with no relation to the practice as visual artist	Continuous	Survey
Company	The artist is self-employed	1 = yes; 0 = no	Register data, Statistics Denmark and survey
Dep. partner	The artist's private economy is also dependent on partner's income (self-assessed)	1 = yes; 0 = no	Survey
Dep. loan	The artist's private economy is also dependent on loans (self-assessed)	1 = yes; 0 = no	Survey
Time art	Percentage of working time as a visual artist	Continuous	Survey
Time related	Percentage of working time devoted to activities where skills from practice as a visual artist are used	Continuous	Survey
Time other	Percentage of working time with no relation to the art	Continuous	Survey
Full-time	How the artist perceives himself/herself	1 = Full-time Artist; 0 = Part-time Artist	Survey
Class membership			
Gender	Gender of the artist	1 = Male; 0 = Female (base variable)	Register data, Statistics Denmark
Age	Age of the artist	Continuous	Register data, Statistics Denmark
Retired	The artist is a retiree (living mainly on pensions)	1 = yes; 0 = no	Register data, Statistics Denmark
Education	The artist has completed a visual art education from an art academy	1 = yes; 0 = no	Register data, Statistics Denmark

Table 1 (continued)

Variable	Description	Type	Source
Member Artists' Society	The artist is a member of the Danish Artists' Society (Kunstnersamfundet)	1 = yes; 0 = no	Member register from Danish Artists' Society
Received grant	The artist received grants from the Danish Arts Foundation in the period 2010–2015	1 = yes; 0 = no	Registers from the Danish Arts Foundation

The model is estimated with Stata 15, which estimates the parameters by the maximization of the overall log-likelihood function, using the EM (expectation–maximization) algorithm. Denoting the total number of observations with N, and assuming each observation i is conditionally independent of the other observations, the overall loglikelihood function is given by:

$$L(\theta) = \sum_{i=1}^{N} \sum_{k=1}^{K} \lambda_{ik} \left[\log \pi_{k|x_i} + \sum_{j=1}^{J} \log f_k(y_{ij}|\boldsymbol{x}_i, \theta_{jk}) \right]. \tag{4}$$

here λ_{ik} is an indicator variable equal to 1 if individual i belongs to class k, 0 otherwise.

Having specified different distributions according to the type of variable, the estimated parameters for continuous and categorical indicators are different: for the former, we estimate the mean value for each class; for the latter, we estimate the coefficient of the underlying logistic regression for each class.

The number of classes is not decided a priori, but determined by statistical criteria. The Bayesian information criterion (BIC) and Akaike information criterion (AIC) are usually used as a guide to determine the number of classes that fit the data best. These criteria are calculated as follows:

$$\text{AIC} = -2\text{LL} + 2p$$
$$\text{BIC} = -2\text{LL} + \text{Ln}(N)p$$

where LL is the value of the log-likelihood function, p the number of parameters, and N the sample size. These criterions are calculated for different models with different numbers of classes. The final number of classes selected is the one for which the value of the test is the smallest.

5 Data and variables

For our research, we have considered the population of visual artists in Denmark, defined as those individuals who meet at least one of the following criteria: being a member of one or both of the main arts organizations in Denmark (namely, Danish Artists' Society (Kunstnersamfundet) and Danish Visual Artists' Association (BKF)); having an artistic education from an arts academy; and/or having received government grants from The Danish Arts Foundation during the period 2006–2016. Each of these in total 3028 visual artists were sent a long questionnaire, electronically via Statistics Denmark, to be answered online. Several reminders were made, in writing and by telephone, in order to increase the response rate. A total of 1071 replies were received, giving a response rate of 35%. Of these, 892 have fully completed the questionnaire.[3]

These survey data have been merged with microdata from the official registers held by Statistics Denmark.[4] From Statistics Denmark, we have used a combination of labor, income and education data for the period 2010–2015. Via the artists' civil registration numbers,[5] it is possible to link the survey data with information from the public registers held by Statistics Denmark.

The combination of register data and survey data offers several advantages. Firstly, register data from Statistics Denmark provides a wide range of variables, which provide concrete information about, e.g., income and demographics. On the other hand, a questionnaire allows for a more detailed examination of the living and working conditions of visual artists than does the information available from Statistics Denmark. Secondly, merging the two sets of data provides special options for analyses of drop-outs. As register data from Statistics Denmark provide a large amount of basic information on those who have not answered the questionnaire, we have examined the representativeness of the study by comparing the distribution of a number of key variables for those who answered the questionnaire with the entire population of visual artists. In particular, we have implemented both chi-square goodness of fit and z-test respectively for the categorical and continuous variables. We found that there are no significant differences between the final sample and the population for the variables: income, grants, membership of artist associations and retired. For the variable related to arts education we found no significant difference only at a 10% level, while in the final sample women are overrepresented by almost four percentage points compared to the population. In addition, the average age in the sample is significantly different.

Thus, the sample can be assumed to be representative of the population except for age and gender (see Appendix) and we don't expect any bias in our result. Concerning gender, it is a common finding that women are overrepresented as they are more likely to participate in surveys (Curtin et al. 2000; Moore and Tarnai 2002).

Informed by the literature review, we want to explore arts as a profession (artists' income and working conditions), and how it relates to our indicators of quality (high professional standards). Therefore, the variables used to identify the latent class refer to artists' income, how they spend their working time and their self-evaluation of being an artist. Concerning income, from Statistics Denmark we have details of the annual income before taxes for each artist.[6] In the survey, we have asked the respondents to provide information about the percentage of their income derived from: art work (*pct income art*), job related to arts (*pct income related job*) in which the respondent uses skills from their work as visual artist, government subsidies

[3] 179 individuals have not reported how their income is divided between jobs with more or less connection to the arts and/or how their working time is divided between these jobs. Because of these missing values, we have excluded them from the analysis.

[4] Statistics Denmark is a governmental organization collecting and maintaining statistical data on Danish society.

[5] In Denmark, every resident has a Central Person Register number.

[6] This variable comes from information from the tax authorities.

(pct income gov),[7] and other income, including income from jobs not related to art *(pct income other)*. We know which respondents have registered a company *(own company)*, and the variable takes the form of a dummy equal to 1 if the artist is self-employed. In addition, we consider the private economy of the artist: thus, we ask the artists whether they are dependent on other sources, such as his/her partner's income *(dep partner)* or loans *(dep loans)*. In the latter case, we consider loans either with security in property or without collateral (bank credit, etc.). This information takes the form of two dummy variables.

Concerning working time, the artists reported the percentage of working time spent on art (*timeart*), on arts-related jobs (*time related job*), and for other income not related to art (*time other*). These are continuous variables. Finally, we ask the artists about their perception of being an artist: We use a dummy variable (*full time*) equal to 1 if the respondent perceives himself/herself as a full-time artist, otherwise equal to 0.

Clarification is needed concerning the percentages reported by respondents to the variables related to sources of income and how artists allocate their working time. In the sample considered, 639 out of 892 individuals (71.6%) answered in such a way that the sum of their percentages is 100%. All the others provided logically inconsistent responses. We decided to normalize the responses of this latter group, such that each sum of percentages adds up to 100%: this decision derives from the assumption that people give a gut-feeling estimate for the income and time categories, tending to be more aware of the size of income/time relative to each other than to each part to the total. In this perspective, normalization of the percentage data to a sum of 100% would seem to be the ideal solution.

These variables aim to describe the artists' incomes and working conditions, whereas the variables used for the membership function fulfill a different aim. Indeed, as we cannot directly identify the latent class to which a particular artist belongs, the membership function needs some "external" variables, related to the respondents' characteristics but not directly related to the artists' income and working condition, that allow for prediction of class membership probabilities. Such variables are normally related to sociodemographic characteristics. In the membership function, we use the following variables: A dummy variable denoting gender and a dummy variable indication of whether the artist has an education from an arts academy (human capital approach). Career stage is measured by age as a continuous variable, with a dummy variable indicating if the respondent is a retiree. Moreover, we include two dummy variables that can characterize the professional standards of the artist: membership of The Danish Artists' Society[8] and receipt of working-grants from The Danish Arts Foundation (grants from the government arts scheme). Table 1 summarizes the variables used in the Finite Mixture Analysis.

[7] This includes Danish students' Grants and Loans Scheme, sick leave benefits, unemployment benefits, and cash benefits. Pensions are excluded from this income category.

[8] For membership of the Danish Artists' Society (Kunstnersamfundet), a jury assesses the quality of a candidate's artistic production and qualifications. Membership therefore depends solely on the person's artistic skills and the quality of the artistic works.

6 Results

For the model selection, we fit the data with finite mixture models that include from 2 to 6 number of classes. Table 2 summarizes the statistics for the models tested.

We have opted for the model with six classes as it provides the smaller values of AIC and BIC, thus this model fits the data better. These values suggest that increasing the number of classes leads to a better model-fit: Indeed the seven-class model provides even better values of both AIC (62,286.29) and BIC (62,928.62). However, we have chosen the 6-class model as the fit improves relatively little from six classes onward; moreover, contrary to the 7-class model, the 6-class model produces reasonable sample size (>5% of the sample), which makes the estimated parameters more stable, and allows for an easier interpretation of the model.

We have also calculated the entropy, which is a type of statistics that assesses the accuracy with which the individuals are assigned their most likely profile. Its value ranges from 0 (classification is no better than random guessing) to 1 (perfect classification). The entropy is calculated as follows:

$$E = 1 - \frac{\sum_{i=1}^{n} \sum_{k=1}^{K} \left[-\widehat{\pi_{ik}} \ln(\widehat{\pi_{ik}}) \right]}{n \log (K)}$$

where n indicates the number of observations and $\widehat{p_{ik}}$ is the estimated probability for individual i to be assigned to class k.

As a value larger than 0.70 is considered acceptable (Jung and Wickrama 2008), we can claim that all the models provide a clear classification of individuals, with the 6-class model providing the greatest value of entropy.

We have conducted a finite mixture analysis based on the dataset. Table 3 shows the estimated parameters of the model.

The last column of Table 3 shows the value of the Wald test, with the respective p value in brackets. The Wald test is a test for the equality of effects of the covariates between classes, indicating whether a variable is equal across classes, and thus class independent.

The results of the Wald test show that artistic education (in accordance with earlier research such as Alper and Wassall 2006; Throsby 1996; Bille and Jensen 2016)

Table 2 Criteria for determining the optimal number of classes

No. of classes	No. of observations	Log-likelihood value	Degree of freedom	AIC	BIC	ENTROPY
2	892	–34,081.13	39	68,240.26	68,427.20	0.8569
3	892	–33,257.93	58	66,631.86	66,909.88	0.8981
4	892	–32,485.15	77	65,124.30	65,493.39	0.8914
5	892	–31,590.11	96	63,372.21	63,832.38	0.9054
6	892	–31,280.37	115	62,790.74	63,341.99	0.9087

Table 3 Estimation of the finite mixture model

	CLASS1	CLASS 2	CLASS 3	CLASS 4	CLASS 5	CLASS 6	WALD test
Percentage	0.21	0.14	0.11	0.16	0.26	0.12	
Income	28.55****	16.55****	18.98****	29.06****	22.82****	29.44****	
	(2.20)	(2.67)	(3.04)	(2.56)	(2.01)	(3.01)	
Pct income art	80.48****	11.29****	33.54****	8.58****	11.40****	7.10****	
	(1.22)	(1.28)	(1.58)	(1.26)	(1.01)	(1.45)	
Pct income related job	6.25****	7.01****	50.00****	4.84****	2.09****	88.08****	
	(0.70)	(0.84)	(1.19)	(0.85)	(0.63)	(1.01)	
Pct income government	1.50**	68.39****	4.23****	2.24***	0.20	1.08	
	(0.71)	(0.90)	(1.01)	(0.81)	(0.64)	(0.95)	
Pct income r	11.77****	13.32****	12.23****	84.34****	86.31****	3.74**	
	(1.30)	(1.42)	(1.67)	(1.41)	(1.21)	(1.57)	
Time art	85.81****	56.81****	55.53****	28.04****	90.09****	29.10****	
	(1.51)	(1.86)	(2.11)	(1.83)	(1.46)	(2.12)	
Time related job	18.50****	26.31****	34.90****	14.87****	26.22****	68.32****	
	(1.78)	(2.20)	(1.92)	(2.38)	(2.28)	(1.93)	
Time other	3.77***	28.97****	10.58****	64.65****	2.04*	4.58***	
	(1.23)	(1.53)	(1.71)	(1.61)	(1.17)	(1.67)	
Full-time	2.90****	0.71****	2.09****	− 0.92****	0.92****	− 0.42**	
	(0.33)	(0.19)	(0.34)	(0.19)	(0.15)	(0.21)	
Own company	1.02****	− 1.63****	0.28	− 1.02****	− 0.93****	− 0.62***	
	(0.17)	(0.24)	(0.21)	(0.20)	(0.15)	(0.21)	
Dep. partner	− 0.65****	− 1.13****	− 0.35*	− 0.99****	− 0.19	− 0.81****	
	(0.15)	(0.21)	(0.21)	(0.19)	(0.14)	(0.22)	
Dep. loan	− 1.84****	− 1.20****	− 1.74****	− 1.86****	− 1.74****	− 2.12****	
	(0.21)	(0.21)	(0.28)	(0.25)	(0.19)	(0.32)	
Class membership							
Male	–	− 0.52**	− 0.33	0.001	− 0.51**	− 0.33	8.23
		(0.26)	(0.26)	(0.24)	(0.25)	(0.26)	(0.144)

Table 3 (continued)

	CLASS1	CLASS 2	CLASS 3	CLASS 4	CLASS 5	CLASS 6	WALD test
Age	–	−0.10**** *(0.01)*	0.01 *(0.01)*	− 0.01 *(0.01)*	0.04** *(0.01)*	0.01 *(0.01)*	84.86 (0.000)
Retired	–	1.59**** *(0.49)*	− 1.51** *(0.62)*	− 1.55*** *(0,57)*	2.08**** *(0.37)*	− 1.88*** *(0.67)*	89.69 (0.000)
Education	–	− 0.28 *(0.42)*	− 0.1 *(0.29)*	0.41 *(0.26)*	0.24 *(0.29)*	0.21 *(0.28)*	7.79 (0.168)
Member Arts Society	–	− 0.40 *(0.42)*	− 0.21 *(0.32)*	− 1.01*** *(0.36)*	− 0.75** *(0.30)*	− 1.21*** *(0.41)*	16.47 (0.005)
Received grant	–	− 1.15**** *(0.30)*	0.30 *(0.28)*	− 1.14**** *(0.28)*	− 0.53* *(0.32)*	− 0.66** *(0.29)*	35.42 (0.000)
Constant	–	4.53**** *(0.63)*	− 1.06 *(0.77)*	0.55 *(0.63)*	− 2.36*** *(0.82)*	− 0.24 *(0.69)*	102.05 (0.000)

$^{*}p < 0.1$; $^{**}p < 0.05$; $^{***}p < 0.01$; $^{****}p < 0.001$

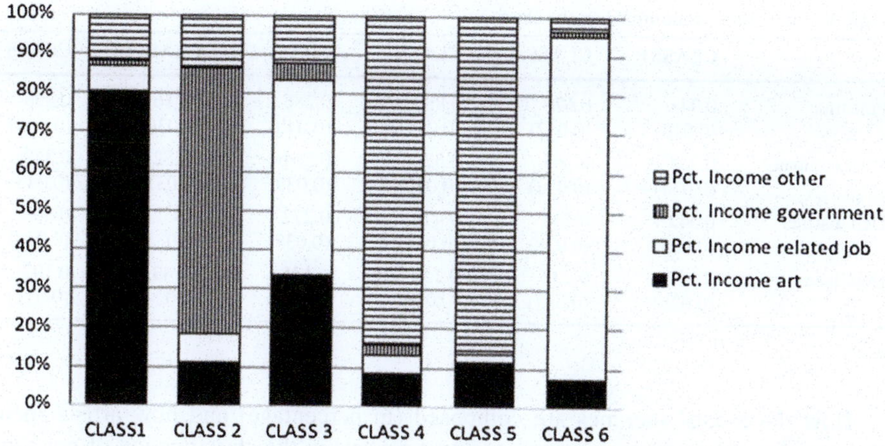

Fig. 1 Estimated mean (in percentage) related to income sources across classes

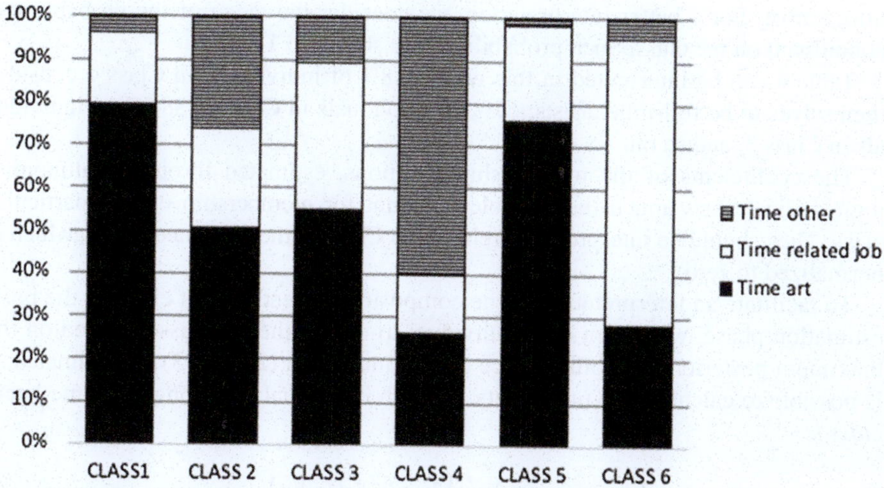

Fig. 2 Estimated mean (in percentage) related to working time across classes

and gender do not differ significantly among latent classes; so, these variables cannot be used to predict the class to which an individual belongs.

As already mentioned, for the continuous observed variables, the estimated parameters represent the class-specific mean values. For example, members of Class 1 have an estimated mean income of 3806 EUR (28,550 DKK[9]), on average 80.48% of their income derives from an art job, 6.25% from activities related indirectly to art, etc.

[9] Exchange rate: 1 EUR = 7.5 DKK (June 28, 2020).

Table 4 Probabilities conditional on the class

	CLASS1	CLASS 2	CLASS 3	CLASS 4	CLASS 5	CLASS 6
Full-time	0.948 (0.016)	0.670 (0.042)	0.889 (0.034)	0.286 (0.040)	0.716 (0.030)	0.396 (0.050)
Own company	0.734 (0.033)	0.163 (0.033)	0.570 (0.051)	0.264 (0.039)	0.282 (0.031)	0.349 (0.048)
Dep. partner	0.342 (0.035)	0.244 (0.038)	0.413 (0.051)	0.272 (0.038)	0.452 (0.034)	0.308 (0.046)
Dep. loan	0.137 (0.025)	0.232 (0.037)	0.150 (0.036)	0.135 (0.029)	0.149 (0.024)	0.107 (0.031)

How the artists' incomes are composed (in percentage) and how artists spend their working time represent two important aspects in the classification of our sample of artists. Figures 1 and 2 summarize the comparison of the different classes.[10]

Concerning the binary variables, the reported coefficients are not particularly informative. For a better interpretation, we consider the mean of the probabilities, conditional on the class. Such probabilities are shown in Table 4.

Table 4 can be interpreted in this way: 94.8% of individuals in Class 1 consider themselves to be full-time artists; 67% of individuals in Class 2, 88.9% of individuals in Class 3, and so on.

The coefficients of the membership functions, estimated through multinomial logit, indicate how much the variables account for membership of that particular class. They should be interpreted in relation to Class 1 (the reference class), which is normalized to zero).

To facilitate an interpretation of the composition of each latent class, in the post-estimation phase, we assign each individual to one of the six classes, based on the maximum posterior probability. Once the parameters in (2) and (3) are estimated, it is possible to calculate the probability for each individual of belonging to the latent *class k*:

$$\pi_{k|y_i,x_i} = \frac{\pi_{k|x_i} \prod_{j=1}^{J} f_k(y_{ij}|\mathbf{x}_i, \theta_{jk})}{\sum_{k=1}^{K} \pi_{k|x_i} \prod_{j=1}^{J} f_k(y_{ij}|\mathbf{x}_i, \theta_{jk})}. \tag{4}$$

Finally, each individual is assigned to the class c that provides the maximum value of (4).

[10] Notice that, for each class, the sum of the percentage of income equals 100. For some classes, the sum of the percentage of working time does not equal 100: this is because Stata treats each individual working time indicator as independent of the other two in the set. Even if this seems to violate the conditional independence assumption, in our estimation it has been relaxed by allowing the error terms to be correlated. In Fig. 2, for visualization purposes, we have normalized the percentages such that all the vertical bars add up to 100.

Such assignment, based on the posterior probability analysis, will be useful for the interpretation of the latent classes, summarized in the following section.[11]

7 Interpretation of the latent classes

The analysis identifies six different typologies of Danish visual artists.

Class 1 (21%). *Devoted to arts or Professional.* This class is composed of people who are professional artists, in both the acceptations mentioned in Sect. 3. Most members of this class (73%) are self-employed, and their income derives mainly from artistic work (mean value of 80.5%). 95% perceive themselves as full-time artists. They devote their working time almost exclusively to art (85.81% of working time as mean value). From the posterior probability analysis, we find that this class is the most heterogeneous from an income perspective: more than half of its members earn less than 27,000 EUR (200,000 DKK); however, almost all artists with an income above one million DKK belong to this class. The latter contribute to raise the mean annual income. This seems to confirm Rosen's theory (Rosen 1981) of the skewness of artists' earnings. Members of this class are professional, given that this class has the highest share of members of the Danish Artists' Society (32%) and, with the exception of Class 3, the highest share of individuals who have received grants from The Danish Arts Foundation (41%). This can be deduced by looking at the coefficients of the covariates and by considering that Class 1 is the reference class: The values of the variable *Member Artists Society* are negative for all the other classes, whereas the values of the variable *Received grant* are only positive for Class 3.

Class 2 (14%). *Subsidized artists.* Members of this class receive most of their income from government subsidies (on average 68.4% of their total income) and only 11.3% from their artistic work. This class is characterized by its age composition: more than 60% of members of this class are under 39 years of age, and 60% of all the 18–29-year-old individuals in our total sample belong to this class. Moreover, it is the only class that does not include individuals over the age of 67. It makes sense that this class comprises mostly young people who receive a large share of their income from government subsidies. These subsidies consist of Danish students' Grants and Loans Scheme, sick leave benefits, unemployment benefits and cash benefits. It is difficult to live on these subsidies for years on end, which means that those who are older have probably found other means of support. Members of this class devote just over half (56.8% on average) of their working time to

[11] Many contingency tables (not reported here) are built crossing the assigned class with the variables used, in order to analyze the main characteristics of each class. Concerning the continuous variables of income and age, we have converted these into categorical variables with 11 categories for the income variable (from less than 100.000 DKK to over one million DKK, with a range of 100.000 DKK for each level of income), and six categories for the age variable (from the category 18–29 to over 67, with a range of 9 years for each level of age).

art, and the other half is split between activities in which they use skills from the work of a visual artist and activities not related to arts. Most of them (67%) perceive themselves as full-time artists. From an income perspective, this class has the lowest average income: the posterior analysis shows that individuals in this class are concentrated in the low-income categories, and no artists in this class earn more than 53,000 EUR (400,000 DKK) per annum. In addition, this class has the highest share of members whose private economy depends on a loan, but the lowest share of individuals dependent on a partner's income (probably because of their young age). Most members of this class (84%) do not have a company registered in their own name. Finally, this class has the lowest share (10%) of individuals who have received a grant from the Danish Arts Foundation.

Class 3 (11%). *Aspiring artists*. This is the smallest class in terms of size. It is composed of individuals who cannot support themselves exclusively from their visual arts practice. Members of this class have heterogeneous sources of income: on average, half of their income is derived from art-related activities, 33.5% from their art job, and 12.2% from activities not related to art. Despite more than half of their income being derived from activities related to art, they only devote 34.9% (on average) of their working time to such activities, whereas most of their working time is devoted to artistic work (55.5% on average). A majority of members (57%) are self-employed, and 88.9% perceive themselves as full-time artists. Most are low–medium income individuals (86% earn less than 40,000 EUR (300,000 DKK) per annum, and the overall average income is slightly higher than that of Class 2. A relatively large share (41.3%) depend financially on a partner's income. This class is mainly composed of middle-aged individuals (65% between 40 and 59 years old), with very few retirees (4%), and it has the highest share of individuals (50%) who have received grants from the Danish Arts Foundation. Overall, it seems that members of this class would like to live exclusively from their visual arts practice, but they struggle to achieve this goal and are forced to find alternative sources of income, either by working with activities in which they can use their artistic skills, by relying on a partner's income, or by applying for grants.

Class 4 (16%). *Arts as a hobby (or secondary activity)*. This class is composed of people who do not consider art to be their main activity. Most (83.6%) are not self-employed, and a few (28.6%) see themselves as part-time artists. Members of this class receive a lower share (8.6% on average) of their income from art jobs. Instead, their income mainly derives from activities not related to arts (84.3% on average). Overall, compared to the other classes, they dedicate fewer working hours to art jobs or to activities related to art and more working hours to activities not related to art. In comparison with the other classes, fewer individuals in this class have a very low income (under 27,000 EUR (200,000 DKK)) and more individuals earn a middle income (between 27,000 and 80,000 EUR (200,000 DKK—600,000 DKK). This class has a low share (3.5%) of retirees, as well as a low share of members of the Danish Artists' Society (only 11%) and beneficiaries of grants (21%).

Class 5 (26%). *Senior*. The main characteristic of this class is given by the fact that members devote almost all their working time (90.08% on average) to artistic practice, but this only generates a minor part (11.4%) of their income. Most of their income is derived from sources not related to art, probably from pensions. Indeed, approximately 77% of individuals in this class are retired, and 82% are over 60 years of age. From the income perspective, this class, much like Class 1, is heterogeneous: 50% earn less than 27,000 EUR (200.000 DKK) and 80% earn less than 40,000 EUR (300.000 DKK), and as many as 45% rely on a partner's income. However, the few individuals who have a very high income are found in this class, as well as in Class 1. The majority of individuals of this class (71.6%) consider themselves a full-time artist, and a few (28.2%) are self-employed.

Class 6 (12%). *Workers related to arts*. This is a small-sized class. The main characteristic of this class is that most of the income and most of the working time are dedicated to activities related indirectly to art: 88.1% on average of income, and more than 68% of working time; only 29.10% of working time is devoted to artistic practice. Only 39.6% perceive themselves as a full-time artist, and 34.5% are self-employed. This class has the lowest share of individuals whose private economy depends on loans. Although having the highest average income, in this class distribution is not skewed as in the case of Class 1: like Class 4, few individuals have a very low income (less than 27,000 EUR) and more individuals have a middle income (between 27,000 and 80,000 EUR). This class has the lowest share of retirees (less than 3%) and is composed mainly of middle-aged individuals (between 40 and 59 years old). Furthermore, very few people in this class are members of the Danish Artists' Society (only 4%).

Table 5 summarizes the characteristics of the six latent classes identified by the model.

8 Discussion and conclusion

The purpose of this article is to explore heterogeneity among artists, and it aims at making a distinction between professional artists and amateurs, and thereby a definition of arts as a profession. We have shown how a finite mixture model can be used to investigate heterogeneity among artists and their incomes and working conditions. We find six distinctive groups of artists. Each of the groups includes between 11 and 26% of the artists in the population studied. The six distinctive groups can be used to make a distinction between professional artists and amateurs.

Of our artists' population, we find only 21% to be "professional artists." This is the only class that meets both the expected criteria for being in the profession, as the class members work full time with their visual arts practice and are mostly able to live from this work, and at the same time they meet high professional standards (as measured by our quality proxies).

Members of three other groups consider themselves in the main to be full-time artists, namely "aspiring artists," "subsidized artists," and "seniors." "Aspiring artists" (11%) are striving to be artists. They are middle-aged and have on average

Table 5 Summary of classes

	Class 1 Professionals	Class 2 Subsidized artists	Class 3 Aspiring artists	Class 4 Arts as a hobby	Class 5 Senior	Class 6 Workers related to arts
Share	21%	14%	11%	16%	26%	12%
Full-time artist	Full-time	Full-time	Full-time	Part-time	Full-time	Part-time
Pct of income from art jobs	High	Low	Heterogeneous source of income	Low (mostly activities not related)	Low (mostly pensions)	Arts related
Self-employed	Yes	Few	Half	Few	Few	Few
Government subsidies	Low	High	Low	Low	Low	Low
Time spend on art	High	Half	Half	Low	High	Arts related
Annual total income	Heterogeneous (skewed)	Low income	Low-medium income	Medium income (high average)	Heterogeneous (skewed)	Middle income (highest average)
Economy depending on loans		High				Low
Economy depending on partner's income		Low	High			
Age	Heterogeneous	Young	Middle-aged	Heterogeneous	Old—retired	Middle-aged
Member of the Danish Artists' Society	High			Low		Low
Received art grants	High	Low	High	Low		

a low income. They are not able to live from their visual arts practice, and they have multiple jobs. In this sense, they are not professional artists, but many have received national art grants, and thereby meet professional standards (quality stamp). Then we have the subsidized artists (14%), who are young and largely live on government subsidies. They would seem to be struggling to establish a career in the arts and enter the profession.

Career stages emerge as an important aspect to be considered in relation to professional artists. As pointed out in earlier literature (Matheiu 2012), it takes time to become established as a professional artist, and as a formal education don't seem to be of significance in establishing a career, "learning by doing" and finding your own stile as an artist seems to be of immense importance. While "subsidized" artists are young and at an early stage in their careers, "aspiring artists" are mid-career, have multiple incomes, and have achieved some recognition.

"Seniors" represent the late career stage, and it is highly interesting that this class represents the largest group in our population of artists, namely 26%. This group is composed of retired/old individuals, living mainly on their pensions. In this sense, they cannot be considered part of the profession (a retired lawyer is no longer part of the legal profession), but many of the retired artists consider themselves to be full-time artists. Our analysis does not indicate whether or not they are professional in terms of meeting high professional standards. One hypothesis could be that they are former members of Class 4 (Arts as a hobby) or Class 6 (Workers related to arts), who no longer have day jobs, and can devote all their time to their art hobby, but the "seniors" class might of course also include former professionals. The fact that a tiny fraction of this class has a very high income, points in the direction of former members of Class 1 (Professional artsits). In other similar studies, it is not uncommon to find a large share of old people/retired artists. In Throsby and Petetskaya (2017), 18% of the artists in their study are 65 + compared to 3% of the labor force in Australia. Retired artists have not received much attention in prior literature, and it would be an interesting topic for further research. If a substantial number of the seniors/retired artists are former "professionals," their ongoing contribution to the art markets could be a constraint on the ability of younger "subsidized" and "aspiring" artists to enter the market.

The last two groups cannot be considered professional artists in any definition of the word. Members of the "arts-as-a-hobby" group (16%) mostly work full time in other jobs, and their income is high compared to the other classes. Likewise, the "workers related to arts" (11%) are mainly working in jobs related to arts, and they have the highest average income.

To sum up, we find that a little less than half of the population (46%) of visual artists in Denmark can be considered professional artists (Classes 1, 2 and 3). 26% are seniors (Class 5), and about 28% have other careers outside the arts or related to the arts (Classes 4 and 6). With a total population of 3,028 visual artists in Denmark, we estimate that about 636 are fully professional and are able to live from their visual arts practice, and about 757 artists are subsidized or aspiring, still struggling to make a career in the arts. 787 artists are seniors, and, in that sense, they are out of the profession, and 848 artists cannot be considered professional artists ("art-as-a-hobby" and "workers related to arts"). It is interesting to note that gender and a formal artist education have no significant impact on class membership. The nonsignificant impact of an arts education is in accordance with prior research (Towse 2006).

Our "classes" cut across previous classifications and demarcations of visual artists, and thereby problematize the classification of visual artists as a category in earlier research. It is evident that none of the criteria relating to occupation (income from arts, working hours and being self-employed) can be used solely to define the population of professional artists. In that case we will lose a big share of artists—especially early career artists, working seriously with their careers, some of whom might already have received recognition among peers.

Likewise, our analysis shows that differentiating between full-time and part-time artists is not an efficient way in which to differentiate between professional artists and amateurs: "part-time artists" in particular will be a heterogeneous group including aspiring artists, who are not able to live fully from their arts practice even though they are striving to do so, and amateurs/non-professionals such as those in Class 4 and Class 6; similarly, the group of full-time artists will include a large section of "seniors" who can be considered to be out of the profession.

It is necessary to differentiate between *ex ante* population selection criteria and analytical subgroups *ex post*. For our research, we have considered the population of visual artists in Denmark based on the satisfaction of at least one of the following conditions: membership of one or both of the main arts organizations in Denmark, an artistic education from a recognized arts academy, and/or receipt of government grants from The Danish Arts Foundation during the period 2006–2016. This is a quite common way in which to delimit a population of artists, as we have used the *ex ante* available criteria, as in similar studies. Our results show that the initial criteria for inclusion in the survey have led to a broad and heterogeneous population of visual artists. Furthermore, our results show that several criteria are required in order to differentiate between professional and amateurs. Variables measuring profession (income and working time) are not enough. Indicators of the quality of the art works (professional standards) are necessary in order to make a meaningful demarcation. Finally, it is important to include career stages, both in terms of early career artists and seniors at the other end of the career spectrum. Therefore, *ex post* analytical groups are needed in order to differentiate between mutually exclusive groups of artists in terms of professionalism.

In this article, we have proposed a theoretical and empirical based and argued definition of arts as a profession and a demarcation between professional artists and amateurs/non-professionals. Such a clear demarcation is important for several reasons.

A clear definition of "professional artist" is important for the branch of the literature aimed at gaining knowledge about artists' and creative workers' employment, working conditions, careers, income, and so forth (e.g., Alper and Wassall 2006; Throsby and Petetskaya 2017; Heian et al. 2012; Bille et al. 2018; Bille 2020). The choice of the criteria to determine who is an artist has major consequences for the number of identified artists as well as their income levels. The existing empirical studies of artists' income conditions have not considered the impact of delimitation criteria on the results concerning the artists' average income. An exception is Bille and Fjællegaard (2018), which demonstrates how the application of various criteria has a huge impact on results concerning Danish authors' income. Furthermore, a coherent and universal agreement on a definition would enable comparisons across countries and creative industries (visual arts, music, performing arts, etc.). We hope our methods and results may help to redefine and lead to greater consensus among scholars about the definition of "professional artist" as a profession. From our research follows several concrete suggestions to improve future research in artists' income and working conditions. Firstly, we suggest ex ante criteria, where occupation as well as indicators of quality are included. These criteria cut across simple demarcations like part/time full time artists and must be carefully considered. Secondly, our research shows that career stages are just as important as the hobbyist/professional delineation. On the one hand, early career artists may fall outside most definitions of professional artists but can still be an important part of professional artists as they are building their careers on truly little income (Alacovska and Bille 2020a, b). On the other hand, senior artists on pension may be considered outside the profession (at least for policy purposes). Finally, there are a large group of artists that can be considered amateurs and workers related to the arts. Both these groups are not striving for a career in the arts, and we suggest them to be considered outside the profession. This will leave us with a much smaller population of artists with a different income-profile, than the population original considered.

Therefore, the definition of artists and the results in the article have important when it comes to policy implications. The prior lack of consensus on who should be included in artists' professions means that it has been difficult to develop appropriate policy measures (Abbing 2002). With the proliferation of floating boundaries between what is art and non-art, new art forms and new kinds of producers (Zolberg 1997), the issue becomes ever more present. The justification of arts subsidies or policy intervention is mostly based on the public good nature of artistic works and human capital, both in terms of their present realizations and future contribution. With this in mind, justification for subsidy can mainly be found for "aspiring" artists and "subsidized" artists, summing up 25% of the total population initially surveyed. For these two classes, we could expect some of their members to produce great works of art in due course, but without subsidies they may not be able to stay in the profession. On the other hand, class 4 (Arts a hobby) and class 6 (Workers related to arts) can be considered outside the artists' profession. The same goes for the seniors. When it comes to class 1 (professional artists) they are already able to live from their arts, and public support may not be necessary to any large extent for this group of artists. This leave us with a much smaller are clearer delimited population of artists where support schemes and policy measures can more easily be developed, and the support can be targeted more directly.

Funding The project has been financially supported by Ny Carlsbergfondet, Bikubenfonden and the Danish Arts Council.

Appendix: The representativeness of the research sample

Variable	Group	N	% of sample	% of population	Test
Gender	Male	386	43.27	46.90	$\chi^2=4.72$; $df=1$;
	Female	506	56.73	53.10	p value = 0.029
Received grants	Yes	234	26.23	24.21	$\chi^2=1.99$; $df=1$;
	No	658	73.77	75.79	p value = 0.158
Arts education	Yes	317	35.45	38.65	$\chi^2=3.65$; $df=1$;
	No	575	64.46	61.35	p value = 0.056
Members of Artists society	Yes	190	21.30	20.31	$\chi^2=0.54$; $df=1$;
	No	702	78.70	79.69	p value = 0.462
Retired	Yes	227	25.45	27.18	$\chi^2=1.35$; $df=1$;
	No	665	74.55	72.82	p value = 0.245

The p value is for the Chi-squared test under the null hypothesis of no difference between the distribution in the sample and in the population

Variable	Sample	Population	Test
Income	Mean = 244,514.2 SD = 307,100.6	Mean = 243,780.4 SD = 449,872	$z=0.0487$ p value = 0.9612
Age	Mean = 52.05 SD = 14.86	Mean = 50.88 SD = 16.19	$z=2.1502$ p value = 0.0315

The p value is for the z-test under the null hypothesis that the sample mean is equal to the population mean

References

Abbing, H. (2002). *Why are artists poor. The exceptional economy of the arts*. Amsterdam: Amsterdam University Press.

Abbott, A. (1988). *The system of professions—Essay on the division of expert labor*. Chicago: University of Chicago Press.

Alacovska, A., & Bille, T. (2020). A heterodox re-reading of creative work (2020: The diverse economics of Danish visual artists, *Work Employment and Society* (forthcoming)

Alper, N., & Wassall, G. H. (2006). Artists' careers and their labor markets. In V. A. Ginsburgh & D. Throsby (Eds.), *Handbook of the economics of the arts and culture* (pp. 813–864). Amsterdam: Elsevier Science.

Bakhshi, H., Freeman, A., & Higgs, P. (2013). *A dynamic mapping of the UK's creative industries*. London: NESTA.

Becker, H. (1982). *Art Worlds*. California: University of California Press.

Berlin, K. S., Williams, N. A., & Parra, G. R. (2014). An introduction to latent variable mixture modeling (part 1): Overview and cross-sectional latent class and latent profile analyses. *Journal of Pediatric Psychology, 39*(2), 174–187.

Bille, T. (2012). Creative labor: Who are they? What do they do? Where do they work? A discussion based on a quantitative study from Denmark. In C. J. Mathieu (Ed.), *Careers in Creative Industries* (pp. 36–65). London: Routledge.

Bille, T. (2020). Artists' labour markets. In R. Towse & T. Navarrete (Eds.), *A handbook of cultural economics* (3rd ed.). Cheltenham: Edward Elgar.
Bille, T., & Fjællegaard, C. B. (2018). Hvornår er man forfatter? Om afgrænsning af og levevilkår for danske forfattere og oversættere. *Nordisk Kulturpolitisk Tidsskrift, 21*(1), 121–146.
Bille, T., & Olsen, F. (2018). Measuring the quality and impact of arts and culture. In K. O. Eliassen, et al. (Eds.), *Contested qualities. Negotiating value in arts and culture* (pp. 229–256). Oslo: Fagbokforlaget.
Bille, T., & Jensen, S. (2016). Artistic education matters: Survival in the arts occupations. *Journal of Cultural Economics, 42*(1), 23–42.
Bille, T., Alacovska, A., Baldin. A, Horndrup, S.N., Mikuta, R.H. (2018): *Billedkunstens økonomiske rum—Danske billedkunstneres økonomiske arbeids - og levevilkår*, Copenhagen Business School, Copenhagen, 276 pages
Bille, T., Løyland, K., & Holm, A. (2017). Work for passion? Labor supply of artists. *KYKLOS, 70*(3), 347–380.
Casacuberta, C., & Gandelman, N. (2012). Multiple job holding: The artist's labor supply approach. *Applied Economics, 44,* 323–337.
Collins, L. M., & Lanza, S. T. (2010). *Latent class and latent transition analysis with application in the social, behavioral, and health sciences*. Hoboken, NJ: Wiley.
Cummingham, S., & Potts, J., et al. (2015). Creative industries and the wider economy. In C. Jones (Ed.), *The Oxford handbook of creative industries*. Oxford: Oxford University Press.
Curtin, R., Presser, S., & Singer, E. (2000). The effects of response rate changes on the index of consumer sentiment. *Public Opinion Quarterly, 64,* 413–428.
Dickie, G. (1974). *Art and the aesthetic*. New York: Cornell University Press.
Eliassen, K. O., et al. (2018). *Contested qualities. Negotiating value in arts and culture*. Oslo: Fagbokforlaget.
Frey, B. S., & Pommerehne, W. W. (1989). *Muses and markets. Explorations in the economics of the arts*. Oxford: Basil Blackwell.
Heian, M. T., Løyland, K., & Mangset, P. (2012). Stability and change: Work and income conditions for Norwegian artists. *Nordic Journal of Cultural Policy, 15*(1), 46–76.
Higgs, P. L., Cunningham, S. D., & Bakshi, H. (2008). *Beyond the creative industries: Mapping the creative economy in the United Kingdom*. London: NESTA.
Jung, T., & Wickrama, K. A. S. (2008). An introduction to latent class growth analysis and growth mixture modelling. *Social and Personality Psychology Compass, 2,* 302–317.
Lena, J. C., & Lindemann, D. J. (2014). Who is an artist? New data for an old question. *Poetics, 43,* 70–85.
Mathieu, C. J. (Ed.). (2012). *Careers in creative industries*. London: Routledge.
Menger, P. M. (1999). Artistic labor markets and careers. *Annual Reviews, 25,* 541–574.
Menger, P. M. (2001). Artists as workers: Theoretical and methodological challenges. *Poetics, 28,* 241–254.
Menger, P. M. (2006). Artistic labor markets: Contingent work, excess supply and occupational risk management. In V. A. Ginsburgh & D. Throsby (Eds.), *Handbook of the economics of art and culture* (pp. 765–811). Amsterdam: Elsevier Science.
Moore, D. L., & Tarnai, J. (2002). Evaluating nonresponse error in mail surveys. In R. M. Groves, D. A. Dillman, J. L. Eltinge, & R. J. A. Little (Eds.), *Survey nonresponse* (pp. 197–211). New York: Wiley.
Robinson, M. D., & Montgomery, S. S. (2000). The time allocation and earnings of artists. *Industrial Relations, 39*(3), 525–524.
Rosen, S. (1981). The economics of superstars. *American Economic Review, 71*(5), 845–858.
Throsby, D. (1992). Artists as workers. In R. Towse (Ed.), *Cultural economics. The arts, the heritage and the media industries*. Cheltenham: Edward Elgar.
Throsby, D. (1994). A work-preference model of artist behaviour. In A. Peacock & I. Rizzo (Eds.), *Cultural economics and cultural policies* (pp. 69–80). Dordrecht: Kluwer Academic Publishers.
Throsby, D. (1996). Disaggregated earnings functions for artists. In V. Ginsburgh & P.-M. Menger (Eds.), *Economics of the arts: Selected essays* (pp. 331–346). Dordrecht: Kluwer Academic Publishers.
Throsby, D., & Petetskaya, K. (2017). *Making art work*. Australia Council for the Arts: An economic study of professional artists in Australia.
Towse, R. (2006). Human capital and artists' labour markets. In V. A. Ginsburgh & D. Throsby (Eds.), *Handbook of the economics of the arts and culture* (pp. 865–894). Amsterdam: Elsevier Science.

Vermunt, J. K., & Magidson, J. (2002). Latent class cluster analysis. *Applied Latent Class Analysis, 11*, 89–106.

Wilensky, H. L. (1964). The professionalization of everyone? *American Journal of Sociology, 70*(2), 137–158.

Zolberg, V. (1997). *Outsider art: Contesting boundaries in contemporary culture*. Cambridge: Cambridge Cultural Social Studies.

Journal of Cultural Economics (2021) 45:557–576
https://doi.org/10.1007/s10824-021-09413-8

ORIGINAL ARTICLE

What Makes an Artrepreneur?

An Exploratory Study of Artrepreneurial Passion, Personality and Artistry

Robert Hoffmann[1] · Bronwyn Coate[1] · Swee-Hoon Chuah[2] · Pia Arenius[1]

Received: 30 September 2020 / Accepted: 15 March 2021 / Published online: 12 April 2021

Abstract
We present an exploratory study to examine the antecedents of artrepreneurship, the decision of artists to commercialise the fruits of their practice. We hypothesise and test the influence of three key drivers using a questionnaire-based study with 93 practicing artists. While a number of factors from individual difference psychology are significant explanators, objective characteristics associated with several aspects of artistic practice (such as career stage, income, recognition and time intensity) provide little evidence to explain what makes an artist become an artrepreneur. We also measure the concept of *artrepreneurial passion* adapted from the business entrepreneurship literature but find no evidence that this drives artrepreneurship. Overall the results, while tentative based on a modest sample size, support a disconnect between artistic identity and business venturing as suggested in the previous work. Instead, individual difference characteristics associated more generally with business entrepreneurship seem to make the artrepreneur.

Keywords Artists · Entrepreneurship · Artrepreneur · Personality · Passion

JEL Classification B40 · C90 · D90 · Z10

✉ Robert Hoffmann
robert.hoffmann@rmit.edu.au

Swee-Hoon Chuah
sweehoon.chuah@utas.edu.au

1 Behavioural Business Lab, College of Business, RMIT University, Melbourne, Victoria 3000, Australia

2 Tasmanian School of Business and Economics, University of Tasmania, Hobart, Tasmania 7001, Australia

1 Introduction

As a response to the perpetually challenging funding environment in the arts and cultural sector, arts entrepreneurship, or *artrepreneurship*, has been proposed as an alternative funding source allowing an independent living from creative practice (e.g. Beckman 2007; Bridgstock 2013; Brown 2005; Henry 2007). Artrepreneurship is defined as the process of brining the fruits of artists' creative endeavours to the market for commercial gain. It results from the blending of artists' aesthetic and economic logics (Eikhof and Haunschild 2007) and encourages a more businesslike approach to creative production (Engelmann et al. 2012) to "translate creativity into money" (Brink 2011, p. 75).

Artrepreneurship has been advocated by governments as a career path for artists that educational institutions should promote (Carey and Naudin 2006; Pollard 2013): Successful commercialisation of creative ideas and practice requires particular skills and competencies that may, to an extent, be acquired. In response, entrepreneurial training as part of fine arts education aims to raise the professional prospects of artists by developing artists' "more intangible, behavioral aspects of entrepreneurship" (Pollard 2013). Two approaches to artrepreneurship education exist, one aimed at the artist's new venture creation, and the other at professional employment (Beckman 2007; Bridgstock 2013).

Artrepreneurship can benefit both the economic viability of the individual artist and the cultural industries more generally (Roberts 2012). For many artists wishing to make a living from their creative practice, entrepreneurism presents new opportunities that can sustain their creative careers. (Lingo and Tepper 2013, p. 337) describe artists as "masters of navigating across historically disparate domains" who increasingly must embrace "self-directed entrepreneurialism".

Moreover, beyond the individual artist, the economic importance of the creative economy, i.e. goods and services based on creative intellectual capital, is considerable and rising. In the UK, for example, cultural industries contribute around 8% of GDP, employ around 6% of the workforce (Carey and Naudin 2006) and are rising faster than any other economic sector (Brown 2005; Henry 2007; Bridgestock 2013). According to evidence from United Nations (2019), the global market for creative goods has more than doubled between 2002 and 2015 to over $500 billion. The importance from this sector comes from "the fact that creativity, knowledge and access to information are increasingly recognised as powerful engines driving economic growth and promoting development in a globalizing world" (United Nations 2019). As an alternative funding source, artrepreneurship can help stimulate the cultural economy.

The potential importance of artrepreneurship both for individuals and the economy more generally highlights the need to understand the drivers of artists' business venturing behaviours. This issue mirrors an equivalent, long-standing debate in the business discipline of entrepreneurship. The identification of the antecedents of entrepreneurship allows policymakers to target and/or develop individuals in order to raise entrepreneurship, and to create suitable institutions and policies to support their activities. This literature has identified an array of antecedent factors including institutional structures and prevailing economic environment and general culture that promote entrepreneurship within the economy (e.g. see Woronkowicz and Noonan 2019). On the other hand, individual-level variables are also important. These include opportunity from personal circumstances, training, upbringing and sheer luck. In addition, a range of psychological variables such as individual personality traits (Carland et al. 1984), motivations (Shaver and Scott 1992) and decision-making styles (Busenitz and Barney 1997) have also been explored (see Frese and Gielnik 2014, for an overview). While results have been mixed, more recent meta-analyses have been able to confirm some of the proposed relationship between individual psychological variables and entrepreneurial behaviour (e.g. Zhao and Seibert 2006; Pekkala Kerr et al. 2017).

This paper is intended to contribute to our understanding of the drivers of artrepreneurship, which is itself an important driver of the cultural economy yet has not enjoyed the same policy focus as other economically important sectors (Caust 2019). In the following, we examine the antecedents of artrepreneurship using a study with 93 practicing artists. Notwithstanding our relatively modest sample size, we believe ours is a first exploratory attempt to study this issue empirically. Our approach to this issue is the following. First, because of the overlap between artrepreneurial and entrepreneurial behaviour along with similarities between processes and environment, we apply relevant insights from entrepreneurship research to inform our research model and hypotheses, and, in turn, data collection.

Overall, we focus on three sets of individual antecedents. First, we pay attention to art-specific factors related to artistic practice, informed by research in cultural economics. In particular, we use established indicators of the artistic career (such as creative income and time allocated to creative practice) to examine its influence on artrepreneurship. The second is the individual passion to engage in entrepreneurial activities related to one's artistic practice. The third comprises certain psychological individual difference characteristics underlying artrepreneurship including general personality and motivation.

The remainder of the paper proceeds as follows. The next section outlines the research model based on prior literature and the hypotheses we derive. Section 3 contains details of the data collection and the result of their analysis. Section 4 concludes with a discussion of the findings, the limitations of our study and concluding remarks.

2 Theoretical model and hypotheses

The research question that motivates the current study relates to the individual-level drivers of artrepreneurial behaviour. Our study was designed to identify the individual professional and psychological characteristics that underlie an artist's decision to become an artrepreneur, i.e. to leverage their artistic practice for commercial gain. We now outline our research model in terms of the variables and their hypothesised relationships that we derived based on relevant existing literature (see Fig. 1). The details of how we measure these are contained in Sect. 3.1.

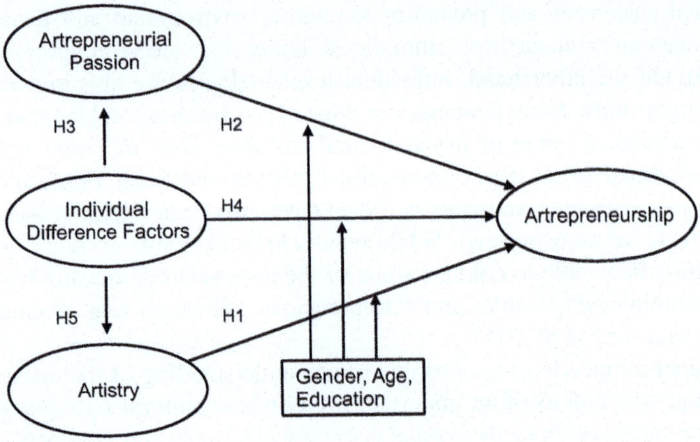

Fig. 1 Research model

2.1 Artistry

A first and necessary condition for artrepreneurship is to be an artist, i.e. someone engaging in creative practice that is suitable for commercialisation. The question who may be called an artist in this sense of the term is not clear cut. Artists' labour market behaviour has been much-studied in cultural economics (for an overview see: Alper and Wassall 2006; Bille 2020). The idiosyncrasies of this market mean that no definitive criteria of what precisely constitutes professional artistry exists. Multiple job holdings are one aspect, as is the varying and subjective nature of the quality of artistic output. Frey and Pommerehne (1989) propose a host of qualifying criteria including time spent on creative practice, income derived from it, recognition among peers and the public, self-image, training, professional memberships and the quality of artistic works.

We term this group of factors artistry, the intensity and importance of artistic practice in an artist's life. Artistry consists of commitment to creating art and the standing it has in an artist's life. It is therefore an important driver of willingness to commercialise art as it positively affects the prospect of success and the enjoyment it brings compared to alternative career choices. We expect this variable to be related to artrepreneurship as it contains both the ability and willingness to create art that may be leveraged commercially.

Hypothesis 1 *Artistry is positively associated with artrepreneurship status.*

2.2 Artrepreneurial passion

We next consider an affective factor underlying an individual's artrepreneurial decisions that we adapt from recent entrepreneurship literature. Several seemingly non-rational aspects of entrepreneurial behaviour, such as excessive optimism, risk taking and intense commitment as well as drive, have long been attributed to strong emotional forces. This led to the conceptualisation of entrepreneurial passion, argued to be one of the most central phenomena of entrepreneurial activity (Cardon et al. 2009).

Cardon et al. (2009) conceptualise entrepreneurial passion as those consciously accessible intense positive emotions resulting from entrepreneurial activity that provide the individual concerned with the motivation to deal with the attendant challenges of uncertainty, with meaning and with self-identity. In the empirical development of the concept, entrepreneurial passion has been identified as a key driver of decisions to engage in entrepreneurship generally (Cardon et al. 2013).

Due to the centrality of passion to entrepreneurship and the existence of more psychological similarities between artists and entrepreneurs (Arenius et al. 2020; Coate et al. 2021), we examine a role for an equivalent construct underpinning an artist's decision to venture creatively: We conceptualise the notion of artrepreneurial passion as a driver of artrepreneurship. However, in contrast to entrepreneurs, artists contemplating leveraging their creativity for commercial gain are potentially faced with a dilemma. For many, turning art into business is akin to "selling out" and is associated with losing artistic integrity and control (Abbing 2008; Bridgstock 2013).

Another point of difference is that the entrepreneurial passion of artists involves a greater amount of identification with their venture (Darmer 2008). In artrepreneurship, the commercialised venture simultaneously creates an experience in consumers (of consuming art) and producers (of venturing) that overlap significantly. Similarly, Beckman (2007) and Bridgstock (2013) argue that the drivers of artrepreneurship differ from business in the greater importance of identity compared to financial motives.

We therefore adapt the entrepreneurial passion scale developed by Cardon et al. (2013) to the particular context of commercialising art. Using this scale, we focus on domains of artrepreneurship identified previous literature as sources of strong positive feelings. These include novelty, searching for new opportunities and overcoming challenges as well as the pursuit of success, reputation and income. In particular, we conceptualise two dimensions of artrepreneurial passion. The first, which we term *commercial artrepreneurial passion* (AP-COM) reflects the commercial motive behind artrepreneurial passion including an element of networking and collaboration for expressly extrinsic reasons. The second, which we call *innovative artrepreneurial passion* (AP-NEW), speaks to change and innovation—the excitement from the development and success of new opportunities beyond the artist's comfort zone. We posit that entrepreneurial passion, in the context of artists commercialising their creative practice, consists of two separate dimensions: The artistic passion for innovation and change, and another one for commercial success.

Hypothesis 2 *Artrepreneurial passion is positively associated with artrepreneurship status.*

2.3 Individual difference factors

By individual difference factors, we mean person-specific psychological characteristics including personality, motivations and cognitive styles. Among the vast array of individual difference factors established in research, we select those that have been shown in the previous literature as predictive of behaviour *either* in the entrepreneurial or artistic realm, i.e. part of the artrepreneurial behaviour profile as artrepreneurs are *both* artists and entrepreneurs. For this reason, individual difference factors are contained in our model in that they are hypothesised to influence all the other constructs. We consider two types: personality and motivational factors.

First, personality consists of stable tendencies that shape an individual's typical actions, thoughts and feelings. They commonly include five to six dimension including openness to experience, conscientiousness, extraversion, agreeableness and neuroticism. An additional factor of honesty–humility is also argued to exist (Ashton and Lee 2009).

Certain personality aspects have been found to be predictive of being an artist. Studies using different personality inventories have been conducted with artists since the 1950s not least to test the stereotypical artistic personality. While the evidence is mixed it suggests that artists are less emotionally stable and extravert but also more open to change (Drevdahl and Cattell 1958; Cross et al. 1967; Götz and Götz 1979; Kemp 1996). On the other hand, the evidence overall is mixed and associations tend not to be strong potentially because of other external influences such as opportunity and environmental and institutional factors (Abuhamdeh and Csikszentmihalyi 2014; Feist 1998).

We also hypothesise personality to be an influence on artrepreneurship. We take our cue from plentiful literature in entrepreneurship that attests to the importance of underlying psychological characteristics that affect someone's intention and decision towards, as well as success in business venture creation (e.g. Busenitz and Barney 1997). Among these, generalised personality has been the subject of many studies. Overall, studies have documented some significant personality drivers of entrepreneurship including conscientiousness, openness to experience, emotionality and extraversion (Zhao and Seibert 2006). We hypothesise that similar personality dimensions drive artists' decisions to commercialise the fruits of their practice.

There is evidence that psychological and personality attributes are linked to entrepreneurial passion in business. For example, Obschonka et al. (2019) find that a person's overall entrepreneurial profile, i.e. entrepreneurial tendencies across all fundamental personality dimensions, is positively associated with entrepreneurial passion. We therefore make a corresponding hypothesis for artrepreneurial passion.

Hypothesis 3 *Artrepreneurial passion is positively associated with certain personality dimensions.*

In addition to general personality, we also consider two specific psychological characteristics known to be associated with *both* artistry and business entrepreneurship, and therefore relevant to our study of artrepreneurship. The first is intrinsic motivation. An intrinsically motivated person performs an action for its own reward rather for some external (and especially material) reward. Such people seek self-actualisation and higher purposes, characteristics often attributed to artists who pursue their passions and creative drive (Abbing 2008).

The second is a complex of symptoms known as attention deficit hyperactivity disorder (ADHD), including inattention, hyperactivity and impulsiveness. Historical research suggests historical figures in the arts world like Leonardo may have been afflicted (Catani and Mazzarello 2019). More generally, artists tend to be relatively impulsive (Feist 1998), distractible (Honos-Webb 2010) and sensitive, signs of ADHD also associated with creativity and intuition (Simonton 2014). Similarly, existing research suggests that those in self-employment or with entrepreneurial intentions manifest these symptoms more (Verheul et al. 2015; Lerner et al. 2018). ADHD symptoms may confer benefits for the entrepreneurial career (Wiklund et al. 2017). We refer to this dimension as impulsivity and ADHD interchangeably in the following.

Hypothesis 4 *Artrepreneur status is positively associated with certain personality dimensions and impulsivity and intrinsic motivation.*

Hypothesis 5 *Artistry is positively associated with certain personality dimensions and impulsivity and intrinsic motivation.*

Finally, our model considers various demographic influences that may affect the constructs or their relationships. Rather than developing hypotheses about such effects, we control for three demographics in our analyses, namely gender, age and educational attainment.

Our model of artrepreneurship, including both its constructs and their interrelationships, is in line with current models of entrepreneurship. For instance, Frese and Gielnik (2014, p. 429) provide a comprehensive framework including personality, motivational factors, cognitive antecedents and social preconditions as causes of entrepreneurial success. These four groups of factors, in that order, correspond closely to ours of individual difference factors, artrepreneurial passion, artistry and our demographic moderators, respectively. Because Frese and Gielniks (2014) framework is both general and conceptual it also includes both broader (national culture, economic environment) and more specific (entrepreneurial behaviours and activities) factors not present in our empirical model that relates to the specific data we collected. For instance, we do not include institutional variables because our sample of artists operates under the same economic and cultural conditions in Australia.

3 Methods and results

We conducted a study to measure these artistic, psychological and occupational variables in order to test their hypothesised relationships. In particular, we measured a raft of psychological constructs in a diverse group of 93 artists with different artistic profiles and experience that we elicit by questionnaire. We ask whether their decisions to engage in artrepreneurship are explained with reference to the different aspects of their artistic practice and measured psychological traits as well as artrepreneurial passion.

3.1 Measures

Our main dependent variable, artrepreneurship (ARTE), was measured based on participants' self-assignment to occupation categories as either freelancing (46%), "self-employment akin to cultural entrepreneurship" (37% of participants), paid employment (12%) or "other" (5%). We generated a dummy variable to denote those artists who declared themselves to be self-employed cultural entrepreneurs on response to this question (ARTE = 0 or 1).

We also measure artistry, the depth of an artist's profile. Artistry captures the importance of artistic practice to an artist's life in terms of longevity of career to date, commitment, recognition and income derived from practice. Based on the factors identified by Frey and Pommerehne (1989), we focus on recognition, time and income as defining and readily measurable aspects of artistic practice but added career stage.

We therefore conceptualise artistry as a multi-dimensional measure of a person's artistic profile in terms of the intensity of their commitment to practice, its importance to their financial income and the history of their practice. Artistic standing (STAND) is an ordinal variable ranging from future artist, hobbyist, professional to peer-recognised professional. We measure time spent on creative practice (TIME) as an ordinal variable ranging from 8 hours to 38 or more hours a week. Career stage (STAGE) is measured as an ordinal variable from emerging, to mid-career and established artist. Finally, INCOME measures the contribution artistic earnings make to an artist's overall income.

In terms of the psychological constructs, we measured six major personality traits using the 60-item version of HEXACO (Ashton and Lee 2009) as honesty–humility (HEX-H), emotionality (HEX-E), extraversion (HEX-X), agreeableness (HEX-A), conscientiousness (HEX-C) and openness to experience (HEX-O). Intrinsic motivation is composed of different dimensions. Learning goal orientation is the motivation to achieve mastery by acquiring new skills and competences. We measure learning goal orientation (VandeWalle 1997) to measure intrinsic motivation (INT-MOT). We administered six screening questions of the Attention deficit hyperactivity disorder (ADHD) Scale (ASRS-v1.1, Kessler et al. 2005) which is used to screen adults for symptoms including inattention, hyperactivity and impulsiveness Table 1.

3.2 Data Collection

Of the 93 artists who participated in our study, 53 identified as female and 38 as male. Their average age was 35.2 years. For 94%, English was the mother tongue. We recruited using ads in online and physical fora frequented by artists as well as through invitation emails sent by participating artists organisations that we approached. Individuals qualified if some part of their income came from artistic practice. Different fields of practice were represented including film, music, dance,

Table 1 Study variables

Variables	Description	Mean	StDev
Demographics			
Education	Highest educational qualification (high school, diploma, undergraduate degree, higher degree, other)		
Female	Participant identifying as female (yes/no)	0.57	
Age	Age in years	35.15	11.654
Artistry			
TIME	Average weekly hours currently dedicated to art/creative practice (>38, 19–38, 8–19, <8)	2.96	0.855
STAGE	Career stage (emerging, mid-career, established, former artist)	1.46	0.621
STAND	Artistic Self-Image (non, previous, student, hobbyist, professional, recognised)	3.38	1.042
INCOME	Proportion of income generated from art/creative practice (All, majority, half, small, no)	2.73	1.143
EMPLOY	Employment as freelancer, cultural entrepreneur or paid employment		
ARTE	Dummy variable for cultural entrepreneurs		
Artrepreneurial Passion (AP)			
AP-COM	Factor 1: Commercialisation	2.51	1.041
AP-NEW	Factor 2: Innovation	1.57	0.493
Personality and Psychological Factors			
HEX-H	Humility	3.61	0.667
HEX-E	Emotionality	3.29	0.668
HEX-X	Extraversion	3.43	0.631
HEX-A	Agreeableness	3.24	0.660
HEX-C	Conscientiousness	3.81	0.499
HEX-O	Openness to experience	4.40	0.387
INTMOT	Intrinsic motivation	4.54	0.532
IMPULS	Impulsiveness	2.99	0.567

Table 2 Spearman rank correlations between the four dimensions of artistry. p values in brackets

	INCOME	STAGE	TIME
STAGE	0.2049 (0.0778)		
TIME	0.4964 (0.0000)	0.2334 (0.0438)	
STAND	0.0982 (0.4020)	0.0778 (0.5072)	0.2592 (0.0247)

literature and visual art, the latter accounting for more than half of participants. In some of our analyses below, the number of observations falls below this number due to incomplete responses.

The study was conducted in a university laboratory in central Melbourne, Australia. Multiple sessions were conducted with between 5 and 20 participants seated at partitioned computer terminals. The artist sessions were part of a larger study with different occupational groups performing tasks not reported here but in our companion paper (Arenius et al. 2020). Sessions lasted 90 minutes on average. Participants received financial compensation in cash and by bank transfer averaging 42 AUD for all tasks. Participants completed questionnaires on their computer screens. Biographical questions about artistic practice and experience were followed by demographic questions and psychological measures.

We now examine to what extent artrepreneurship is determined by a person's artistry, underlying psychological individual difference variables and artrepreneurial passion, controlling for relevant demographic factors.

3.3 Artistry

We begin by examining artistry, the artistic profile that artrepreneurs seek to commercialise. There are (as expected) significant inter-correlations between the four aspects of the artistic profile that we measure (Table 2). We use the nonparametric Spearman approach as the variables concerned are ordinal in nature. While TIME is positively related to all the other dimensions, STAND relates to none of the other dimensions. Our inclusion of career stage is supported by the association of this variable with the other measures we derived from the literature. From this, we derive an overall measure of artistic profile (ARTISTRY) as the average of the four dimensions of artistry (INCOME, STAND, STAGE, TIME), which is normally distributed (Shapiro–Wilk $p = 0.119$).

What determines individual artistry? We previously discussed the psychological determinants of the artistic personality examined in previous psychometric studies that compared artists with non-artists. In contrast to those studies, our focus on artist participants allows us to examine the degree of artistry between them. Models 1 to 3 in Table 3 contain ordinary least squares regressions with robust errors where ARTISTRY is the dependent variable. Models 1 and 2, respectively, enter the HEXACO fundamental dimensions and the other two traits separately. The reason is that both intrinsic motivation and impulsivity are known to be highly correlated with multiple personality dimensions, potentially measuring the same parts of some of the underlying psychological constructs. When entered alone, none of the personality dimensions significantly explain differences in artistry between our artist participants. Model 2 shows that ADHD symptoms and intrinsic motivation (marginally) explain artistry. In order to examine the combined effects of all individual difference factors considered in this study, we employ a general-to-specific approach (Campos et al. 2005) in model 3 where insignificant explanators are iteratively eliminated. The final model shows extraversion and openness to experience now are significant along with ADHD symptoms and intrinsic motivation. All coefficients' variance inflation factors are below 1.3, suggesting no multicollinearity problems exist. These results control for demographic variables (gender, age and education level).

Result 1 *Artistry is significantly and positively associated with impulsivity and intrinsic motivation as well as with openness to experience and extraversion, partly confirming* H5.

The fact that individual difference factors explain the intensity of an artistic profile goes beyond existing findings of characteristics that distinguish artists from non-artists (see Sect. 2.3). The particular influences we identify (intrinsic motivation, impulsivity and extraversion) and the direction of the effects are also in line with those findings. However, the negative significant coefficient for openness to experience is unexpected as this personality dimension has been shown to be more typical for artists than other professions in other studies.

3.4 Artrepreneurial Passion

We now examine the hypothesised role of the two dimensions of artrepreneurial passion in our model. The 13 items we adapted from the entrepreneurial passion instrument of Cardon et al. (2013) are shown in Fig. 2. The first, commercial artrepreneurial passion (AP-COM, Cronbach $\alpha = 0.75$), comprises items 1 and 8 to 10. The second, innovative artrepreneurial passion, consists of items 2 to 7 and 11 to 13 (AP-NEW, $\alpha = 0.65$). The two are moderately correlated (Pearson $r = 0.233$, $p = 0.044$).

We next examine whether these two different factors underlying artrepreneurial passion are linked to psychological characteristics as hypothesised. Models 4 and 5 in Table 3 show the results for AP-COM. None of the individual difference factors generate significant coefficients. In marked contrast, artrepreneurial innovative passion (AP-NEW) is related to a number of individual difference factors (model 7). Intrinsic motivation is a significant negative influence, as are extraversion and humility.

Result 2 *Innovative, but not commercial artrepreneurial passion is significantly associated with some individual difference factors, partly confirming* H3.

These results speak to the psychological correlates of emotions that artists may experience when commercialising their practice. It is noteworthy that the relationships are negative in that commercially passionate artrepreneurs are relatively low

Table 3 Regression results for artistry (ARTISTRY, Ordinary Least Squares) as well as commercial and innovative artrepreneurial passion (AP-COM and AP-NEW, Ordinary Least Squares). Standardised beta coefficients with standard errors in parentheses

	(1) ARTISTRY	(2) ARTISTRY	(3) ARTISTRY	(4) AP-COM	(5) AP-COM	(6) AP-COM	(7) AP-NEW	(8) AP-NEW	(9) AP-NEW
HEX-H	–0.163			–0.079			–0.235**		
	(0.371)			(0.285)			(0.0705)		
HEX-E	–0.062			0.019			0.027		
	(0.435)			(0.235)			(0.0537)		
HEX-X	0.096		0.230*	–0.151			–0.233***		
	(0.466)		(0.432)	(0.196)			(0.0571)		
HEX-A	0.232			–0.171			–0.120		
	(0.459)			(0.245)			(0.0574)		
HEX-C	0.056			–0.013			0.096		
	(0.548)			(0.330)			(0.0909)		
HEX-O	-0.155		–0.258**	0.157			0.024		
	(0.663)		(0.591)	(0.411)			(0.101)		
Education	0.179	0.141	0.116	-0.047	0.038	–0.028	0.197**	0.249*	0.247*
	(0.332)	(0.339)	(0.347)	(0.207)	(0.172)	(0.163)	(0.0604)	(0.0851)	(0.0879)
Female	0.221**	0.166*	0.158*	–0.046	0.038	0.087	0.080	–0.028	–0.015
	(0.357)	(0.315)	(0.308)	(0.235)	(0.177)	(0.152)	(0.0592)	(0.0817)	(0.0815)
Age	0.024	0.089	0.143	–0.076	–0.094	–0.162	–0.039	–0.132	–0.144
	(0.0217)	(0.0180)	(0.0196)	(0.00910)	(0.00835)	(0.00839)	(0.00325)	(0.00458)	(0.00469)
INTMOT		0.205*	0.263**	–0.092			–0.631***		
		(0.465)	(0.455)	(0.290)			(0.0654)		
IMPULS		0.255**	0.309***	–0.044			–0.141		
		(0.411)	(0.411)	(0.279)			(0.0823)		
ARTISTRY					–0.475***			–0.180	
					(0.0507)			(0.0263)	

Table 3 (continued)

	(1) ARTISTRY	(2) ARTISTRY	(3) ARTISTRY	(4) AP-COM	(5) AP-COM	(6) AP-COM	(7) AP-NEW	(8) AP-NEW	(9) AP-NEW
STAGE						0.181*			0.091
						(0.154)			(0.0852)
TIME						−0.204			−0.285**
						(0.170)			(0.0765)
STAND						0.022			0.095
						(0.254)			(0.124)
INCOME						−0.493***			−0.049
						(0.103)			(0.0518)
N	75	75	75	75	75	75	75	75	75
R^2	0.162	0.178	0.256	0.112	0.228	0.344	0.671	0.084	0.137

$^*p < 0.10$, $^{**}p < 0.05$, $^{***}p < 0.01$

1. It is exciting to figure out new ways to solve unmet artistic/creative challenges that can be commercialized.
2. Searching for new ideas to express in my artistic/creative practice is enjoyable to me.
3. I am motivated to figure out how to make my existing artistic/creative practice more innovative.
4. Scanning the environment for new artistic/creative opportunities really excites me.
5. Embarking upon a new artistic/creative project or venture excites me.
6. Having artistic/creative and expressive freedom energizes me.
7. Nurturing a new artistic/creative venture through its emerging success is enjoyable.
8. Commercializing my artistic/creative practice to generate profit or income is important.
9. I actively seek out the right people to network with in order to build my artistic/creative reputation.
10. As part of my artistic/creative practice I collaborate with others.
11. Pushing myself beyond my comfort zone excites and better motivates me.
12. Nurturing and growing my artistic/creative practice is an important part of who I am.
13. Art/creative practice is pursued as a calling and should be pursued for its own sake.

Fig. 2 Artrepreneurial Passion Instrument

in humility. This dimension is associated with greed, lack of modesty, sincerity and fairness (Ashton and Lee 2009). Similarly, the negative relationship to intrinsic motivation is rooted in the extrinsic nature of commercial passion. The negative relationship of passion to extraversion, gratification from social interactions, is not clear.

We did not hypothesise a relationship between artistry and artrepreneurial passion but our data provide an opportunity to explore this link. AP-COM is significantly negatively associated with artistry overall (model 5), perhaps supporting the idea of a conflict between artistic integrity and commercial motives. It is also supported by the significant relationship between artistry and intrinsic motivation we find in this study. When we break artistry down, advanced career stage is a positive and income a negative influence (model 6). The latter finding suggests that entrepreneurs rely on other forms of earnings to complement their artistic venture. Overall artistry is not related to AP-NEW (model 8) but when we break this construct down (model 9), a different aspect, time spent of practice, is negatively associated with innovative passion. While the reason for this result is not definitive, it may again reflect a disconnect between the intrinsic motivation behind art and artrepreneurial passion generally.

Result 3 *Commercial, but not innovative artrepreneurial passion is significantly and negatively associated with artistry.*

3.5 Artrepreneurship

We finally turn to our key interest, the factors that drive artrepreneurship, which we measure in terms of self-reported employment status. Hypotheses 1, 2 and 4 propose artistry, passion and individual difference factors as such drivers.

We first use univariate tests for difference between the three artistic occupational groups, i.e. artrepreneurs, freelancers and employees. We do not include the fourth group ("other") due to its small number and ambiguous interpretation. Kruskal–Wallis tests show that the three groups differ significantly only in emotionality ($p=0.009$), marginally in conscientiousness ($p=0.055$) and impulsivity (p=0.053). In particular, among the three groups, artrepreneurs have the highest scores for conscientiousness and the lowest for emotionality as well as impulsivity. There were no significant group differences for any of the other psychological characteristics, artistry or the two artrepreneurial passion factors.

These results reflect other studies that find conscientiousness and low emotionality to be more associated with entrepreneurs than other occupational groups (e.g. Zhao and Seibert 2006). For impulsiveness, the literature provides no clear guide because, as discussed, this construct is related to both being an artist and being an entrepreneur.

Table 4 shows the regression results which confirm artistry overall is not a significant explanator of artrepreneurship. Drilling down to the constituent parts of artistry we see that artistic standing alone is associated with artrepreneurship, but the relationship is negative. There is therefore no evidence that artistry positively affects artrepreneurship suggesting other, non-artistic factors may be driving entrepreneurial spirit among artists.

Result 4 *There is no evidence supporting* H1: *Artistry is not a significant driver of artrepreneurship.*

We next examine the role individual difference factors play in artrepreneurship. Controlling for personal demographics, half of the HEXACO-dimensions are significantly related to artrepreneurship. Compared to the other artists, artrepreneurs tend to be less emotional, less impulsive and less agreeable but more conscientious. These results are in line with our univariate findings above. The former two results also support previous findings that business entrepreneurs are significantly less emotional and impulsive than artists (self-citation, 2020).

Result 5 *Artrepreneurship is significantly associated with certain individual difference factors including low emotionality and impulsivity and agreeableness and conscientiousness, supporting* H4.

We finally examine to what extent artrepreneurial passion drives artrepreneurship. The results are contained in model 5 of Table 4. It shows that neither dimension has a significant effect on artrepreneurship.[1] This finding is unexpected because of the evidence that passion significantly explains entrepreneurial behaviour in a business context. The validity and/or reliability of our new construct is a potential explanation. On the other hand, we saw that it relates significantly (and in the expected directions) to other measures.

Result 6 *There is no evidence supporting* H2: *Artrepreneurial passion is not a significant driver of artrepreneurship.*

[1] This finding does not depend on our two-dimensional approach to artrepreneurial passion. When we enter AP as a single dimension as an average of all 13 questionnaire items the coefficient fails to achieve statistical significance. The Pearson correlation coefficient between artrepreneurship and artrepreneurial passion is only 0.0301.

Table 4 Regression results for artrepreneur status (ARTE, Probit). Standardised beta coefficients with standard errors in parentheses

	(1) ARTE	(2) ARTE	(3) ARTE	(4) ARTE	(5) ARTE
ARTISTRY	−0.005		−0.113	0.141	
	(0.0780)		(0.0801)	(0.0878)	
Education	−0.360	−0.531*	−0.488	−0.336	−0.385
	(0.204)	(0.216)	(0.213)	(0.203)	(0.210)
Female	−0.128	−0.004	0.286	−0.172	−0.148
	(0.246)	(0.253)	(0.290)	(0.252)	(0.247)
Age	0.970***	1.116***	1.044***	0.814**	0.959***
	(0.0130)	(0.0135)	(0.0147)	(0.0135)	(0.0131)
INCOME		−0.374			
		(0.177)			
STAGE		0.450			
		(0.294)			
TIME		0.526			
		(0.223)			
STAND		−0.870**			
		(0.464)			
HEX-H			0.247		
			(0.269)		
HEX-E			−1.191***		
			(0.285)		
HEX-X			−0.192		
			(0.278)		
HEX-A			−0.800**		
			(0.283)		
HEX-C			1.025***		
			(0.406)		
HEX-O			−0.150		
			(0.431)		
INTMOT				0.055	
				(0.304)	
IMPULS				−0.695**	
				(0.309)	
AP-COM					−0.235
					(0.145)
AP-NEW					0.087
					(0.328)
N	75	75	75	75	75
χ^2	9.431	16.529	29.394	14.538	9.982

$^*p < 0.10$, $^{**}p < 0.05$, $^{***}p < 0.01$

4 Discussion and conclusions

This study attempted to identify the individual-level factors resulting in an artist's decision to commercialise their art as an artrepreneur. Our study is, to our knowledge, the first to measure artrepreneurship in individuals and therefore also the first to examine the individual-level antecedents of it.

Based on existing relevant literature, we hypothesised the effect of three groups of factors. The first two involved several psychological individual differences and artistic profile antecedents. The third was a new a measure of artrepreneurial passion that we hypothesised to be a factor based on relevant theory in entrepreneurship. Our overall finding is that the psychological constructs have the greatest explanatory power, with both artistry and artrepreneurial passion not exerting a significant influence on artrepreneurship. We now discuss these results.

The overall impression from our results is tentative support for a disconnect between the intrinsic motivations of artists, as in art for art's sake, and the commercial aspects of business venturing using one's creative practice. Several facts speak to this. Artistry was not related to artrepreneurship even though, in a sense, it provides the business case for the venture. Artistic standing is negatively associated with artrepreneurship. Intrinsic motivation was negatively related to one dimension artrepreneurship. Overall the profile of the artrepreneur compared to other artists (high conscientiousness, low emotionality and impulsivity) reflects the difference between artists and the general population. This raises the question whether artrepreneurs are less typically artistic in nature. It may be that the same underlying source of artistry at the same time motivates resistance to sell it: What makes a person artistic may be also make them perceive and resist the idea of "selling out". We feel that this possibility warrants a closer look in future research because if true, it would constitute a major impediment to artrepreneurship.

We made a first, exploratory step to the development of an artrepreneurial passion instrument, based on an equivalent construct in entrepreneurship. The two dimensions we identified stand for distinct sources of artrepreneurial passion, a commercial and an innovative passion. Both have modest but acceptable internal consistency. Neither was a significant explanator of artrepreneurship. Future work may improve the adaptation of the entrepreneurial passion instrument to artrepreneurship with a larger sample size.

We should note that in terms of our main dependent variable the bar is set high. We measure actual artrepreneurship rather than aspirational or intended commercialisation of an artist's creative practice. Our dichotomous measure is therefore rather blunt. Also, some business-minded artists may have chosen to commercialise albeit within the more predictable environment of a salaried artistic occupation. A more fine-grained measure may be a desirable development of our work. We should also note the modest sample size occasioned by logistical challenges. Future work with a greater number of artists of different types and experiences would no doubt improve the reliability and validity of results.

The policy implications from our work come from a better understanding of the individual difference characteristics that influence what type of artist a person typically becomes. Such insight is important for cultural policy and artistic professional development. Self-awareness has been identified as an important skill in managing the artistic career in an increasingly adverse funding environment. Policy and artrepreneurial education programmes may be targeted towards the drivers of artrepreneurship not associated with the typical artist (e.g. Roberts 2012; Brown 2005).

Our findings speak to the explanatory power of personality and motivation-based individual difference factors that have fallen out of fashion within entrepreneurship. A number of authors have cast doubt on the personality approach to entrepreneurship that may also limit what such approaches can reveal about artrepreneurship (e.g. Duening 2010). Our results echo the sentiment of Zhao and Seibert (2006, p. 259) "that this conclusion is premature and may truncate theory development in the field of entrepreneurship by unnecessarily precluding personality variables".

A number of limitations of the current study should be noted. The first is the relatively modest sample occasioned from the logistical challenges associated with recruiting artists for a laboratory-based study. We believe our findings have to be interpreted in this light. Our exploratory results nonetheless provide hypotheses for future work to examine using larger samples. In addition, there are limits on the number of questionnaire items that can be elicited before fatigue or demotivation to participate set in, further challenging recruitment. Future studies with larger and different samples should be conducted to replicate our results to further support our conclusions. Larger sample sallow for more sophisticated statistical tools to assess the possibility of autocatalytic relationship between artrepreneurship and artrepreneurial passion, equivalent to such relationships detected in entrepreneurship research. Here, entrepreneurial passion has been found to be simultaneously a cause and an effect of entrepreneurial behaviour (Gielnik et al. 2015).

We close by observing that individual difference factors are one of a complex set of internal and external factors that should be evaluated in the context of other findings. Similarly, while the human psychology may give a fatalistic impression of constant suitability to commercialise art and venture out, this is far from the case. Self-reflection, development of behavioural competencies and personalities that adapt to experience provide plenty of room for improving artrepreneurship that is partly determined by individual difference factors.

References

Abbing, H. (2008). *Why are artists poor? The exceptional economy of the arts*. Amsterdam: Amsterdam University Press.

Abuhamdeh, S., & Csikszentmihalyi, M. (2014). The artistic personality: A systems perspective. In *The systems model of creativity* (pp. 227–237). Springer.

Alper, N. O., & Wassall, G. H. (2006). Artists' careers and their labor markets. *Handbook of the economics of art and culture, 1*, 813–864.

Arenius P, Chuah SH, Coate B, & Hoffmann R (2020). The economic psychology of creating and venturing: A comparative behavioural portrait of artists and entrepreneurs. *Small Business Economics*, published 3 November. https://doi.org/10.1007/s11187-020-00420-1.

Ashton, M. C., & Lee, K. (2009). The HEXACO-60: A short measure of the major dimensions of personality. *Journal of Personality Assessment, 91*(4), 340–345.

Beckman, G. D. (2007). "Adventuring" arts entrepreneurship curricula in higher education: An examination of present efforts, obstacles, and best practices. *The Journal of Arts Management, Law, and Society, 37*(2), 87–112.
Bille, T. (2020). Artists' labour markets. In *Handbook of Cultural Economics*. Edward Elgar Publishing, Camberley.
Bridgestock, L. (2013). Graduate jobs: What employers look for. *QS Top Grad School Guide*, 2013–2014.
Bridgstock, R. (2013). Not a dirty word: Arts entrepreneurship and higher education. *Arts and Humanities in Higher Education, 12*(2–3), 122–137.
Brink, E. (2011). *The Artrepreneur: Financial success for artistic souls*. Bergen: Papy Publishing.
Brown, R. (2005). Performing arts creative enterprise: Approaches to promoting entrepreneurship in arts higher education. *The International Journal of Entrepreneurship and Innovation, 6*(3), 159–167.
Busenitz, L. W., & Barney, J. B. (1997). Differences between entrepreneurs and managers in large organizations: Biases and heuristics in strategic decision-making. *Journal of Business Venturing, 12*(1), 9–30.
Campos, J., Ericsson, N. R., & Hendry, D. F. (2005). *General-to-specific modelling*. Camberley: Edward Elgar.
Cardon, M. S., Gregoire, D. A., Stevens, C. E., & Patel, P. C. (2013). Measuring entrepreneurial passion: Conceptual foundations and scale validation. *Journal of Business Venturing, 28*, 373–396.
Cardon, M. S., Wincent, J., Singh, J., & Drnovsek, M. (2009). The nature and experience of entrepreneurial passion. *Academy of Management Review, 34*(3), 511–532.
Carey, C., & Naudin, A. (2006). *Enterprise curriculum for creative industries students*. Education+ Training.
Carland, J. W., Hoy, F., Boulton, W. R., & Carland, J. A. C. (1984). Differentiating entrepreneurs from small business owners: A conceptualization. *Academy of Management Review, 9*(2), 354–359.
Catani, M., & Mazzarello, P. (2019). Grey Matter Leonardo da Vinci: A genius driven to distraction. *Brain, 142*(6), 1842–1846.
Caust, J. (2019). The continuing saga around arts funding and the cultural wars in Australia. *International Journal of Cultural Policy, 25*(6), 765–779.
Coate, B., Hoffmann, R., Arenius, P., & Chuah, S.-H. (2021). A behavioural approach to understanding the artist as entrepreneur. In E. Lazzaro, N. Moureau, & A. Turpin (Eds.), *Researching Arts Markets: Past, Present and Tools for the Future*. Routledge.
Cross, P. G., Cattell, R. B., & Butcher, H. J. (1967). The personality pattern of creative artists. *British Journal of Educational Psychology, 37*(3), 292–299.
Darmer, P. (2008). Entrepreneurs in music: The passion of experience creation. In J. Sundbo (Ed.), *Creating experiences in the experience economy* (p. 6). Ch: Edward Elgar Publishing.
Drevdahl, J. E., & Cattell, R. B. (1958). Personality and creativity in artists and writers. *Journal of Clinical Psychology, 14*, 107.
Duening, T. N. (2010). Five minds for the entrepreneurial future: Cognitive skills as the intellectual foundation for next generation entrepreneurship curricula. *The Journal of Entrepreneurship, 19*(1), 1–22.
Eikhof, D. R., & Haunschild, A. (2007). For art's sake! artistic and economic logics in creative production. *Journal of Organizational Behavior: The International Journal of Industrial, Occupational and Organizational Psychology and Behavior, 28*(5), 523–538.
Engelmann, M., Grünewald, L., & Heinrich, J. (2012). The new artrepreneur-how artists can thrive on a networked music business. *International Journal of Music Business Research, 1*(2), 31–45.
Feist, G. J. (1998). A meta-analysis of personality in scientific and artistic creativity. *Personality and Social Psychology Review, 2*(4), 290–309.
Frese, M., & Gielnik, M. M. (2014). The psychology of entrepreneurship. *Annual Review of Organizational Psychology and Organizational Behavior, 1*(1), 413–438.
Frey, B. S., & Pommerehne, W. W. (1989). *Muses and Markets: Explorations in the Economics of the Arts*. Hoboken: Blackwell.
Gielnik, M. M., Spitzmuller, M., Schmitt, A., Klemann, D. K., & Frese, M. (2015). "I put in effort, therefore I am passionate": Investigating the path from effort to passion in entrepreneurship. *Academy of Management Journal, 58*(4), 1012–1031.
Götz, K. O., & Götz, K. (1979). Personality characteristics of successful artists. *Perceptual and Motor Skills, 49*(3), 919–924.
Henry, C. (2007). *Entrepreneurship in the creative industries: An international perspective*. Cheltenham: Edward Elgar Publishing.

Honos-Webb, L. (2010). *The gift of ADHD: How to transform your child's problems into strengths*. New Harbinger Publications.
Kemp, A. E. (1996). *The musical temperament: Psychology and personality of musicians*. Oxford: Oxford University Press.
Kessler, R. C., Adler, L., Ames, M., Demler, O., Faraone, S., Hiripi, E., et al. (2005). The World Health Organization adult ADHD Self-Report Scale (ASRS): A short screening scale for use in the general population. *Psychological Medicine, 35*(2), 245.
Lerner, D. A., Hunt, R. A., & Verheul, I. (2018). Dueling banjos: Harmony and discord between ADHD and entrepreneurship. *Academy of Management Perspectives, 32*(2), 266–286.
Lingo, E. L., & Tepper, S. J. (2013). Looking back, looking forward: Arts-based careers and creative work. *Work and Occupations, 40*(4), 337–363.
Obschonka, M., Moeller, J., & Goethner, M. (2019). Entrepreneurial passion and personality: The case of academic entrepreneurship. *Frontiers in Psychology, 9*, 2697.
Pekkala Kerr, S., Kerr, W. R., & Xu, T. (2017). *Personality traits of entrepreneurs: A review of recent literature*. Cambridge: National Bureau of Economic Research.
Pollard, V. (2013). The "entrepreneurial mindset" in creative and performing arts higher education in Australia. *Activate, 3*(1), 53–63.
Roberts, J. S. (2012). Infusing entrepreneurship within non-business disciplines: Preparing artists and others for self-employment and entrepreneurship. *Activate, 1*(2), 53–63.
Shaver, K. G., & Scott, L. R. (1992). Person, process, choice: The psychology of new venture creation. *Entrepreneurship Theory and Practice, 16*(2), 23–46.
Simonton, D. K. (2014). Historiometric studies of genius. *The Wiley Handbook of Genius*, 87–106.
United Nations. (2019). *Creative economy outlook: Trends in international trade in creative industries 2002–2015*.
VandeWalle, D. (1997). Development and validation of a work domain goal orientation instrument. *Educational and Psychological Measurement, 57*(6), 995–1015.
Verheul, I., Block, J., Burmeister-Lamp, K., Thurik, R., Tiemeier, H., & Turturea, R. (2015). ADHD-like behavior and entrepreneurial intentions. *Small Business Economics, 45*(1), 85–101.
Wiklund, J., Yu, W., Tucker, R., & Marino, L. D. (2017). ADHD, impulsivity and entrepreneurship. *Journal of Business Venturing, 32*(6), 627–656.
Woronkowicz, J., & Noonan, D. S. (2019). Who goes freelance? The determinants of self-employment for artists. *Entrepreneurship Theory and Practice, 43*(4), 651–672.
Zhao, H., & Seibert, S. E. (2006). The big five personality dimensions and entrepreneurial status: A meta-analytical review. *Journal of Applied Psychology, 91*(2), 259.

Journal of Cultural Economics (2021) 45:577–611
https://doi.org/10.1007/s10824-021-09415-6

ORIGINAL ARTICLE

Flocking to the crowd: Cultural entrepreneur mobility guided by homophily, market size, or amenities?

Douglas S. Noonan[1] · Shiri M. Breznitz[2] · Sana Maqbool[2]

Received: 14 August 2020 / Accepted: 26 March 2021 / Published online: 16 April 2021

Abstract

Economic activity and innovation clusters in urban areas. Urban economics points to important knowledge and productivity spillovers in cities, in addition to other factors like thicker markets, lower transportation costs, and consumptive amenities. Yet thus far little work has analyzed how these different factors drive migration decisions of arts-related entrepreneurs, especially when they work in online platforms for fundraising. We use data on the largest US crowdfunding platform to identify relocating creators, allowing us to identify which kinds of regions are attracting and retaining more of this sort of talent. We test for the influence of clustering based on homophily, migration to larger markets, and relocation toward particular geographic amenities. Overall we find the strongest evidence for homophily and some distinct tendencies favoring certain regional amenities. Importantly, we both identify general relocation patterns among crowdfunding creatives and break down the attracting features for different types of creators. An examination of (net) migration by different categories of projects, such as musicians or filmmakers, reveals important heterogeneity in the attractors. For example, musicians are drawn stronger music sectors, while writers seek more isolation from other writers. This helps inform the interregional competition for talent and "creative class," especially among a group of relatively footloose arts- and culture-intensive entrepreneurs.

Keywords Crowdfunding · Cultural entrepreneurs · Migration · Regional competition · Clustering · Knowledge spillovers

JEL Classifications Z10 · L26 · R23 · R11 · L82

✉ Sana Maqbool
sana.maqbool@mail.utoronto.ca

1 Center for Cultural Affairs, Indiana University-Purdue University Indianapolis, Indianapolis, USA

2 Munk School of Global Affairs and Public Policy, University of Toronto, Toronto, Canada

1 Introduction

Amidst a rising tide of urbanization, uneven trajectories in the growth and economic vitality of cities draw attention to the underlying conditions and forces influencing these dynamics. The observed clustering of human capital and innovation in certain urban regions are set against a backdrop of globalization and increasing use of online and digital technologies. Regions compete to attract and retain talent. While high-skilled labor and entrepreneurs in innovative or high-tech sectors receive much attention, arts and culture can play a role, too, directly producing innovation or indirectly supporting innovation and growth (Florida, 2002; Rodríguez-Pose & Lee, 2020). The "creative class" and "creative industries" are often touted as catalysts for innovative hubs and contributors to the economic engine (Lee, 2014; Sleuwaegen & Boiardi, 2014). Yet, if creative and cultural entrepreneurs are valuable ingredients to vibrant regional economies, then rather little is known about the factors that attract or retain this creative talent. Attracting cultural entrepreneurs, especially in a digital age, may not follow traditional clustering patterns.

Human capital is one of the most important factors in today's knowledge economy and is an essential part of any industrial cluster (Porter, 1990). Hundreds of scholars around the world emphasize the importance of co-location of related industries (Piore and Sable, 1984, Porter, 1990). Initially, clusters were based on the location of their basic resources, mostly natural resources such as energy and access to transport. Over time, as the industrial process became flexible, transportation costs went down, and markets became increasingly important, industrial clusters specialized in parts of the production chain such as research, design, development, and manufacturing. Today, in the global economy, most advanced companies focus on R&D rather than manufacturing their own product. Subsequently, the ability of highly skilled human capital to transfer knowledge, by leveraging their social capital, became the most important resource that determines the ability of industries and regional development (Granovetter, 1973; Putnam, 1995). As cities compete for resources, the most sought-after resource became human capital.

According to Moretti (2012), the polarized US has some cities attracting more high-skilled workers than others, leading to winning and losing cities. On one side, "brain hub" cities include those with the largest share of workers with college degrees (e.g., Samford, CT; Boston, MA; San Jose, CA). On the other side are cities with the lowest share of workers with college degrees (e.g., Flint, MI; Yuma, AZ; Merced, CA). These cities have higher unemployment rates and outmigration. Moretti's winning cities depend on a balance between the supply of labor and the availability of jobs. Companies want to locate in winning cities to ensure access to the top talent while workers want to reside in winning cities to secure the best jobs. Policymakers promote their city's economic status by attracting either employers or workers.

At the same time, the creative class literature (Florida, 2002) highlights how winning cities can attract innovative workers by investing in amenities, such as culture and environment. In addition, workers in the arts and cultural sector may themselves directly contribute to innovation and revitalize a local economy

(Rodríguez-Pose & Lee, 2020). Importantly, artists contribute to local economy directly through their own innovative work as well as help make places more attractive for other high-human-capital workers to live, work, and innovate in (Tubadji et al., 2015). In the words of Markusen and Schrock, "regional artists can enhance the quality and saleability of products and services of other businesses in the region who are customers of or suppliers to artists" (Markusen & Schrock, 2006, p. 1662). Artists do well in larger cities due to demand for their work and the agglomeration of related art fields (Blau, 1989; Holcomb, 1999; Judd, 1999; Scott, 2005), most of which correlate with wealthier and larger cities. Cities compete to attract the creative class (Buettner & Janeba, 2016), yet what drives success is not well established.

Entrepreneurship plays a crucial role in job creation and economic development (Acs, 1992, Minniti and Levesque, 2008) as entrepreneurship is a tool that fosters innovation and economic growth (Acs et al., 2008). Thus, it is important to understand the factors that create a fruitful entrepreneurial environment. According to Hoffmann (2007), there are six major determinants of entrepreneurship: access to resources, specifically technology and finance; the capabilities and access to skilled labor; market conditions which lead to opportunities, including access to customers; the regulatory framework; and cultural factors, such as a collaborative environment where entrepreneurs support each other. We are particularly interested in the market access and collaborative environment aspects of a region's influence on entrepreneurship. Entrepreneurs may choose to relocate, either permanently or temporarily, to take advantage of the entrepreneurial ecosystem in a different region in an effort to minimize the risk associated with launching a new venture (Mittelstädt and Cerri, 2008). Entrepreneurs' use networks of support and access to finance or customers often to generate employment and value in a region. As cities compete to attract entrepreneurs, it is important to decipher the attributes that attract entrepreneurs to start a business in one city over another.

The emergence of the platform economy raises questions around the relevance of winning and losing cities. When high-skilled workers can work from anywhere as long as they have internet connection, we might see limited movement of platform users between cities. However, this is not the case. Our analysis of a large database of crowdfunding entrepreneurs in the creative sector shows fairly frequent relocations. Our sample, for instance, shows an interstate annual mobility rates of 2.9%, which is substantially greater than Basso and Peri show (2020). Hence, this paper asks: what regional attributes explain which metros attract more online creators? We leverage this novel database of creators using a crowdfunding platform to fundraise to trace their relocations and assess which regions are attracting more of this talent. We test alternative hypotheses regarding tendencies to migrate near others like them (leveraging spillovers in their area of economic activity), to move to better markets, or to relocate to regions with nicer (consumptive) amenities like climate. We find strong and consistent evidence in support of the homophily hypothesis, although important differences arise across different types of creatives (e.g., those in fine arts vs. filmmakers). Despite fundraising in a cloud-based platform, local market size and environmental amenities still play roles in attracting entrepreneurial projects and migrants.

Recent attention to "gig workers," the "platform economy," and freelance work in the creative sector raises questions about recent dynamics in supporting and growing innovative talent. In an arts and cultural sector characterized by diverse work (e.g., full-time vs. part-time, primary job vs. secondary/hobby, employee vs. self-employed), many datasets and analyses can overlook entrepreneurial efforts undertaken as "gigs" or side projects. Our analysis addresses this gap by using a dominant crowdfunding platform to essentially capture snapshots over time of cultural entrepreneurs on the platform. Our focus on crowdfunding creators contributes insight into where these potentially more transitory creative efforts are relocating. This complements other studies of cultural entrepreneurs with more persistent or conventional funding. And without directly observing cultural entrepreneurs' relocations and their motivations, focusing on the cities that gain or lose these projects reveals systematic patterns in the data. Our novel approach allows us to track the relocating of projects by the same creator, revealing where new creative ventures are moving. This is important as online platform-based creative work may decouple where an entrepreneur lives from where they work.

We start by discussing several bodies of literature. We examine studies on city attractiveness, the literature on entrepreneurial mobility, and studies related to factors influencing relocation decisions of artists and creative talent. Next, we describe the data on crowdfunding creators and other region-specific data. We then introduce our model and empirical estimation technique, taking account of dual processes that may underlie region's net migration. After presenting the results, we discuss them in light of the alternative hypotheses about which forces are most important for attracting this potentially footloose group of creative entrepreneurs. Finally, we review these findings in the context of policy implications for regional competition and development.

2 Literature review

Cities are attractive due to a variety of advantages they provide to workers and firms in general. Strong agglomeration forces can arise from locational advantages for firms in larger markets, such as larger scales with more productivity-enhancing capital and better access to consumers. In such circumstances, workers who migrate to cities immediately benefit from a wage premium (Krupka & Noonan, 2013). Knowledge-based explanations for clustering in cities—such as human capital that is enhanced by proximity to and spillovers from others in the city (the 'city air' as Alfred Marshall called it)—receive considerable attention in urbanization and migration literatures (e.g., Ellison et al. 2010). Glaeser (2010) notes that at the center of agglomeration economies lies the knowledge gained from interactions in urban areas that enhances the development of human capital and increases the flow of ideas. Further, Glaeser maintains that despite being the most expensive regions, the opportunities to share networks and resources makes cities extremely desirable and advantageous to work in. Brail (2020) states that some of the benefits from working near other firms within agglomeration economies include the provision of strong networks of such shared knowledge, research activity, labor pools, and training programs. These opportunities come from the co-location of supporting institutions, universities, and governance structures that encourage economic development.

While there may be a taste for certain urban centers that correlates with high-skill workers and artists, other factors beyond sorting support agglomeration. Larger cities provide thicker markets for specialized inputs and better labor matching. These forces, much like benefits from knowledge spillovers, encourage clustering in urban centers. These findings align with the work of Chen and Rosenthal (2008) who demonstrate that workers with higher human capital tend to migrate to productive regions, where they can take advantage of their skills. In general cities specializing in industries with stronger agglomeration economies will experience greater economic gains from a larger population density. Krupka and Noonan (2013) leverage differences in experience and tenure to show how a mix of knowledge spillovers and better matching helps explain urban advantages, especially for the largest and smallest cities. Thus we might expect to see arts-related entrepreneurs migrate to or between cities in search of better access to customers or funders (better markets), better potential job matches or complementary productive partners (better matches), or better spillover opportunities (better networks and learning). Relocation can bring arts entrepreneurs to better markets or spillovers as they "flock together."

In his work on *The New Geography of Jobs*, Moretti (2012) defines unique cities that attract top talent as "Brain Hubs." His analysis indicates that "stars" prefer some cities over others due to homophily: people's desire to be with similar people. Thus, according to Moretti, highly skilled workers prefer cities with people who possess similar interests and level of knowledge. Nevertheless, studies have shown that cities can attract top talent using other strategies, beyond homophily, such as promoting culture and providing certain amenities (Florida, 2002). Glaeser and Maré (2001) argue that there are four critical urban amenities which contribute to the desirability of a city. These include a rich variety of services and consumer goods, aesthetics and physical setting, good public services, and the ease of movement. They argue that if cities are to continue to be prosperous, they must attract workers through appealing quality-of-life factors and higher wages. Moreover, a greater variety of cuisines and cultural amenities such as museums and preforming arts contribute to cities' development and attraction of human capital (Schiff, 2015; Glaeser & Maré, 2001). Glaeser and Maré's (2001) findings suggest that cities with greater amenities have grown at faster rates than low amenity cities.

The approaches that give primacy to amenities or tolerant cultures in explaining urban growth and migration have generated large literatures and several critiques. That critiques of Florida's "creative class" thesis are well-rehearsed at this point (e.g., Borén & Young, 2013a) underscores the ongoing interest in the drivers of migration of creative and talented workers. Storper and Scott (2009) argue for a primacy of production and jobs—the dynamics of job creation—rather than amenities, tastes, or changing factor mobility. They see high-skilled workers as ultimately following employment opportunities. Although amenities can accelerate urban growth, the inflow of high skilled workers will cease if the supply of jobs dries up. Chen and Rosenthal (2008) find that cities with growing business environments attract more workers, particularly higher skilled, highly educated, and younger workers, while cities with growing amenities typically attract retired persons, regardless of education level. Specifically examining the impact of cultural workers, Rodriguez-Pose and Lee's (2020) research highlights the need for diverse knowledge within cities. They examine the contribution of scientific and creative activity to innovation in cities. They find that innovation in US cities results from both STEM workers and creative workers' activities. Tubadji et al. (2015) argue for the importance of arts workers in supporting growth and in attracting immigration in the US, though their work looks only at international immigration and does not focus on migration of artists themselves.

Studies in economics examining artists' relocation decisions are rare. Kelly and O'Hagan (2007) investigate the global pattern of geographic artist clustering by birth location, the labor migration patterns and internal clustering of Italian Renaissance artists, and the internal and external labor migration of artists in France in the nineteenth century. They identify four sets of factors to consider for formation of clusters in particular regions: wealth, artistic freedom, chance events, and factor conditions. Wealth is seen as a necessary condition for a city to generate artistic clustering, as high income translated to high artistic demand and a competitive market. Factors of production, capital resources, and infrastructure also determine cluster locations and migration patterns for artists. Lopez (2019) models sorting between urban areas in the presence of mobile cultural producers who can serve high-income residents with high demand while struggling to afford to live in affluent cities. His model emphasizes the tensions of congestion and cost of living for cultural producers in cities with agglomeration economies while also highlighting equilibria with cultural workers moving to smaller markets and the importance of diversity in a region's cultural offerings.

Regional amenities can have distinct draws on migrating artists. Regional attributes like learning opportunities, labor markets, and professional networks (rather than outdoor amenities) matter most for migrating creatives (Borén & Young, 2013b; Hansen & Niedomysl, 2009). Markusen (2013) uses older data from the U.S. Census Public Use Microdata Series and American Community Survey data to explore the location of U.S. artists and their migration patterns to and from major metropolitan areas. The author finds that artists actively move among cities of all sizes but are pulled to centers of metros as their presence is low in suburban areas. While she hypothesizes cities gaining in migrating artists to be those with better complementary factors and learning opportunities, better scale economies, higher incomes, lower costs-of-living, and better lifestyle amenities, Markusen (2013) does not formally test these hypotheses. She finds artists to be distributed widely across the country, moving frequently, and exhibiting different migration patterns among visual artists, performing artists, and writers. Housing supply and cost of living surely helps explain the presence of artist clusters in smaller markets (Lopez, 2019; Markusen, 2013). Berlin and Detroit (after the 2008 financial crisis) are examples of cities with large concentrations of arts-related employment and artists who were drawn to these cities partly because of housing availability and cost of living (Ewing and Grady, 2012). Buettner and Janeba (2016) find subsidizing a local cultural public good to be effective in attracting a highly productive mobile creative class in Germany.

It is difficult to distinguish a set of variables that create agglomeration economies as they arise due to a combination of historical momentum—regional growth rooted in path-dependent economic evolution (Scott, 2006; Storper & Manville, 2006)—and policies that attract high skilled workers to a region (Storper & Scott, 1995). More recent migration patterns of entrepreneurial artists should reflect major technological and labor market shifts. The rise of the "platform economy" and "gig workers" in the US (Kenney & Zysman, 2020) may increase self-employment rates, reduce locational dependency on a single employer, and empower more mobility among artists. This may be especially true for more solitary creators like visual artists and writers (Markusen, 2013). In addition, the rise of online crowdfunding to provide new ways to earn revenue (Lazzaro & Noonan, 2020; Regner, 2020) may entail different relocation pressures. We contribute new evidence on this emerging topic of platform-based (or "platform-dependent") entrepreneurs, especially their geography, which thus far has not received much attention (Kenney & Zysman, 2020). Crowdfunding allows potential entrepreneurs to raise funds irrespective of location. As a result, as Sorenson et al. (2016) show, we see far less spatial concentration of crowdfunding activity than we do for traditional financial support for entrepreneurs. Yet decisions to stay or go can affect one's social network, critical to new forms of cultural participation (Peukert, 2019). For instance, moving may cost an individual access to their prior local network while improving their access to a new local network. Distance to potential funders matters for crowdfunding success (Mendes-Da-Silva et al. 2016), so entrepreneurs may relocate to gain proximity to the "crowd" of funders. If crowdfunding entrepreneurs' relocation decisions relate to their past or future crowdfunding activity, then it raises questions about what kind of places they tend to seek or remain at. Some locations may provide a more supportive environment or market than others.

3 Data

We analyze which regions attract more online platform-dependent, creative entrepreneurs, and which regions are losing them, after combining several data sources. Detailed data on artistic entrepreneurs' mobility, at a national scale, can be scarce in terms of the geography or classification of "arts related." The prevalence of arts-related ventures by entrepreneurs outside of their primary occupation further limits the usefulness of most large-scale public datasets. To address this, we employ a rich dataset from Kickstarter—a reward-based crowdfunding platform, notable for its arts- and culture-intensive portfolio of campaigns and for being the dominant crowdfunding platform in the United States (Dalla Chiesa & Handke, 2020; Lazzaro & Noonan, 2020). We use this platform to indirectly track the relocation of projects of creative entrepreneurs who use the platform multiple times yet change locations between campaigns. The Kickstarter platform is arguably the world's largest crowdfunding platform—thus far with over $5 billion raised from over 18 million backers for almost 200,000 successful projects—and remains the dominant platform of its kind in the US market. The great majority of Kickstarter campaigns related to artistic and creative ventures, reflecting Kickstarter's mission "to help bring creative

Table 1 Frequencies of crowdfunding campaigns by Kickstarter category

	Among repeat-creators only		All projects
	Count	% Share	% Share
Art	2048	7.95	10.72
Comics	1812	7.03	3.79
Crafts	540	2.10	3.37
Dance	429	1.66	1.64
Design	2016	7.82	3.84
Fashion	1018	3.95	5.54
Film & Video	3792	14.71	13.79
Food	988	3.83	7.90
Games	3651	14.16	6.75
Journalism	169	0.66	2.29
Music	3537	13.72	13.71
Photography	625	2.42	3.43
Publishing	2820	10.94	10.08
Technology	1323	5.13	10.33
Theater	1007	3.91	2.81
Total	25,775	100	100

projects to life" (Kickstarter, 2020). Reflecting their commitment to art and creative expression, most campaigns fall into top-level categories related to arts (see Table 1).

Using data scraped from all Kickstarter projects (successful or not) launched from its start through 2016 (Li, 2019), we identify the subset of all project creators with multiple campaigns. This amounts to over 25,000 repeat creators in the Kickstarter data. Almost 24% of these creators list different locations for their successive campaigns. To be clear, the data do not track actual migration of the project creators, but rather the location of the project itself. Thus, although we refer to this as relocating entrepreneurs or creators, it is actually their projects or ventures that relocate in our data. When the locations entrepreneurs' residences and ventures diverge, this approach has the advantage of focusing on where the economic activity or project is located. Using the locations for each project, we map the full set of projects to their urbanized region (Core-Based Statistical Area, or CBSA), including 942 metropolitan and micropolitan regions across the US. CBSAs capture regional economies and can vary widely in terms of demographic, economic, and environmental characteristics in the US. Further, aggregating to the CBSA level allows us to focus on major relocations and not local moves.

A number of publicly available datasets that capture the characteristics of the CBSAs complement the Kickstarter data. We gather additional data on employment (by NAICS code, for Creative Class), demographics, the presence of arts-specialty schools, and climate at the CBSA level. This includes socioeconomic indicators like total population, average household income, the number of residents with a college degree or higher, and the number of residents with employment, as well as the cost of living in each CBSA. We add information about the employment concentrations by sector for CBSA residents. The Martin Prosperity Institute Local IDEAs database (2010) provides data on the proportion of creative class workers. In addition, we use 2010 employment data from the Bureau of Labor Statistics based on NAICS codes at the CBSA level to estimate employment concentration in sectors related to Kickstarter categories. We also control for "brain hub" CBSAs from Moretti (2012), related to the proportion of employed with graduate degrees, and for CBSAs around "platform hubs" (Kenney & Zysman, 2020) like Seattle and San Francisco. Additionally, we join data related to regional characteristics like climate attributes (McGranahan, 1999), land area, and whether the CBSA contains a coastline. Lastly, we also use data on the number of arts-specialty schools located in each CBSA (Breznitz & Noonan, 2018). Table 2 contains details on variable definitions. See the "Appendix" for additional information on how employment data were linked to Kickstarter categories.

Assembling the data for each metropolitan and micropolitan region allows a focus on which regions better attract relocations of creative entrepreneurs, controlling for factors describing the region's conditions. This helps inform the inter-regional competition for talent and "creative class," especially among a group of relatively footloose arts- and culture-intensive entrepreneurs. (This approach tells us little about why an arts entrepreneur would pick one city or one neighborhood over another. It focuses on inter-regional competition.) Almost half of the relocating repeat creators actually move their venture to a location outside of their original CBSA. Even with almost a quarter million distinct crowdfunding projects, and 25,000 repeat creators using this platform, the number of relocating creatives in the data dwindles—partly reflecting the specialized nature of this subgroup. The descriptive statistics in Table 3 show CBSA characteristics and how those attributes differ for those CBSAs experiencing nonzero net migration. Focusing on *net* migration implies a mean net migration value near to zero because, except for some 'leakage' involving locations outside of CBSAs in the US, it is a zero-sum measure. The shaded rows in Table 3 indicate net migration of particular subsets of creators based on the Kickstarter category of their initial project. More CBSAs naturally experience nonzero net migration for broader categories of creators (e.g., Arts) than narrower categories (e.g., Technology). Comparing the set of all CBSAs with just those experiencing nonzero net migration (i.e., 'winners' and 'losers'), Table 3 shows how the regions with more churn in these creative entrepreneurs tend to be larger, more educated, more coastal, more urban, and home to more Kickstarter projects overall. Among the many regions experiencing nonzero net migration of these creators, Table 4 indicates the CBSAs with the greatest positive and negative net migration. While some of the biggest 'winner' metro areas (e.g., San Francisco, Seattle, Nashville) may not be very surprising, other 'loser' metro areas (e.g., Boston, Austin, San Diego) suggest that simple narratives received from the more general literature on the new geography of jobs or general entrepreneurial mobility might not capture well the dynamics among these relatively footloose creative entrepreneurs.

Table 2 Variable descriptions

Variable	Description
NetMigration	Number of Kickstarter repeat-creators with project in CBSA *and* prior project not in CBSA minus number of repeat-creators with project in not in CBSA *and* prior project in CBSA
Local	*NetMigration* of only creators with initial projects in a Local subcategory
FineArts	*NetMigration* of only creators with initial projects in Kickstarter category of Art, Dance, Theater
Arts	*NetMigration* of only creators with initial projects in Kickstarter category of Art, Dance, Theater, Film & Video, Music
Music	*NetMigration* of only creators with initial projects in Kickstarter category of Music
Film & Video	*NetMigration* of only creators with initial projects in Kickstarter category of Film & Video
Publishing	*NetMigration* of only creators with initial projects in Kickstarter category of Publishing
Technology	*NetMigration* of only creators with initial projects in Kickstarter category of Technology
AllProjects	Number of Kickstarter projects located in the CBSA, excluding projects by repeat-creators whose prior projects were outside the CBSA
OwnProjects	*AllProjects* counting only projects of the same type as the dependent variable
Pop[a]	Total population residing in CBSA in millions, 2010
Income[a]	ln(Average household income within CBSA in 2010)
College[a]	Proportion of working-age population with a college degree or higher within the CBSA in 2010
GradsperJob[a]	Number of college degrees divided by number of jobs in CBSA in 2010
ArtSchools	Number of arts-speciality schools in CBSA
CostofLiving[b]	Cost of living index, 2009, with national average = 100; missing values for micropolitan areas imputed using either lowest *CostofLiving* in that state or 100, whichever is less
PlatformHub	Dummy variable equal to 1 if CBSA intersects Silicon Valley or Seattle, 0 otherwise
CreativeClass[c]	Proportion of working population employed in the creative class jobs in the CBSA; 0 if missing
East	Dummy for CBSA is in New England, Mid-Atlantic or South Atlantic census divisions
West	Dummy for CBSA is in Pacific or Mountain census divisions, 0 otherwise
Coast	Dummy for CBSA has a coast
JanTemp	Average temperature (F) in January in the CBSA
JulyTemp	Average temperature (F) in July in the CBSA
Humidity	Average levels of humidity in July in the CBSA
PopDensity[a]	Number of residents per square meter in CBSA in 2010
BrainHub	Dummy for CBSA is amongst the 20 CBSAs with highest share of workers with a college degree (Moretti, 2012)
Metro	Dummy for CBSA is a metropolitan area (0 if CBSA is a micropolitan area)
OwnJob	Proportion of employed individuals in the CBSA working in the same category (see Table A5 in "Appendix") as the dependent variable; 0 if missing

Sources: [a]United States Census Bureau. (2011). Comparing 2011 American community survey data. Available online at: https://www.census.gov/programs-surveys/acs/guidance/comparing-acs-data/2011.html

[b]Bureau of Economic Analysis. Regional Price Parities by State and Metro Area. https://www.bea.gov/data/prices-inflation/regional-price-parities-state-and-metro-area

[c]Martin Prosperity Institute. (2010). Copy of 3Ts and Class Data for 2010. Toronto, Canada

[d]United States Census Bureau. (2010). *Metropolitan Combined Statistical Areas—2010 Census*. https://tigerweb.geo.census.gov/tigerwebmain/Files/bvp20/tigerweb_bvp20_metro_cbsa_2010_us.html

Table 3 Summary statistics

Variable	All CBSAs ($N=942$)		CBSAs with NetMigration$\neq$0				
	Mean	Standard deviation	No. of observations	Mean	Standard deviation	Min	Max
NetMigration	0.0011	2.8526	430	0.0023	4.2247	−15	54
Local	0.0159	0.7950	121	0.1240	2.2232	−7	12
FineArts	−0.0064	0.8336	165	−0.0364	1.9966	−5	12
Arts	−0.0340	1.8865	341	−0.0938	3.1375	−16	25
Music	−0.0212	1.2874	229	−0.0873	2.6143	−16	23
Film	−0.0064	0.9866	218	−0.0275	2.0544	−5	13
Publishing	−0.0318	0.7427	184	−0.1630	1.6777	−7	7
Technology	0.0287	0.7084	95	0.2842	2.2249	−3	17
AllProjects	189.2081	974.3074	430	380.1791	1415.8450	0	23,734
Pop	0.3076	1.0363	430	0.5339	1.3623	0.0167	18.9200
Income	10.6646	0.2357	430	10.7043	0.2063	9.8820	11.3875
College	0.2038	0.1615	430	0.2615	0.1924	0.0281	2.1988
GradsperJob	0.4429	0.2572	430	0.5481	0.2299	0.0981	0.9198
ArtSchools	0.9947	4.0798	430	1.9209	5.3766	0	45
CostofLiving	90.0216	7.4083	430	92.6974	7.6099	73.8	122.6
PlatformHub	0.0074	0.0859	430	0.0093	0.0961	0	1
CreativeClass	0.1780	0.0688	430	0.2083	0.0476	0.1032	0.4262
East	0.3142	0.4645	430	0.3465	0.4764	0	1
West	0.1773	0.3821	430	0.2116	0.4089	0	1
Coast	0.0648	0.2462	430	0.0791	0.2702	0	1
JanTemp	34.3926	12.3119	430	34.4677	12.5902	3.1	72.0
JulyTemp	75.6346	5.6947	430	75.2717	5.7850	55.9	91.1
Humidity	56.4469	15.4613	430	55.9942	16.2627	14	81
PopDensity	0.0001	0.0017	430	0.0001	0.0001	9.34×10^{-7}	0.0009
BrainHub	0.0212	0.1442	430	0.0419	0.2005	0	1
Metro	0.3885	0.4877	430	0.6000	0.4905	0	1

4 Model and estimation methods

To contribute to the literature on entrepreneurial migration and which regions gain or lose particular components of a "creative class," we test a set of hypotheses regarding the roles of homophily, market size, and amenities. Urbanized areas with more economic activity of a type similar to the relocating entrepreneurs may be more likely to attract more of this relocation as workers seek greater 'peer effect' spillovers or thicker markets (Krupka & Noonan, 2013). We test for this tendency for people to be attracted to others like them—homophily—by estimating whether net migration increases with more crowdfunding projects of the same category or more jobs in related sectors. Alternatively, these relocating creators may seek to

Table 4 Top- and bottom-ranked metro areas based on net migration

Bottom CBSAs	Net	Top CBSAs	Net
Austin-Round Rock-San Marcos, TX	−15	San Francisco-Oakland-Fremont, CA	54
Boston-Cambridge-Quincy, MA-NH	−11	Nashville-Davidson–Murfreesboro–Franklin, TN	25
San Diego-Carlsbad-San Marcos, CA	−10	Seattle-Tacoma-Bellevue, WA	20
Kansas City, MO-KS	−10	Denver-Aurora-Broomfield, CO	17
Minneapolis-St. Paul-Bloomington, MN-WI	−9	Atlanta-Sandy Springs-Marietta, GA	13
Provo-Orem, UT	−8	Indianapolis-Carmel, IN	11
Baltimore-Towson, MD	−8	Detroit-Warren-Livonia, MI	11
Albany-Schenectady-Troy, NY	−7	Las Vegas-Paradise, NV	11
Bridgeport-Stamford-Norwalk, CT	−7	Milwaukee-Waukesha-West Allis, WI	9
Raleigh-Cary, NC	−6	Asheville, NC	8
Charlottesville, VA	−6	Cleveland-Elyria-Mentor, OH	8
Hartford-West Hartford-East Hartford, CT	−6	Rochester, NY	7
Worcester, MA	−6	Albuquerque, NM	6
St. Louis, MO-IL	−6	Buffalo-Niagara Falls, NY	6

avoid local competition. We hypothesize that net migration increases with larger, wealthier markets. Thus, we expect that regions with greater population, income, education will experience greater net migration. Comparing tests of the homophily and market-size hypotheses help identify whether proximity to "crowds" of peers or backers is more important, especially in the context of entrepreneurs who use an online platform for fundraising. The online nature of these ventures also suggests that amenities like climate or regional location may play an important role. We expect net migration to be greater for regions with favorable conditions, though we remain agnostic about which sorts of weather or rural lifestyle these creators favor.

Our approach emphasizes migration or changes in location for entrepreneurial projects rather than the overall level of entrepreneurial activity or financing in a region. Some metro areas host more crowdfunding activity or have stronger histories of or infrastructures for funding cultural activity. Yet affluent cities with robust funding resources for cultural ventures (e.g., New York City, Los Angeles, San Francisco) may not be the same that attract these entrepreneurs' projects. Neither New York nor Los Angeles have a positive net migration, while San Francisco's prominent position in Table 4 may be offset by cultural hubs with strong traditional funding such as Boston and Minneapolis on the left side of Table 4. Still, in case a region's affluence and traditional support of cultural activity may crowd out crowdfunding, we control for income and creative-class employment levels.[1]

[1] The strength of a region's traditional cultural funding infrastructure might crowd-out crowdfunding as conventional funding sources can be more readily found, although conversely it might crowd-in alternative fundraising via crowdfunding as more entrepreneurial activity flourishes. Either way, considering dynamics (i.e., relocation) rather than more static, overall "levels" of crowdfunding shifts our attention to the decision to relocate *conditional on having already completed an initial crowdfunding campaign*. From this perspective, it is less clear how the strength of a region's traditional funding infrastructure would make the second project more or less likely to relocate. An entrepreneur in a traditionally stronger

To test these hypotheses about which metro areas are attracting more of these creative entrepreneurs, we set up a model to explain net migration flows as a function of factors describing the attractiveness of a metro area. Clearly, analyzing relocation patterns at the aggregated, metro-level do not directly reveal motivations for or mechanisms shaping individual relocations, even though the hypotheses derive from microfoundations. Akin to the linear modeling of Neal (2012) and Cebula et al. (2020), our basic empirical model also explains migration to a region based on its demographics, regional economy, and amenities. Our initial model then takes the form:

$$\text{Net migration} = \omega + \beta H + \mu M + \alpha A + \varepsilon \tag{1}$$

where *H* represents homophily related variables, *M* describes market size and conditions, and *A* indicates amenities. Though this model is linear in parameters (ω, β, μ, α), including population as a quadratic term (*Pop*, Pop^2) allows identification of nonlinear effects of metropolitan market size. Such an approach is necessary to properly test for market-size effects and whether marginal effects of increases in regional "crowd size" differ with the size of the population center. Other variables describing the regional market conditions include the average wealth (*Income*), share of the population with college degrees (*College*), the number of arts-specialty schools (*ArtsSchools*), and a regional cost-of-living index (*CostofLiving*). As shown in Breznitz and Noonan (2018), arts schools can be important to arts-related job growth and may be direct contributors to out-migration of early stage arts entrepreneurs who graduate and leave the market. An interaction term for *Cost of Living* and *ArtsSchools* better accounts for this possibility, testing whether arts schools "export" more crowdfunding creators when cost-of-living is higher. Further, following Moretti (2012), regional market conditions include the ratio of the number of residents with college degrees to the number of jobs (*GradsperJob*) and an indicator for the top-20 metro areas in terms of share of jobs with college degrees (*BrainHub*), which Moretti describes as the US's "brain hubs" (p. 92) and especially attractive and productive. The amenities variables include geographic factors like regional fixed effects (*Eastern*, *Western*, *coastal*), population density (*PopDensity*), and climate (*JanTemp*, *JulyTemp*, *Humidity*).

The model in Eq. (1) also includes factors related to the homophily hypotheses. First, employment conditions are characterized by the region's share of jobs in creative-class occupations (*CreativeClass*) and whether the region is located in one of the platform-economy hubs (*PlatformHub*) identified by Kenney and Zysman (2020). Regions with strong clusters in the creative class or platform economy hubs may be especially attractive to relocating creatives on a crowdfunding platform. To account for the possible attraction to others working on the same platform,

Footnote 1 (continued)
area might relocate their project to traditional funding deserts ahead of their second campaign to take advantage of a crowdfunding's comparative advantage there. Conversely, they might relocate to traditional funding hotspots in search for positive spillovers and diversified funding sources (e.g., regular employment).

the number of other (i.e., not associated with a creator who relocated there) projects in the region (*AllProjects*) in included. When examining migration of subgroups, such as those creating music projects or fine arts projects, broader measures of creative-class employment or general platform-based activity may not capture a sufficiently precise peer group. In subgroup migration models, we also include the count of crowdfunding projects in the same category as the migrants (*OwnProjects*). Likewise, subgroup-specific migration models include per-capita employment in related industry sectors (*OwnJob*). This enables identification of whether the more general or narrow measures explain net migration, and whether migrants are drawn to peers as complements to their work or are moving away from their competitors. Controlling for broader labor-market conditions (e.g., *CreativeClass*, *OwnJob*) especially helps identify whether related employment prospects better explain relocation patterns or whether attractiveness to other unrelated crowdfunders (*AllProjects*) or related crowdfunding projects (*OwnProjects*) predict relocation for different subgroups. Conducting the analysis at the metro-level prevents us from making inferences about individual-level motivations and mechanisms, but focusing on drivers of regional attractiveness does show the relocation tendencies at the metro-level.

Thus, we estimate a model to explain net migration of these creative entrepreneurs across regions (CBSAs) in order to test our competing hypotheses of homophily, market size, and amenities as potential attractors for these creative entrepreneurs. Interregional competition to attract the "creative class," "hipsters," or "geeks" (Rodríguez-Pose & Lee, 2020) hinges on strategies related to this kind of creative entrepreneur. We hypothesize regional factors appealing to or retaining these creatives as shown in Eq. (1): homophily, market size, and amenities. Estimating Eq. (1) via ordinary least squares (OLS) regression techniques suffers from a problem when very many regions have zero net migration. The high frequency of regions with zero net migration includes some regions with offsetting in-migration and out-migration and many more that simply experience neither arrivals nor departures.[2] To account for this zero-inflated distribution of the dependent variable, a finite mixture model (FMM) is estimated via maximum likelihood. In short, the finite mixture model assumes two latent classes—regions that do and do not experience migration—and allows for different densities for these two different classes of regions. This approach allows the estimator to adjust for the clustering of data at zero, much like a zero-inflated count model would. This more general approach importantly allows for negative values in the dependent variable, which we commonly observe among regions "exporting" or "losing" migrants. The estimator here fits a two-component model with a point mass density at zero and a linear regression for Eq. (1). The finite mixture model also allows for different sets of parameters for each component. For simplicity, as much as possible here we estimate the two component models with the same independent variables. For comparison, the "Appendix" includes the equivalent net migration models estimating using only OLS. Because our interest lies with

[2] Of the 512 CBSAs with zero net migration, 104 had offsetting in-migration and out-migration (e.g., New Orleans had 28 in-migrants and 28 out-migrants) while 408 had no migration in this sample. A full 90% of all CBSAs had at least one Kickstarter project launched.

the component of the finite mixture model explaining net migration, our discussion of results emphasizes that component and treats the point-mass model largely as a control.

Initially, we present results for all relocating, creative crowdfunding-based entrepreneurs. Then, we deconstruct the aggregation of these creative entrepreneurs into different groupings based on the categories of their initial projects. This allows us to examine how musicians, filmmakers, and others might migrate differently, and whether different sorts of metro areas might attract them. Our interest here follows from the heterogeneity identified by Markusen (2013). The possibility that the disconnect between an entrepreneur's locations of residence and project also motivates estimating separate models by different subgroups if this disconnect is more severe for, say, musicians. We differentiate these creators based on their (initial) campaign's self-reported category (see Table 1). We also reconstruct the "Local" (i.e., location-based projects) categories from Breznitz and Noonan (2020) in order to assess the factors attracting these creators to different urbanized regions.[3] After examining the factors attracting more locally-based migrants to regions, we then explore the factors explaining net migration for subgroups based on other artistic categories like the fine arts, film and video, and others.

5 Results

Table 5 exhibits the results for net migration across all movers in the data. The full set of results for the finite mixture models includes estimates for belonging to the set of regions with zero net migration *and* (conditionally) how much net migration regions experience. We focus our discussion on parameter estimates for this second stage of the model because our primary interest lies in explaining nonzero net migration. See the "Appendix" for the full results that include estimates of the parameters explaining the point mass at zero. Those results indicate that regions with zero net migration tend to be in the East and have fewer Kickstarter projects overall.[4]

Several interesting patterns emerge for predictors of net migration in these models in Table 5. In terms of amenities, we can see that there is a strong attraction to western regions away from eastern ones. Regions with higher humidity tend to have more positive net migration. In terms of market size, population has

[3] "Local" or more location-based projects are identified based on their subcategories, including architecture, community gardens, dance, festivals, installations, plays, public art, spaces, residencies, restaurants, theater, residencies, and workshops.

[4] See the "Appendix" (Tables 7, 8) for the estimates of the first-stage of the point mass at zero net migration. The results for different categories of creators generally resemble those for All movers, with a few key differences. First, having more projects of the same type (not just any type) tends to be associated with nonzero net migration. In addition, more wealth and less creative class employment tend to be associated with greater likelihood of zero net migration. Yet differences across creator categories remain, such as an insignificant role of income for Music, Publishing, and Technology. Like the results for All movers, in general total population in the region is not significantly associated with the likelihood of having zero net migration of Local or Music creators. For the other categories of movers, however, it appears that very populous metro areas tend to be more likely to have zero net migration.

Table 5 Finite mixture model estimates for net migration by CBSA

	All	Local	Fine arts	Arts
OwnProjects		0.0157***	0.0037	0.0113***
		(0.0052)	(0.0037)	(0.0023)
OwnJob			−6.8288	−0.3205
			(8.7170)	(9.1513)
AllProjects	0.0050***	−0.0007	0.0004	−0.0042***
	(0.0043)	(0.0006)	(0.0005)	(0.0013)
Pop	−0.2223	0.0255	−0.1489	0.4538
	(0.4393)	(0.2977)	(0.2751)	(0.4693)
Pop^2	−0.2227***	−0.0900***	−0.0567**	−0.1344***
	(0.0282)	(0.0302)	(0.0251)	(0.0339)
Income	−0.9945	0.3726	0.0470	−0.1494
	(0.9597)	(1.0945)	(0.9117)	(0.8901)
College	−0.6943	0.0556	0.2233	−0.5692
	(1.0673)	(0.2833)	(0.6281)	(1.1721)
GradsperJob	−0.5460	−0.3426	−0.6398	−0.4954
	(0.8897)	(1.0744)	(1.0584)	(1.0184)
ArtSchools	2.4897***	0.6693**	0.3869	1.2663***
	(0.4396)	(0.2833)	(0.2493)	(0.3735)
CostofLiving	−0.0339	−0.0745**	−0.0422	−0.0504
	(0.0342)	(0.0375)	(0.0292)	(0.0321)
CostofLiving × ArtSchools	−0.0273***	−0.0066**	0.2456	0.5898**
	(0.0042)	(0.0027)	(0.5048)	(0.07494)
CreativeClass	−2.1870	3.1330	1.6553	1.2984
	(4.0487)	(3.7596)	(2.9383)	(3.5012)
East	−1.2282***	−0.7414**	−0.3403	−0.7416**
	(0.3650)	(0.3481)	(0.2772)	(0.3146)
West	2.2763***	3.3902***	2.5489***	2.5734***
	(0.7933)	(0.9016)	(0.7099)	(0.7088)
JanTemp	−0.0222	−0.0662***	−0.0646***	−0.0440**
	(0.0232)	(0.0249)	(0.0190)	(0.0208)
JulyTemp	0.0238	0.0890*	0.1173***	0.0619
	(0.0504)	(0.0477)	(0.0401)	(0.0443)
Humidity	0.0474***	0.0756***	0.0534***	0.0472***
	(0.0168)	(0.0195)	(0.0159)	(0.0154)
Constant	9.9816	−7.0693	−0.0041*	−0.0129***
	(9.8595)	(10.3334)	(0.0024)	(0.0036)
Regional controls[a]	Yes	Yes	Yes	Yes
No. of observations	942	942	942	942
Log Likelihood	−1551.4	−418.9	−571.2	−1206.1

(a) Regional controls include *PopDensity* and *Coast*, *Metro*, *BrainHub*, and *PlatformHub* dummy variables. Also includes dummies indicating missing values for *CreativeClass* and, when included in model, *OwnJob*. Standard errors in parentheses.

* $p<0.10$; ** $p<0.05$; *** $p<0.01$

a strong nonlinear effect, such that the most populous metro regions tend to have lower or more negative net migration. These mobile creators are being drawn out of the metropolises.

Market conditions in the region also significantly predict net migration. A consistent and important market factor includes the interaction term between cost of living and the number of art schools. Metro areas with many art schools tend to be net exporters of these creators when they also have high cost of living. Lower cost of living, conversely, helps attract these creators when many art schools occupy the region. Also consistent with the homophily hypothesis, metro areas with larger numbers of other Kickstarter projects in the region draw more net migration to the region. Employment in the creative class, in general, does not seem to be a significant factor.

The remainder of the results shift the focus to various subgroups of crowdfunding creators. The remaining columns in Table 5 show model estimates for net migration only among subgroups of Kickstarter creators. The first broad category, Local, highlights attractors for more location-based projects, perhaps differing from the bulk of other projects in a more digital space. The next two groupings build on Kickstarter's explicitly arts-related categories for crowdfunding projects: Fine Arts (Art, Dance, Theater) and Arts (Fine Arts, Film & Video, Music). For these FMM estimates of subsets of the full crowdfunding database, we can control for other projects in the same grouping. For example, the Fine Arts estimates include a variable measuring the number of other Fine Arts projects on Kickstarter in that CBSA (*OwnProjects*). Contrasting that parameter with the control for all projects of any type (*AllProjects*) allows us to identify whether it is a general crowdfunding community that attracts movers or whether it is a more specialized group of peers. Likewise, for the arts-related categories, we can control for employment concentrations in related industries (*OwnJob*) to see if more jobs in relevant sectors attracts movers. For instance, estimated effects for *OwnJob* in the Fine Arts model can contrast how fine-arts related job intensity predicts net migration with the broader *CreativeClass* employment measure.

Differentiating among factors relevant to various subgroups of crowdfunding creators is especially important given the substantial variation among Kickstarter creators. Examining subgroups of relocating creators allows us to identify which CBSAs better attract different types of entrepreneurs. For example, the migrants in more location-based categories show somewhat different patterns, as can be seen in the Local column of Table 5. Local creators are drawn to regions with many other Local project creators on Kickstarter, rather than just all projects on Kickstarter in general. Further, they are also drawn out of metro areas with very high populations, drawn out of platform-hub economy regions, and drawn to regions with more art schools. Notably, the positive effect of art schools declines in cost of living, suggesting that expensive cities with many art schools tend to export Local creators while cheaper regions with art school attract them. In terms of amenities, a similar story holds for relocating Kickstarter creators in general as for Local ones, except that we see a significant negative effect of winter temperatures.

Table 5 breaks down some different arts-related categories among the movers in the Kickstarter data. For the narrower definition (Fine Arts), we see particularly strong climate-related amenity factors explaining net migration, the continued negative role of very populous metro regions and of the platform economy hubs, and otherwise no significant effects of any of our homophily indicators. Art schools do not play a significant role, and these fine-arts creators do not appear to be particularly drawn to or away from metros with strength in the fine arts or even creative class jobs or crowdfunders. When we broaden the definition of arts to also include Music and Film & Video productions, we see another significant shift in the results. Arts-related creators tend to relocate projects toward metros with more Arts crowdfunding creators, not towards more crowdfunding activity in general or Arts-related jobs. The tendency for regions to export (import) creators when they have more art schools and cost of living is high (low) returns. There is also a strong westward push, an appeal of colder winters and higher humidity, and little impact of regional socioeconomic indicators like income and education.

The Music category and the Film & Video category comprise almost 30% of all Kickstarter campaigns. Table 6 shows results that investigate those two categories separately. Homophily results are strong here, particularly for other projects related to their own category and not for all Kickstarter projects in general. Music migrants, unlike any of the other categories, tend to be drawn to regions with more music-related employment. Except for the westward attraction to moving musicians, neither relocating musicians nor filmmakers show a very strong role for the amenity factors in explaining which cities tend to attract more net migration. The attractiveness of regions with both high concentrations of art schools and low cost of living remains for Film & Video, but these effects are much weaker for Music. In addition, musicians do not appear to be drawn to or away from regions based on the size of their population.

Table 6 shows the results for two more subgroups of the migrating creators' data. The migrating creators in the Publishing category show rather different patterns compared to the other groups. Not only are Publishing migrants being drawn away from coastal regions and being drawn towards platform-economy hubs, they also tend toward areas with higher education levels—the only subgroup examined here that does so. They also seem to be drawn towards high-density regions. The most important difference for Publishing movers, however, involves homophily, as they are drawn *away* from regions with more publishing-related Kickstarter campaigns. This contrasts with what is observed for other subgroups.

The final set of results in Table 6, for Technology-category movers, provides some contrast against the more traditionally artistic or arts-related projects in Kickstarter. More populous regions tend to lose these crowdfunding Technology creators, though they are drawn to high population density regions. Most notably, Table 6 shows how regions with more Kickstarter projects—both overall and specifically those related to Technology—tend to attract more Technology-project migration. These results importantly differ from more arts-related Kickstarter categories, which show more specialized interest of the artistic entrepreneurs. Attractions to smaller metros and those with lower cost-of-living and including more arts schools remain generally consistent. But, like the Film & Video category (and unlike the others and

Table 6 Additional finite mixture model estimates for net migration by CBSA

	Music	Film & Video	Publishing	Technology
OwnProjects	0.0113***	0.0110***	−0.0101**	0.0111**
	(0.0019)	(0.0036)	(0.0048)	(0.0045)
OwnJob	1635.3810*	200.4007	11.6227	−7.9664
	(973.0785)	(251.5507)	(7.0078)	(11.5085)
AllProjects	−0.0023***	−0.0013*	0.0014***	0.0008**
	(0.0005)	(0.0007)	(0.005)	(0.0004)
Pop	0.0429	0.3840	−0.3322	−0.6427***
	(0.3117)	(0.3069)	(0.2410)	(0.2476)
Pop^2	0.0249	−0.0576*	−0.0126	−0.0255
	(0.0196)	(0.0307)	(0.0158)	(0.0193)
Income	−0.2560	−0.5543	−1.1544	0.8759
	(0.9673)	(0.6211)	(0.7080)	(1.1549)
College	−1.1903	−0.4063	0.9628*	0.2995
	(0.9900)	(0.6798)	(0.5172)	(0.7957)
GradsperJob	−0.3142	−0.1973	−1.0444	0.0632
	(1.1010)	(0.7799)	(0.7036)	(1.6311)
ArtSchools	0.5261	0.5292**	0.4369**	0.5206**
	(0.3201)	(0.2269)	(0.1924)	(0.2480)
CostofLiving	−0.0240	−0.0138	0.0022	−0.0219
	(0.0327)	(0.0225)	(0.0221)	(0.0364)
CostofLiving × ArtSchools	−0.0052*	−0.0052**	0.1763	−1.2642**
	(0.0030)	(0.0022)	(0.4034)	(0.5125)
CreativeClass	−3.1968	2.6173	1.5965	−3.7647
	(3.3092)	(2.4177)	(2.4500)	(3.5275)
East	−0.2718	−0.3532	0.0051	−0.1920
	(0.3116)	(0.2275)	(0.2092)	(0.3148)
West	1.7483**	0.6793	1.0883**	0.9027
	(0.7494)	(0.4766)	(0.4501)	(0.7783)
JanTemp	−0.0023	−0.0098	0.0067	0.0090
	(0.0218)	(0.0134)	(0.0134)	(0.0219)
JulyTemp	−0.0184	0.0164	−0.0042	−0.0083
	(0.0491)	(0.0297)	(0.0284)	(0.0480)
Humidity	0.0258	0.0153	0.0081	0.0248
	(0.0162)	(0.0102)	(0.0095)	(0.0172)
Constant	5.1285	4.4870	−0.0041**	−0.0059**
	(9.7083)	(6.1641)	(0.0018)	(0.0023)
Regional controls[a]	Yes	Yes	Yes	Yes
No. of Observations	942	942	942	942
Log Likelihood	−781.2	−728.8	−590.1	−327.1

(a) Regional controls include *PopDensity* and *Coast*, *Metro*, *BrainHub*, and *PlatformHub* dummy variables. Also includes dummies indicating missing values for *CreativeClass* and, when included in model, *OwnJob*

$^*p<0.10$, $^{**}p<0.05$, $^{***}p<0.01$

Kickstarter projects overall), the Technology net migration does not exhibit tendencies toward wealth, education, or particular amenities.

6 Discussion

The purpose of this paper was to understand whether traditional factors of location apply to online cultural related projects. The analysis finds that though some factors such as homophily are similar to traditional clustering of human capital (Moretti, 2012), the results identify different attractors drawing creative entrepreneurs to launch projects in certain regions. Specifically, humid climates in the west have positive net migration of crowdfunding creators, most populous metro regions tend to have lower or negative net migration, and metro areas with many art schools tend to be net exporters of these creators when they also have high cost of living. These results strengthen studies on the location decisions of artists indicating that they do not follow traditional attraction of population and wealth when it collides with cost of living (Lopez, 2019). These results can help explain the success of cities such as Berlin and the growing art scene in declining cities such as Detroit (Ewing and Grady, 2012).

Overall, we have shown which regional features tend to attract a special population of creative entrepreneurs—those using an online crowdfunding platform to support their creative venture. With a special focus on creators of more arts-related projects, we identified the main factors that lead regions to "gain" creators launching these sorts of projects (or to experience a "drain" of losing these creators to elsewhere). Some regions tend to 'export' these creators, while others tend to attract and retain them. The literature on the economic geography of jobs and entrepreneurship points to three broad forces that can explain migration patterns: market conditions, homophily, and amenities. Testing the relevance of these forces for our population of entrepreneurs—those skewing heavily to artistic activities and relying on an online platform for fundraising—highlights a particularly interesting, mobile, and creative group. Our empirical models show *some* support for all three forces, with the strongest and most consistent effects evidence for homophily, although important differences across types of creators remain. Net migration of these creators tends to be drawn to regions that have many other *similar* crowdfunding creators, not just a generally stronger crowdfunding community, more creative class employment, or more jobs in related sectors. Further, net migration tends toward the west, toward more humid summers, and less populous metro areas. Unlike prior studies, wealth and education levels of regions play insignificant roles here. Combined with the general negative effect of population size, we see little overall support for the hypothesis that market size is an important driver of net migration for these creators.

Because examining creative entrepreneurs working via crowdfunding platforms inevitably pools very different sorts of creators and projects, our analysis decomposes the relocation patterns across different types of creators. The results show some consistency across types of creators as well as substantial heterogeneity. Net migration falls, for instance, with greater regional population, regardless of the category of the ventures. Western regions also tend to have greater net migration for all of these creative types. Interestingly, the null results for income, creative class, brain hub metros, and summer temperatures also persist across all categories. The "brain gain" of regions tends to follow rather narrowly defined peers—i.e., Kickstarter creators are drawn to regions with more Kickstarter projects like theirs, not to regions with more crowdfunding overall or more jobs related to their specialty. Results common to many of the creative types, such as the strength of homophily (in terms of similar Kickstarter creators), negative effect of population, and arts-specialty schools 'exporting' crowdfunding entrepreneurs from markets with higher costs of living, point to the power of conventional theory in explaining migration patterns for these new entrepreneurs. In other cases, certain types of creators prove to be exceptions to the rule. This includes musicians (the only group attracted to regions with more music-related jobs), those in publishing (eschewing others in publishing and coasts), and those in fine arts (drawn to warmer summers, not drawn to similar creators).[5]

Through its focus on creators of crowdfunding projects related to arts and culture, our research raises some questions about creative workers in today's economies. Though creators who fundraise via a crowdfunding platform are not representative of creative workers as whole, and those that undertake multiple fundraising campaigns may be stranger still, studying this group sheds some light on a particularly interesting type of creative worker. The cultural sector has greater frequency of self-employed and more fluidity between employment types (Woronkowicz & Noonan, 2019), and crowdfunding can play a role as cultural entrepreneurs shift between gigs, stable income, and other opportunities. These cultural entrepreneurs operating on a crowdfunding platform might treat their project as a secondary consideration or a hobby, even though we focus our attention on creators who use the platform multiple times. Bringing attention to entrepreneurs undertaking secondary or gig activities raises the possibility some of creatives who relocate their projects may be doing it for reasons unrelated to their cultural entrepreneurship (e.g., their or their partner's employer transfers them to a new location). Uncertainty remains about whether our estimated parameters reflect individual entrepreneurs' preferences or strategies related to their crowdfunding endeavors or something coincidental. This, and our focus on metro-level aggregate analysis, limits our ability to directly attribute our findings to entrepreneurs' motivations or mechanisms shaping relocations. Future work could examine this more directly via surveys and interviews of these entrepreneurs. We see our analysis as capturing regional relocation dynamics for an emerging, potentially important, and often difficult-to-measure sort of cultural entrepreneur. Though that entails some uncertainty in classification and interpretation, the messiness also to some extent reflects a reality for this sort of entrepreneurial activity.

[5] Performers, such as musicians, may have a higher propensity to relocate projects if they tour or temporarily relocate for performances. We split the data by subgroups to help account for this possibility. We remain interested in fundraising for a temporary project that brings economic activity to another city, even if the creator does not permanent relocate.

Our main concern lies with spurious correlations that might arise when it appears that creators "of a feather flock together" for homophily reasons but rather are independently drawn to another particular, unmeasured factor. If these relocations are driven by thicker labor markets, for instance, then what appears as homophily could be just relocation toward better employment prospects. We mitigate against this concern by explicitly controlling for jobs related to the crowdfunding project (*OwnJob*) and to the broader creative sector (*CreativeClass*). That related employment measures explain little of the regional relocation patterns in most of our models, and that *OwnProjects* tends to explain more, is a remarkable finding considering the potentially high incidence of part-time entrepreneurs in our data. Of course, these entrepreneurs may be systematically drawn to employment prospects unrelated to the industries and other factors that we control for in the models. We cannot rule this out. But the diverse findings across the separate analyses by subgroups of projects suggest that *AllProjects* does not simply proxy for a particular unobservable and that different subgroups ("feathers") flock together differently.

Data limitations also restrict our ability to more directly observe when these entrepreneurs move to new homes. Future research would do well to investigate residential locations of these crowdfunders, especially if the disconnect between residential location and workplace is important. While touring artists or those who temporarily exhibit or produce in distant locations may be more common among creative workers than in other sectors of the economy, the rise of the platform economy and online (digital) distribution may entail even greater potential for mismatch between locations of residence and economic activity. After all, the two largest subsectors of the arts and cultural sector of the US economy in 2017 are 'broadcasting' and 'other information services' (Noonan, 2021). More than just crowdfunders, much of the arts and cultural sector's economic activity may be shifting to a digital, cyberspace.

Overall, the identified patterns in net migration suggest potentially useful directions for future research. Similar to Markusen and Schrock (2006), we show strong clustering tendencies among creators using this crowdfunding platform—where certain metro regions with many creators of one type will tend to gain more of that type via migration. The strong overall support for clustering is broadly consistent with much of the prior literature on migration, including artists. While this is true for many arts-related types of projects, it does not hold for those in publishing nor is it significant for those in fine arts. This contrasts with some prior work, especially regarding visual artists (Kelly & O'Hagan, 2007). Given the differences in our sample and the prior work on historical clustering of artists, this raises questions about the roles of modern technology in productivity and location decisions for visual artists, especially when their arts activities are part-time or "gig" work. The weak support for market size hypotheses and the insignificance of income levels raises similar questions about how well those conventional forces explain location decisions today for artists working in an online platform. That sheer size of metro areas does not attract more (net) migration of these creators who operate on online platforms may reflect greater importance of lifestyle amenities (Markusen, 2013) for subpopulation. Finally, the overall importance of our geographic and climate amenity factors in explaining net migration points to the need to better unpack the sources of these tendencies. Whether regional biases reflect differences in "people climate" (Borén & Young, 2013b) or cultural environments (Backman and Nilsson, 2018) and why these arts-related creators tend to be drawn toward colder winters and more humid summers—in contrast to Glaeser and Shapiro (2003)—offer promising avenues for future study.

These results are of particular interest to city and regional leaders seeking to attract certain residents and entrepreneurial activity. Whether they seek to cultivate more of a "creative class," become the next "brain hub," or attract more "hipsters" and "geeks," these results offer some insights as to which sorts of places tend to attract them—and which ones tend to lose them. First and foremost, the findings here point to the need for multifaceted approaches to attract and retain this kind of creative talent. Though similar to the results of Mollick (2014) where the author finds ties between project locations and the nature of projects (such as country music in Nashville, Tennessee), in this analysis the regions that have performed best in attracting (not losing) these creators differ in their characteristics depending on which type of creative activity. Some things, like arts schools or more crowdfunding activity overall can help in general, but different arts appear drawn to different sorts of regions. Musicians are drawn to strong music scenes, but publishing-related creators avoid others like them while favoring denser, more educated regions. Policymakers are unlikely to find a one-size-fits-all solution to a attracting these sorts of creative entrepreneurs. Findings here also offer hope to regions outside of metropolises and with arguably worse weather (more humidity, colder winters). These regions can do well in attracting this sort of arts entrepreneur, especially if they lack infrastructure for selling and exhibiting artistic work and can instead provide the networking and spillovers from other similar creators.

7 Conclusion

The tendency for industry and innovation to cluster in vibrant urban areas is as well-known as it is a key component of many regional economic development strategies. The 'creative class' (Florida, 2002), 'hipsters' (Rodríguez-Pose & Lee, 2020), and other creative or artistic workers are often seen as somewhere between helpful and vital to these processes. Cultivating vibrant clusters of this talent involves a mix of home-grown and in-migrating creatives. In this analysis, we focus on the migration side of this clustering process. We seek to identify factors associated with regions better able to attract and retain creatives who use an online crowdfunding platform. The rapid rise of crowdfunding in the cultural and creative industries (Lazzaro & Noonan, 2020) makes this group of creatives a particularly interesting population. These potentially "footloose" entrepreneurs, less tied to local markets for raising funds and pursuing risky and innovative ventures, exhibit relocation patterns that only partly resemble migration patterns of broader populations. Tracing their relocations reveals a strong tendency for clustering and some attraction to certain regions.

Overall, regional market size and strength does not explain much net migration, but important heterogeneity by artistic type persists. Different categories of creators have different attractors, such as musicians being drawn to music-related employment. Filmmakers appear unconcerned about amenities, while net migration in Fine Arts tends to be influenced more by geography and climate rather than any homophily. In contrast with more technology-oriented creators on the same platform, the arts-related net migration tends to be more influenced by amenities and by the presence of more narrowly defined peers. This heterogeneity highlights the importance of further investigation of how different types of arts entrepreneurs take advantage of networks, markets, and other platforms or institutions. Clearly, peer effects and spillovers from collocation matter even for many of these creators who use an online platform for fundraising. Yet attractive regions in terms of net migration of this sort of creative talent may not translate this "brain gain" into success for the creators or the region.

We have only scratched the surface of better understanding the support needed to develop and sustain a cluster of arts-related entrepreneurs. The hotly debated topics of what drives urban growth and, especially, how to best attract talented, creative workers to a region poses pressing questions for academics and policymakers alike. In this much broader topic, our analysis contributes some empirical evidence on a fairly narrow group of cultural entrepreneurs. Although our crowdfunding creators do not appear to be uniformly and simply chasing employment opportunities, the dynamics observed here do highlight a few important themes. To the extent that these cultural entrepreneurs are or become employers themselves, relocating their projects to metros that already host similar projects reflects the positive-feedback loop or path dependency of urban growth (Storper & Scott, 2009). This "brain gain" associated with urban growth—at least for our cultural entrepreneurs—may not hinge on climate and other amenities, broader creative class employment, or even narrow employment concentrations. Instead, the main drivers here are agglomeration economies, peer effects, and new production systems. The clustering observed follows the use of online crowdfunding platforms rather than traditional labor markets. This raises important questions about how artists and other creative workers sort and cluster outside of conventional classifications and also about how decisions to use crowdfunding platforms and to relocate fit into the life-cycle of these entrepreneurs. Consistent with the effect of arts schools in our models, age and career stage play roles here (Borén & Young, 2013b), especially for an emerging fundraising mechanism and younger entrepreneurs building their networks and reputations. How online platforms fit into cultural entrepreneurs' career paths has implications for which regions they select and what their arrival brings.

Appendix

See Tables 7, 8, 9, 10 and 11.

Table 7 Full results for finite mixture model estimates for net migration by CBSA

Class 1: Point mass at NetMigration = 0

	All	Local	Fine arts	Arts
OwnProjects		−0.0085	−0.0916**	−0.1287***
		(0.0439)	(0.0395)	(0.0494)
AllProjects	−0.0446***	−0.0094*	0.0009	−0.0105
	(0.0152)	(0.0052)	(0.0051)	(0.0162)
Pop	−6.1034	0.7186	0.3881	4.1838
	(6.5477)	(1.6709)	(1.8187)	(2.5848)
Pop^2	2.8491	−0.0382	0.4049*	3.5482***
	(12.8059)	(0.2050)	(0.2230)	(0.9199)
Income	0.6853	2.0236**	2.7275***	1.7647***
	(0.5990)	(0.9039)	(0.8568)	(0.6738)
College	−0.4833	−1.0419	−2.8542	4.9180**
	(56.5800)	(1.2049)	(3.3427)	(1.9155)
GradsperJob	0.9633	0.5013	−0.6482	−2.4576**
	(1.7027)	(1.0250)	(1.6339)	(0.9833)
ArtSchools	−0.6339	0.0583	−0.1725	−0.6485
	(0.5522)	(0.1275)	(0.1484)	(0.4170)
CostofLiving	−0.0238	−0.0198	−0.1100***	−0.0433
	(0.0265)	(0.0358)	(0.0356)	(0.0291)
PlatformHub	1.6302	13.4959	21.0687	1.0776
	(1.3639)	(712.9451)	(14,950.8100)	(1.5059)
CreativeClass	−4.9671	−9.8440***	−7.1298**	−7.7760***
	(3.5174)	(3.7679)	(3.2993)	(2.9000)
Missing	47.5822			
CreativeClass	(562.22)			
East	0.6071**	−0.1935	0.1517	0.3767
	(0.2838)	(0.4138)	(0.3637)	(0.3035)
West	−0.0710	−0.6578	0.0825	−0.6368
	(0.5765)	(0.8443)	(0.7052)	(0.6296)
Coast	0.0070	−0.4724	0.8574	−0.2577
	(0.6196)	(0.7254)	(0.7876)	(0.5910)
JanTemp	−0.0080	0.0387	0.0189	0.0041
	(0.0188)	(0.0244)	(0.0216)	(0.0196)
JulyTemp	0.0094	−0.0227	−0.0421	−0.0447
	(0.0094)	(0.0531)	(0.0480)	(0.0419)
Humidity	−0.0012	−0.0094	0.0054	−0.0166
	(0.01368)	(0.0184)	(0.0159)	(0.0151)
Constant	−3.6021	−13.6984	−12.4850	−7.4611
	(7.4140)	(9.4487)	(9.1048)	(8.2185)

Table 7 (continued)

Class 2: Base outcome of NetMigration

	All	Local	Fine arts	Arts
OwnProjects		0.0157***	0.0037	0.0113***
		(0.0052)	(0.0037)	(0.0023)
AllProjects	0.0050***	−0.0007	0.0004	−0.0042***
	(0.0043)	(0.0006)	(0.0005)	(0.0013)
Pop	−0.2223	0.0255	−0.1489	0.4538
	(0.4393)	(0.2977)	(0.2751)	(0.4693)
Pop^2	−0.2227***	−0.0900***	−0.0567**	−0.1344***
	(0.0282)	(0.0302)	(0.0251)	(0.0339)
Income	−0.9945	0.3726	0.0470	−0.1494
	(0.9597)	(1.0945)	(0.9117)	(0.8901)
College	−0.6943	0.0556	0.2233	−0.5692
	(1.0673)	(0.2833)	(0.6281)	(1.1721)
GradsperJob	−0.5460	−0.3426	−0.6398	−0.4954
	(0.8897)	(1.0744)	(1.0584)	(1.0184)
ArtSchools	2.4897***	0.6693**	0.3869	1.2663***
	(0.4396)	(0.2833)	(0.2493)	(0.3735)
CostofLiving	−0.0339	−0.0745**	−0.0422	−0.0504
	(0.0342)	(0.0375)	(0.0292)	(0.0321)
CostofLiving × ArtSchools	−0.0273***	−0.0066**	−0.0041*	−0.0129***
	(0.0042)	(0.0027)	(0.0024)	(0.0036)
PlatformHub	1.5219	−6.0867***	−4.8304***	−0.6968
	(1.6153)	(1.8005)	(1.7181)	(1.2855)
CreativeClass	−2.1870	3.1330	1.6553	1.2984
	(4.0487)	(3.7596)	(2.9383)	(3.5012)
Missing CreativeClass	−1.2445	0.4557	0.5412	1.2984
	(4597.7)	(5.4992)	(4.4284)	(3.5012)
East	−1.2282***	−0.7414**	−0.3403	−0.7416**
	(0.3650)	(0.3481)	(0.2772)	(0.3146)
West	2.2763***	3.3902***	2.5489***	2.5734***
	(0.7933)	(0.9016)	(0.7099)	(0.7088)
Coast	−0.5880	−0.2070	0.7449	0.5194
	(0.6536)	(0.6118)	(0.5167)	(0.5418)
JanTemp	−0.0222	−0.0662***	−0.0646***	−0.0440**
	(0.0232)	(0.0249)	(0.0190)	(0.0208)
JulyTemp	0.0238	0.0890*	0.1173***	0.0619
	(0.0504)	(0.0477)	(0.0401)	(0.0443)
Humidity	0.0474***	0.0756***	0.0534***	0.0472***
	(0.0168)	(0.0195)	(0.0159)	(0.0154)
PopDensity	4016.8130	3625.8760*	1690.5330	398.6170
	(2510.9670)	(1911.2360)	(1560.5600)	(2113.8110)

Table 7 (continued)

Class 2: Base outcome of NetMigration

	All	Local	Fine arts	Arts
BrainHub	−1.5323*	−0.6151	0.2456	0.5898
	(0.8996)	(0.6074)	(0.5048)	(0.7494)
Metro			−0.0103	0.4827
			(0.4297)	(0.4118)
OwnJob			−83.0821	−92.6761
			(72.5102)	(106.3072)
Missing OwnJob			−0.3137	0.3897
			(72.5102)	(1.7241)
Constant	9.9816	−7.0693	−6.8288	−0.3205
	(9.8595)	(10.3334)	(8.7170)	(9.1513)
AIC	3183.22	917.87	1228.80	2493.39
BIC	3377.14	1111.90	1437.26	2706.71

$^{*}p<0.10$, $^{**}p<0.05$, $^{***}p<0.01$

Table 8 Full Results for Additional Finite Mixture Model Estimates for Net Migration by CBSA

Class 1: Point mass at NetMigration = 0

	Music	Film & Video	Publishing	Technology
OwnProjects	−0.0939***	−0.1594**	−0.0839*	−0.1126
	(0.0283)	(0.0620)	(0.0466)	(0.0686)
AllProjects	0.0084**	−0.0037	−0.0073	−0.0010
	(0.0037)	(0.0077)	(0.0072)	(0.0039)
Pop	−1.4093	1.8381	−0.0073	−1.0971
	(1.6889)	(2.2287)	(1.8497)	(1.2281)
Pop^2	0.2521	1.9485***	1.0112***	0.4451**
	(0.8092)	(0.6435)	(0.3700)	(0.1914)
Income	0.6545	2.4488***	0.1892	0.6681
	(0.7911)	(0.7862)	(0.8103)	(1.1525)
College	0.0944	0.6432	1.3994	−0.3043
	(1.2992)	(1.980)	(1.3022)	(1.1610)
GradsperJob	−2.7581***	0.1310	−1.3350	0.2045
	(0.8953)	(1.0846)	(0.9201)	(1.2075)
ArtSchools	0.2269	0.1211	0.2295	−0.0077
	(0.1414)	(0.1535)	(0.2091)	(0.1382)
CostofLiving	−0.0150	−0.0669**	−0.0209	−0.0709
	(0.0286)	(0.0314)	(0.0326)	(0.0438)
PlatformHub	0.1458	−0.3082	0.2132	12.3327
	(1.3965)	(1.3984)	(1.4579)	(718.3742)
CreativeClass	−20.4912***	−8.1389***	−6.4615*	−11.6266**
	(3.9985)	(3.1481)	(3.3172)	(4.5792)

Table 8 (continued)

Class 1: Point mass at NetMigration = 0				
	Music	Film & Video	Publishing	Technology
East	−0.0134	0.0700	0.2280	0.7004
	(0.3152)	(0.3447)	(0.3703)	(0.7004)
West	−0.3398	−0.1754	0.5969	0.3572
	(0.6566)	(0.6472)	(0.7484)	(1.0801)
Coast	0.3458	−0.2373	−0.7374	−0.0501
	(0.5753)	(0.6318)	(0.5964)	(0.8257)
JanTemp	0.0273	−0.0005	0.0146	0.0398
	(0.0198)	(0.0207)	(0.0227)	(0.0302)
JulyTemp	−0.0718	0.0036	−0.0505	−0.0611
	(0.0439)	(0.0445)	(0.0505)	(0.0715)
Humidity	−0.0215	−0.0031	−0.0027	−0.0190
	(0.0146)	(0.0151)	(0.0159)	(0.0230)
Constant	7.1573	−16.8049*	7.2829	9.0026
	(8.4255)	(8.7876)	(9.0090)	(12.4980)

Class 2: Base outcome of NetMigration				
	Music	Film & Video	Publishing	Technology
OwnProjects	0.0113***	0.0110***	−0.0101**	0.0111**
	(0.0019)	(0.0036)	(0.0048)	(0.0045)
AllProjects	−0.0023***	−0.0013*	0.0014***	0.0008**
	(0.0005)	(0.0007)	(0.005)	(0.0004)
Pop	0.0429	0.3840	−0.3322	−0.6427***
	(0.3117)	(0.3069)	(0.2410)	(0.2476)
Pop^2	0.0249	−0.0576*	−0.0126	−0.0255
	(0.0196)	(0.0307)	(0.0158)	(0.0193)
Income	−0.2560	−0.5543	−1.1544	0.8759
	(0.9673)	(0.6211)	(0.7080)	(1.1549)
College	−1.1903	−0.4063	0.9628*	0.2995
	(0.9900)	(0.6798)	(0.5172)	(0.7957)
GradsperJob	−0.3142	−0.1973	−1.0444	0.0632
	(1.1010)	(0.7799)	(0.7036)	(1.6311)
ArtSchools	0.5261	0.5292**	0.4369**	0.5206**
	(0.3201)	(0.2269)	(0.1924)	(0.2480)
CostofLiving	−0.0240	−0.0138	0.0022	−0.0219
	(0.0327)	(0.0225)	(0.0221)	(0.0364)
CostofLiving × ArtSchools	−0.0052*	−0.0052**	0.1763	−1.2642**
	(0.0030)	(0.0022)	(0.4034)	(0.5125)
PlatformHub	0.6372	0.1175	1.4970*	1.4260
	(1.2747)	(0.7568)	(0.7907)	(1.6696)
CreativeClass	−3.1968	2.6173	1.5965	−3.7647
	(3.3092)	(2.4177)	(2.4500)	(3.5275)

Table 8 (continued)

Class 2: Base outcome of NetMigration

	Music	Film & Video	Publishing	Technology
Missing CreativeClass	−0.4187	0.8409	0.3793	−0.5215
	(9.5734)	(2.2117)	(2.0237)	(5.7178)
East	−0.2718	−0.3532	0.0051	−0.1920
	(0.3116)	(0.2275)	(0.2092)	(0.3148)
West	1.7483**	0.6793	1.0883**	0.9027
	(0.7494)	(0.4766)	(0.4501)	(0.7783)
Coast	0.0409	0.1395	−0.7488**	−0.8754
	(0.5572)	(0.3702)	(0.3281)	(0.5609)
JanTemp	−0.0023	−0.0098	0.0067	0.0090
	(0.0218)	(0.0134)	(0.0134)	(0.0219)
JulyTemp	−0.0184	0.0164	−0.0042	−0.0083
	(0.0491)	(0.0297)	(0.0284)	(0.0480)
Humidity	0.0258	0.0153	0.0081	0.0248
	(0.0162)	(0.0102)	(0.0095)	(0.0172)
PopDensity	1369.0960	−1335.4520	2587.3790**	3840.6510**
	(1895.0500)	(1445.9930)	(1210.9280)	(1551.8410)
BrainHub	0.9298	−0.3411	−0.3332	−0.0901
	(0.6282)	(0.4614)	(0.2988)	(0.7416)
Metro	0.5340	0.3256	1.5865	1.7860
	(0.5340)	(0.3148)	(7.0078)	(0.2376)
OwnJob	1635.3810*	200.4007	11.6227	−7.9664
	(973.0785)	(251.5507)	(7.0078)	(11.5085)
Missing OwnJob	0.1644	0.0381	−0.1969	−0.2549
	(0.4265)	(0.4981)	(0.3661)	(1.2202)
Constant	5.1285	4.4870	−0.0041**	−0.0059**
	(9.7083)	(6.1641)	(0.0018)	(0.0023)
AIC	1648.56	1537.72	1269.58	742.28
BIC	1857.02	1746.18	1487.74	955.60

$^*p<0.10$, $^{**}p<0.05$, $^{***}p<0.01$

Table 9 Full Results for OLS Model Estimates for Net Migration by CBSA

	All	Local	Fine arts	Arts
OwnProjects		0.0118**	0.0014	0.0097
		(0.0051)	(0.0036)	(0.0081)
OwnJob			−5.8291	−12.7253
			(10.2370)	(24.8587)
Missing OwnJob			0.0114	0.0607
			(0.0433)	(0.1401)
AllProjects	0.0034**	−0.0009	0.0002	−0.0039
	(0.0014)	(0.0007)	(0.0006)	(0.0045)
Pop	0.5583	0.2911	0.0392	0.4348
	(0.8574)	(0.3661)	(0.4212)	(1.0208)
Pop^2	−0.1288**	−0.0471*	−0.0175	−0.0845
	(0.0637)	(0.0254)	(0.0295)	(0.0814)
Income	−0.2805	0.0149	−0.0102	−0.1055
	(0.2528)	(0.0782)	(0.0947)	(0.2047)
College	−0.2834	−0.1924	−0.2433	−0.6753
	(1.1629)	(0.5386	(0.5111)	(1.1452)
ArtSchools	3.3159***	0.7128*	0.4657	1.4841*
	(1.2538)	(0.4051)	(0.3411)	(0.7698)
CostofLiving	−0.0220	−0.0030	−0.0063	−0.0211
	(0.0174)	(0.0046)	(0.0059)	(0.0141)
CostofLiving × ArtSchools	−0.0350***	−0.0073*	−0.0049	−0.0149**
	(0.0132)	(0.0044)	(0.0036)	(0.0077)
BrainHub	−0.0461	−0.1354	0.4002	0.7946
	(1.5761)	(0.5556)	(0.5997)	(1.2218)
PlatformHub	1.2792	−0.8180	−0.6523	−0.2133
	(1.9489)	(0.5814)	(0.4971)	(0.7418)
CreativeClass	−2.3746	1.0552	0.4635	−0.7286
	(2.1861)	(1.0148)	(1.0002)	(1.8207)
Missing CreativeClass	−0.1798	0.1877	0.1122	−0.1069
	(0.4025)	(0.1765)	(0.1622)	(0.3592)
Metro	−0.4655*	−0.0399	−0.0069	0.0593
	(0.2491)	(0.1002)	(0.1102)	(0.2309)
PopDensity	22.3981**	1.6718	2.7992	6.2384
	(11.3477	(4.3777)	(4.4333)	(10.4656)
East	−0.7611**	−0.1461*	−0.0854	−0.4106**
	(0.2938)	(0.0854)	(0.0927)	(0.1838)
West	1.4286***	0.3824**	0.4707***	1.2410***
	(0.5249)	(0.1699)	(0.1815)	(0.4082)
Coast	−0.4775	−0.0387	0.2247	0.2228
	(0.4534)	(0.1305)	(0.1514)	(0.2990)
JanTemp	−0.0031	−0.0042	−0.0107*	−0.0160
	(0.0148)	(0.0043)	(0.0053)	(0.0111)

Table 9 (continued)

	All	Local	Fine arts	Arts
JulyTemp	−0.0082	0.0024	0.0165	0.0212
	(0.0310)	(0.0108)	(0.0125)	(0.0231)
Humidity	0.0299**	0.0091**	0.0087*	0.0210**
	(0.0131)	(0.0043)	(0.0045)	(0.0093)
Constant	4.2379	−0.6415	−0.8340	0.7571
	(3.8442)	(1.3203)	(1.6181)	(3.4220)
No. of Observations	942	942	942	942
R−squared	0.0836	0.1530	0.0776	0.1644

Robust standard errors in parentheses. * $p<0.10$; ** $p<0.05$, *** $p<0.01$

Table 10 Full results for additional OLS model estimates for net migration by CBSA

	Music	Film & Video	Publishing	Technology
OwnProjects	0.0116**	0.0073	−0.0095	0.0150
	(0.0056)	(0.0037)	(0.0095)	(0.0102)
OwnJob	580.6636	45.1599	−1.6150	−4.1820
	(567.7886)	(36.1383)	(2.3471)	(7.8423)
Missing OwnJob	0.0740	0.0186	0.0095	−0.0010
	(0.1047)	(0.0539)	(0.0339)	(0.0288)
AllProjects	−0.0020**	−0.0007	0.0013	0.0001
	(0.0010)	(0.0007)	(0.0010)	(0.0004)
Pop	−0.0213	0.0944	−0.1597	−0.3510
	(0.2748)	(0.4052)	(0.2731)	(0.2721)
Pop^2	0.0034	−0.0235	−0.0090	0.0053
	(0.0166)	(0.0309)	(0.0209)	(0.0157)
Income	−0.0061	−0.0859	−0.1120	0.0959*
	(0.1146)	(0.1023)	(0.0742)	(0.0530)
College	−0.6450	−0.2087	0.4233*	−0.0457
	(0.5782)	(0.2479)	(0.2161)	(0.1892)
ArtSchools	0.2499	0.5372**	0.3751	0.8101**
	(0.3903)	(0.2590)	(0.2790)	(0.4018)
CostofLiving	−0.0026	−0.0105	−0.0032	0.00001
	(0.0081)	(0.0074)	(0.0045)	(0.0036)
CostofLiving × ArtSchools	−0.0027	−0.0053**	−0.0036	−0.0086**
	(0.0039)	(0.0024)	(0.0029)	(0.0043)
BrainHub	0.6282	−0.4266	0.3780	−0.5286
	(0.8173)	(0.5508)	(0.3379)	(0.3908)
PlatformHub	0.3560	0.0752	0.7600	0.2970
	(0.7855)	(0.5515)	(0.4685)	(0.3279)
CreativeClass	−1.0616	0.0059	0.0214	−0.8849*
	(1.4250)	(0.8222)	(0.6031)	(0.5115)

Table 10 (continued)

	Music	Film & Video	Publishing	Technology
Missing CreativeClass	−0.1882	0.0656	−0.0080	−0.1316
	(0.2678)	(0.1515)	(0.1042)	(0.0901)
Metro	0.1578	0.0301	−0.1566**	0.0046
	(0.1045)	(0.0945)	(0.0718)	(0.0533)
PopDensity	3.1268	2.7763	7.3280**	5.8785
	(3.6710)	(3.9946)	(3.0330)	(3.8981)
East	−0.1350	−0.1390	−0.0464	−0.0614
	(0.1053)	(0.0860)	(0.0632)	(0.0531)
West	0.4609*	0.3431**	0.2450	0.0406
	(0.2536)	(0.1472)	(0.1513)	(0.1177)
Coast	−0.0185	0.0085	−0.3172**	−0.1790
	(0.1590)	(0.1598)	(0.1298)	(0.1096)
JanTemp	−0.0011	−0.0041	0.0044	0.0056
	(0.0067)	(0.0044)	(0.0041)	(0.0036)
JulyTemp	−0.0015	0.0076	−0.0065	−0.0121
	(0.0130)	(0.0105)	(0.0107)	(0.0095)
Humidity	0.0078	0.0052	0.0023	0.0034
	(0.0053)	(0.0032)	(0.0033)	(0.0026)
Constant	0.1352	1.0114	1.6176	−0.2982
	(1.9506)	(1.6161)	(1.3074)	(0.8712)
No. of Observations	942	942	942	942
R-squared	0.2244	0.2518	0.1111	0.3791

Robust standard errors in parentheses. * $p<0.10$, ** $p<0.05$, *** $p<0.01$

Table 11 Employment sectors associated with each project category grouping

Category of Project	NAICS code	Description
Fine Arts	711510	Independent Artists, Writers, and Performers
	711120	Dance Companies
	711110	Theater Companies and Dinner Theaters
Music	711130	Musical Groups and Artists
Film & Video	512110	Motion Picture and Video Production
	512131	Motion Picture Theaters (except Drive-Ins)
	711310	Promoters of Performing Arts, Sports and Similar Events with Facilities
Publishing	511199	All Other Publishers
	611310	Colleges, Universities and Professional Schools
Technology	332312	Fabricated Structural Metal Manufacturing
	333244	Printing Machinery and Equipment Manufacturing
	334111	Electronic Computer Manufacturing
	334310	Audio and Video Equipment Manufacturing
	334511	Search, Detection, Navigation, Guidance, Aeronautical and Nautical System and Instrument Manufacturing
	541512	Computer Systems Design Services
	811211	Consumer Electronics Repair and Maintenance

Acknowledgements Research support for this paper was provided by Hannah Nadler, Mackenzie Rice, and Michael Weigel. This paper could not have been written without the generous support of the Social Sciences and Humanities Research Council of Canada [Grant number 895-2013-1008], the National Endowment for the Arts [Award#: 1844331-38-C-18]. The opinions expressed are those of the author(s) and do not represent the views of the National Endowment for the Arts Office of Research & Analysis or the National Endowment for the Arts. The Arts Endowment does not guarantee the accuracy or completeness of the information included in this material and is not responsible for any consequences of its use.

Funding Research funding from the Social Sciences and Humanities Research Council of Canada [Grant number 895-2013-1008] and the National Endowment for the Arts [Award#: 1844331-38-C-18].

Availability of data and material All data are publicly available, as referenced in the manuscript.

Code availability (software application or custom code) StataMP v15 used for all calculations.

Declarations

Conflict of interest The authors declare no conflicts of interest or competing interests in this research.

References

Acs, Z. J. (1992). Small business economics: A global perspective. *Challenge, 35*(6), 38–44.

Acs, Z. J., Desai, S., & Klapper, L. F. (2008). What does "entrepreneurship" data *really* show? *Small Business Economics, 31*(3), 265–281.

Backman, M., & Nilsson, P. (2018). The role of cultural heritage in attracting skilled individuals. *Journal of Cultural Economics, 42*(1), 111–138.

Basso, G., & Peri, G. (2020). Internal mobility: The greater responsiveness of foreign-born to economic conditions. *Journal of Economic Perspectives, 34*(3), 77–98.

Blau, J. (1989). *The Shape of Culture*. Cambridge University Press.

Borén, T., & Young, C. (2013a). Getting creative with the 'creative city'? Towards new perspectives on creativity in urban policy. *International Journal of Urban and Regional Research, 37*(5), 1799–1815.

Borén, T., & Young, C. (2013b). The migration dynamics of the 'Creative Class': Evidence from a study of artists in Stockholm, Sweden. *Annals of the Association of American Geographers, 103*(1), 195–210.

Brail, S. (2020). World cities of ride-hailing. *Urban Geography*. https://doi.org/10.1080/02723638.2020.1775030.

Breznitz, S. M., & Noonan, D. S. (2018). Planting the seed to grow local creative industries: The impacts of cultural districts and arts schools on economic development. *Environment and Planning A, 50*(5), 1047–1070.

Breznitz, S. M., & Noonan, D. S. (2020). Crowdfunding in a not-so-flat world. *Journal of Economic Geography*. https://doi.org/10.1093/jeg/lbaa008.

Buettner, T., & Janeba, E. (2016). City competition for the creative class. *Journal of Cultural Economics, 40*(4), 413–451.

Cebula, R. J., Davis, M. L., Koch, J. V., & Saunoris, J. M. (2020). The relationship between entrepreneurial activity and domestic gross state in-migration patterns in the US. *Applied Economics, 52*(41), 4542–4556.

Chen, Y., & Rosenthal, S. S. (2008). Local amenities and life-cycle migration: Do people move for jobs or fun? *Journal of Urban Economics, 64*(3), 519–537.

Dalla Chiesa, C., & Handke, C. (2020). Crowdfunding. In R. Towse & T. Navarrete Hernández (Eds.), *Handbook of Cultural Economics*. (pp. 158–167). Edward Elgar Publishing.

Ellison, G., Glaeser, E. L., & Kerr, W. R. (2010). What causes industry agglomeration? Evidence from coagglomeration patterns. *American Economic Review, 100*(3), 1195–1213.

Ewing, H. & Grady, R. (Directors). (2012). *Detropia* [Film]. Loki Films.
Florida, R. (2002). *The Rise of the Creative Class*. Basic Books.
Glaeser, E. L. (2010). Introduction. *Agglomeration Economics*. (pp. 1–14). University of Chicago Press.
Glaeser, E. L., & Maré, D. C. (2001). Cities and skills. *Journal of Labor Economics, 19*, 316–342.
Glaeser, E. L., & Shapiro, J. M. (2003). Urban growth in the 1990s: Is city living back? *Journal of Regional Science, 43*(1), 139–165.
Granovetter, M. S. (1973). The strength of weak ties. *American Journal of Sociology, 78*(6), 1360–1380.
Hansen, H. K., & Niedomysl, T. (2009). Migration of the Creative Class: Evidence from Sweden. *Journal of Economic Geography, 9*(2), 191–206.
Hoffmann, A. N. (2007). A rough guide to entrepreneurship policy. In D. B. Audretsch, I. Grilo, & R. A. Thurik (Eds.), *Handbook of research on entrepreneurship policy*. (pp. 140–161). Edward Elgar, Cheltenham.
Holcomb, B. (1999). Marketing cities for tourism. In D. Judd & S. Fainstein (Eds.), *The Tourist City*. (pp. 54–70). Yale University Press.
Judd, D. (1999). Constructing the tourist bubble. In D. Judd & S. Fainstein (Eds.), *The Tourist City*. (pp. 35–53). Yale University Press.
Kelly, E., & O'Hagan, J. (2007). Geographic clustering of economic activity: The case of prominent western visual artists. *Journal of Cultural Economics, 31*(2), 109–128.
Kenney, M., & Zysman, J. (2020). The platform economy: Restructuring the space of capitalist accumulation. *Cambridge Journal of Regions, Economy and Society, 13*(1), 55–76.
Kickstarter. (2020). https://www.kickstarter.com/about.
Krupka, D. J., & Noonan, D. S. (2013). City air and city markets: Worker productivity gains across city sizes. *International Regional Science Review, 36*(2), 183–206.
Lazzaro, E., & Noonan, D. S. (2020). A comparative analysis of US and EU regulatory frameworks of crowdfunding for the cultural and creative industries. *International Journal of Cultural Policy*. https://doi.org/10.1080/10286632.2020.1776270.
Lee, N. (2014). The creative industries and urban economic growth in the UK. *Environment and Planning A, 46*(2), 455–470.
Li, G. C. (2019). Kickstarter Structured Relational Databasehttps://doi.org/10.7910/DVN/EOYBXM,HarvardDataverse,V2.
Lopez, J. C. G. (2019). Cultural workers and the character of cities. *The Annals of Regional Science, 62*(1), 211–246.
Markusen, A. (2013). Artists work everywhere. *Work and Occupations, 40*(4), 481–495.
Markusen, A., & Schrock, G. (2006). The artistic dividend: Urban artistic specialization and economic development implications. *Urban Studies, 43*(10), 1661–1686.
McGranahan, D. A. (1999). *Natural amenities drive rural population change*. Agricultural Economic Report No. (AER-781). United States Department of Agriculture, Economic Research Service.
Mendes-Da-Silva, W., Rossoni, L., Conte, B. S., Gattaz, C. C., & Francisco, E. R. (2016). The impacts of fundraising periods and geographic distance on financing music production via crowdfunding in Brazil. *Journal of Cultural Economics, 40*(1), 75–99.
Minniti, M., & Lévesque, M. (2008). Recent developments in the economics of entrepreneurship. *Journal of Business Venturing, 23*(6), 603–612.
Mittelstädt, A. & Cerri, F. (2008). Fostering Entrepreneurship for Innovation, *OECD Science, Technology and Industry Working Papers*, No. 2008/05, OECD Publishing, Paris.
Mollick, E. (2014). The dynamics of crowdfunding: An exploratory study. *Journal of Business Venturing, 29*, 1–16.
Moretti, E. (2012). *The New Geography of Jobs*. Mifflin Harcourt: Houghton.
Neal, Z. (2012). Creative employment and jet set cities: Disentangling causal effects. *Urban Studies, 49*(12), 2693–2709.
Noonan, D. S. (2021). The arts and culture sector's contributions to economic recovery and resiliency in the United States: Technical report. Washington, DC: National Assembly of State Arts Agencies. https://nasaa-arts.org/nasaa_research/the-arts-and-culture-sectors-contributions-to-economic-recovery-and-resiliency-in-the-united-states-technical-report/
Peukert, C. (2019). The next wave of digital technological change and the cultural industries. *Journal of Cultural Economics, 43*(2), 189–210.
Piore, M., & Sabel, C. (1984). *The Second Industrial Divide*. . Basic Books.
Porter, M. E. (1990). *The Competitive Advantage of Nations*. . Free Press.

Putnam, R. D. (1995). Bowling alone: America's declining social capital. *Journal of Democracy, 6*(1), 65–78.
Regner, T. (2020). Crowdfunding a monthly income: An analysis of the membership platform Patreon. *Journal of Cultural Economics*. https://doi.org/10.1007/s10824-020-09381-5.
Rodríguez-Pose, A., & Lee, N. (2020). Hipsters vs geeks? Creative workers, STEM and innovation in US cities. *Cities, 100*, 102653.
Schiff, N. (2015). Cities and product variety: evidence from restaurants. *Journal of Economic Geography, 15*(6), 1085–1123.
Scott, A. J. (2005). *On Hollywood: The Place*. Princeton University Press, Princeton, NJ.
Scott, A. J. (2006). Entrepreneurship, innovation and industrial development: Geography and the creative field revisited. *Small Business Economics, 26*(1), 1–24.
Storper, M., & Manville, M. (2006). Behaviour, preferences and cities: Urban theory and urban resurgence. *Urban Studies, 43*(8), 1247–1274.
Storper, M., & Scott, A. J. (1995). The wealth of regions: market forces and policy imperatives in local and global context. *Futures, 27*(5), 505–526.
Storper, M., & Scott, A. J. (2009). Rethinking human capital, creativity and urban growth. *Journal of Economic Geography, 9*(2), 147–167.
Sleuwaegen, L., & Boiardi, P. (2014). Creativity and regional innovation: Evidence from EU regions. *Research Policy, 43*(9), 1508–1522.
Sorenson, O., Assenova, V., Li, G. C., Boada, J., & Fleming, L. (2016). Expand innovation finance via crowdfunding. *Science, 354*(6319), 1526–1528.
Tubadji, A., Osoba, B. J., & Nijkamp, P. (2015). Culture-based development in the USA: Culture as a factor for economic welfare and social well-being at a county level. *Journal of Cultural Economics, 39*(3), 277–303.
Woronkowicz, J., & Noonan, D. S. (2019). Who goes freelance? The determinants of self-employment for artists. *Entrepreneurship Theory and Practice, 43*(4), 651–672.

Journal of Cultural Economics (2021) 45:613–631
https://doi.org/10.1007/s10824-021-09417-4

ORIGINAL ARTICLE

Economies of scope in artists' incubator projects

Amy Whitaker[1]

Received: 23 June 2020 / Accepted: 5 April 2021 / Published online: 26 April 2021

Abstract

Although economies of scale are relatively well studied in the arts, economies of scope have received less attention. Yet recent trends toward freelancing and technological connectivity make scope economies especially timely in addressing structural challenges to artist-led incubators. This paper offers a conceptual framework for cooperative strategies that employ economies of scope both in the economic sense of joint production and in the financial sense of risk pooling. This framework distinguishes franchise, federation, and resource-sharing organizational structures as developed through case studies of two US-based organizations: ArtBuilt and REC (Resources for Every Creator), placed in a larger context of cooperative organizational strategy in the USA and Europe. The proposed strategies of cooperative networks (quasi-franchises, federations, or resource-sharing networks) also draw on a literature of spatial agglomeration in creative industries. The framework leads to more speculative ideas of "balance-sheet philanthropy" through credit backstopping by foundations, and of novel investment trusts that can be piloted across a range organizations including foundations, grant-makers, artist residency programs, and even for-profit companies engaged in reinsurance. The paper contributes managerial tools and strategies for the creative engagement of capacity building in arts organizations.

Keywords Entrepreneurship · Social innovation · Real estate services · Cultural economics · Creative industries · Property rights (P14) · Economics of art and literature (Z11) · Property and intellectual capital (O34)

> *One day I woke up and realized that everything I love about New York City was possibly endangered….No one would give me money [to fix it] and then I lost my temper and did it myself….We realized they didn't have a clear understanding of the value of arts as an actual business enterprise*
>
> – Esther Robinson

✉ Amy Whitaker
amy.whitaker@nyu.edu

1 Department of Art and Art Professions, Visual Arts Administration, Steinhardt School, New York University, 34 Stuyvesant Street, New York, NY 10003, USA

1 Introduction

Although studies of economies of scale in the arts are relatively longstanding (Baumol and Bowen 1966), economies of scope have received less attention. Yet recent trends in the arts workforce toward freelancing (Woronkowicz and Noonan 2019) make economies of scope particularly timely as a strategy in the creative industries (Caves 2000). This paper analyzes applications of economies of scope to artist-led incubators and co-working spaces. These spaces exist in a wide variety of forms (Essig 2014) but are generally scale-limited in order to protect their sense of community. Because, as Essig finds, these incubators show a wide variety of funding and governance models, this paper's contribution is to assist managers, increase capacity and best use of funds, and inform the academic literature on incubators, co-working spaces, and by extension creative industries. As this paper argues, without economies of scale, these incubators and co-working spaces can benefit strongly from economies of scope in both the economic sense of joint production (Chandler 1994) and the financial sense of risk pooling (Markowitz 1952).

This paper proposes a conceptual framework for cooperative strategies that employ economies of scope. The framework is developed through case studies of two US organizations—ArtBuilt and REC (Resources for Every Creator). ArtBuilt is an artists' studio space in the Brooklyn Army Terminal, New York. REC is a co-working space whose current location is in the Fashion District mall in Philadelphia, Pennsylvania. This paper argues that these venues can benefit from franchise and cooperative organizational structures both operationally and financially. These strategies achieve via scope and risk pooling what cannot in the arts be achieved via scale.

These strategies offer a timely contribution given the continued precarity of artistic labor and the increase in the number of artists who are freelancing. With regard to precarity, relatively recent studies by both Creative Independent (2018) and Arts Council England (2018) show low levels of earnings and high uncertainty around sustainable support for artistic practice. Artists also are freelancers or self-employed at much higher rates than for other occupations, at approximately 35% of artists as compared to 15% of other professions (Woronkowicz and Noonan 2019, at 657).

Although not well studied in the academic literature in the arts, economies of scope and risk pooling in the arts can be placed within organizational architectures of franchise and federation. The Tate in London has a federation structure, analogous to the states that comprise the USA, whereas the Guggenheim had a franchise structure. After the opening of the Guggenheim Bilbao in 1997, the Solomon R. Guggenheim Foundation was approached to create the "Bilbao Effect" in other locations and accepted the offer to brand what were effectively franchise locations worldwide (Whitaker 2021). In contrast, after the opening of the Tate Modern in 2000, Tate was approached to create that effect in other areas of the UK. Instead of creating many Tate Moderns, the organization instead started a federation of the existing local arts organizations and shared resources across a network, occasionally lending reputational endorsement from Tate's central

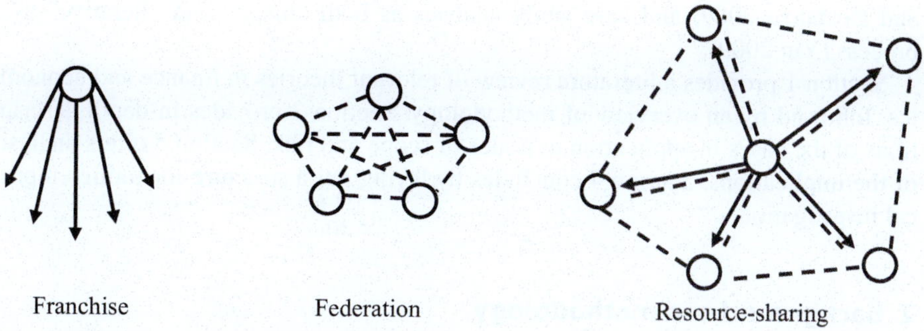

Fig. 1 Diagram of franchise, federation, and resource-sharing network

leadership visiting local events around the UK. The ensuing program, called Plus Tate (Collier and Serota 2015), continued this initiative as a membership body, reinforcing its federation approach. A key differentiation between franchise and federation as governance models is the centralization of decision rights, which are dispersed substantially more in a federated structure.

Other organizations have taken this knowledge-sharing or, more broadly, resource-sharing approach across a network of organizations. Springboard for the Arts, based in St. Paul, Minnesota, USA, has focused on replicating programs in communities, sharing resources out to a network of other organizations in such a way that those other organizations can customize them for their own purposes (author interview, Laura Zabel, Springboard for the Arts, December 7, 2020). This focus on resource-sharing combines some aspects of scale with scope and builds infrastructure to share templates that can then be customized. Gener8tor, a Milwaukee, Wisconsin-based accelerator with a dedicated arts program, has built a distributed model of replicable structures rolled out across other cities (author interview, Maureen Ragalie, Gener8tor, November 20, 2020). (See Fig. 1 for a diagrammatic overview of franchise, federation, and resource-sharing networks.)

These models exemplify different governance structures of franchise in the case of the Guggenheim, of federation in the case of Tate Plus, and of resource-sharing for mass customization in the case of Springboard for the Arts and Gener8tor. These approaches form the basis of the case study analysis of ArtBuilt and REC as projects that consider cooperative and collaborative models that invoke economies of scope in the arts. The method of analysis draws on author interviews with the leaders of these organizations and application of theories described in this literature review section.[1] Because these strategies are relatively new, this paper approaches managerial strategy as an emergent discipline using methods of strategic foresight (MacKay

[1] These interviews include site visits, structured questions, and unstructured follow-up conversations, as well as ideation sessions regarding the needs of the organizations. The interview process also included formal talks by the founders within a graduate course in "hybrid practice."

and Costanzo 2009) and case study analysis as both "linear" and "iterative" as a process (Yin 2009).

Section 1 provides a literature review of relevant theories in finance and economics, followed by an overview of methodology. Section 2 provides in-depth descriptions of the cases in application to issues of scope and risk. Section 3 offers analysis of the implications. Section 4 concludes by laying out a structure for future empirical investigation.

2 Background and methodology

As defined by Alfred Chandler, an economy of scale describes the lowering of per unit cost with the rise in overall level of production (Chandler 1994, at 17). Chandler considers scale in production and distribution as part of the Industrial Revolution and the rise of managerial capitalism. Chandler also describes economies of scope, those advantages that come about from joint production and distribution (Chandler 1994, at 17). Art organizations commonly lack access to economies of scale. They suffer from Baumol and Bowen's "cost disease" because they do not produce uniform goods in quantity and their production costs generally do not decline over time (1966).[2] Many arts organizations are not Coasean firms in the sense that they are not organized by a competitive profit motive, but they can still be understood through a Coasean logic in their need to operate where internal transaction costs are reasonable (Coase 1937).

2.1 Economies of scope and joint production

Economies of scope receive relatively little attention in the literature in arts management and cultural economics. When they do receive attention it is typically in reference to theatre, music, or performing arts. In a standard library database (EBSCO) search of articles published in this journal, only ten articles have included the phrase "economies of scope." (Usage of the phrase in the singular does not add results.) Of these ten articles, one concerns visual art but applies to international art trade not to incubators (Schulze 1999). Two study television (Doyle 2000; van der Wurff 2005), one studies recorded music (Montoro-Pons and Cuadrado-García 2018), one focuses on libraries (Locher 2005), one covers video games (Engelstätter and Ward 2018), and four focus on theatres, symphonies, and other performing arts venues

2 Baumol and Bowen's "cost disease" has been studied contextually given its formative impact on the study of arts administration (e.g., Besharov 2005; Towse 1997). The theory has also been investigated critically, notably in a 1996 plenary of the marking the 30th anniversary of Baumol and Bowen's work, which took place as part of the Ninth Annual Conference on Cultural Economics and which was memorialized in a special issue of the *Journal of Cultural Economics* (Blaug 1996). For critical responses to "cost disease," see in particular Cohen (1996), Peacock (1996), and Throsby (1996). Throsby in particular considers the economic circumstance of the performing artist finding benefits and working conditions to have improved but pay still to be low, as in the Creative Independent (2018) and Arts Council England et al. (2018) studies of visual artists.

(Lange and Luksetich 1993; Fazioli and Filippini 1997; Last and Wetzel 2010; Fernández-Blanco et al. 2019). This last paper by Fernández-Blanco et al. considers marginal cost efficiencies in Warsaw's municipal theaters. Although the authors' central finding, that productions could be 7% less expensive without artistic loss (Fernández-Blanco et al. 2019, at 113), does not pertain here, their related empirical observations do. They found that mounting new productions cost 3.33 times that of presenting works that the theater had already originated (Fernández-Blanco et al. 2019 at 114). Their findings underscore the research and development (R&D) problem that creative work is much more expensive in its formation than its presentation or repetition, creating the central challenge that arts rely on discovery not only efficiency (Whitaker and Grannemann 2019).

Scholars have in fact addressed economies of scope in the creative industries more broadly. The EBSCO library database shows 157 academic articles citing both of these terms. While many of these articles do not pertain to this study of incubators—most still largely focused on performing arts—two further studies bear mention here. Florida et al. (2012) offer a study "geographies of scope," specifically the co-location of organizations in the entertainment industry. Mellander et al. (2018) have mapped geography of music preferences in this journal, but it is the prior (2012) study of geographies of scope that most pertains.

Florida et al. draw on a 1977 paper by Baumol and Bowen to describe this economy of scope experienced across firms. While Baumol and Braunstein (1977) were writing primarily about economies of scale, they approached economies of scope through what they termed "production complementarity." They write, "Economies of scope refers to the efficiency gains and/or cost savings obtained through simultaneous production of many different products by one diversified firm instead of several smaller, more specialized firms." But then they go on to add, "Economies of scope are not limited by the boundaries of the firm, they also extend across space. Geographic economies of scope are different than simple economic diversity" (Florida et al. 2012, at 184). These studies point to network complexities of scope in creative industry ecosystems (Caves 2000). In Florida et al.'s framework, New York City is a "superstar city" for the entertainment industry, drawing a concentration of firms. This work informs the way in which these incubators become part of city infrastructure, with forms of value that may be captured by the organizations or that may remain externalities to their business models (Cheung 1973).

2.2 Agglomeration and positive externalities of co-location

In a related literature on agglomeration—which is to say, spatial advantages or positive externalities of co-location—researchers have found positive effects for creative industries. Borowiecki (2015) studies classical music composers in Europe over the time period 1750 to 1899, a period of great entrepreneurial independence for composers as artists (Borowiecki 2015, at 444). The study finds a U-shaped distribution in which composers benefit from co-location to an extent and then begin to crowd a market and to compete away benefits. Borowiecki's study describes a type of creative interaction akin to Brandenburger and Nalebuff's (1997, 2020) theory of co-opetition, or the simultaneous dynamic of cooperation and competition.

In Borowiecki's study, which measured distance from a musician's birthplace as an endogenous variable, composers were 10% more productive when one additional prominent musician lived in the same city. This effect continued until the concentration of composers was 66% above average and then decreased (Borowiecki 2015, at 445). Borowiecki interprets some benefits from positive externalities of cultural goods to the city overall (at 448) and some to critical mass of arts community to build and share in the use of—but not over-crowd—fixed-cost resources such as concert halls or opera houses (at 446). His argument concerning agglomeration benefits paints a picture of shared reliance on fixed-cost resources, positive externality to the city, and benefit to creators individually from the overall community.

In separate studies of agglomeration, Coll-Martínez (2019) finds that in Barcelona, firms in the creative service industries experience benefits from co-location, especially in industries with "symbolic" knowledge formation—including visual arts—and that these firms in the arts benefit from similarity of firm activity, including within co-working spaces (Coll-Martínez 2019, at 384). In Coll-Martínez et al. (2019), the authors also study agglomeration in Barcelona using distance-based as well as proximity-based measures (at 411) and studying creative industry as well as other organizations (CIs and non-CIs). They find strong agglomeration at very short distances and strong co-agglomeration effects for small firms, i.e., those with fewer than ten employees (Coll-Martínez et al. 2019). This stronger effect for smaller forms and shorter distance, with rapid decay over distance, indicates a likely generalizability of these agglomeration effects in co-working spaces. Overall, these studies reinforce Florida's (2002, 2014) idea of "creative clusters," which Borowiecki and Dahl also study in US artists from 1850 to 2010, finding a migration of clusters from the northeastern USA to broader areas, with some parallel concentration on the west coast (Borowiecki and Dahl 2021).

In contrast to scope, scale is difficult to achieve in arts incubators without growing larger than the size that can support a sense of community. This issue of scale appears to affect all types of artists' incubators in Essig's taxonomy (2014) and to be common across creative industries (Caves 2000). Baumol and Bowen argued that the arts do not scale but instead fall prey to cost disease (1966). Economics often leads to standardization—the uniform number 2 pencil of Leonard Read and Milton Friedman's allegories of the miracle of the pricing system (Read 1958; Friedman 1980). But in the arts, standardization can indicate stagnation even if, as Fernández-Blanco et al. (2019) show, the repetition of performances already in a theater's repertoire is so much more cost effective. Economies of scale require monoculture—the production of a uniform good at scale—to an extent anathema to a diversity of artistic ideas. As Patton Hindle, head of the arts program at Kickstarter, cites the in-house rallying cry, "f*ck the monoculture" (author interview 2020). In contrast, economies of scope can allow for diversity or heterogeneity of practice or output.

2.3 Diversification of investment and risk pooling

While the literature review above pertains to the discipline of economics, a further literature review in finance complements these effects. This literature is addressed here for two reasons, first, because managers of co-working spaces are required to essentially work interdisciplinarily across economics and finance, or in the language of managerial practice, across operating and capital expense. Second, financial methods of institutional collaboration and individual cooperative investment trusts form a unique contribution of this paper and necessarily follow from financial theories of diversification.

While scope is an economic concept applying to the ongoing economic operation of the firm, scope also has this counterpart in the financial management of the organization specifically in the application to risk pooling. Economically and operationally, firms benefit from cost savings via scope. Financially and in an investment sense, firms benefit from risk pooling and diversification. As Markowitz (1952) famously showed, an investor could receive a higher risk-adjusted return by investing in the entire market basket because the internal lack of correlation of returns across instruments provided a kind of internal insurance. In the case of arts organizations, they do not have the scale of investment or capital within which to pool these activities. They often have highly concentrated investment in their own single organization and physical plant. By Markowitz's logic, a group of incubators could arguably receive lower lending rates than a single entity. Thus, operating across a network or constellation of like-sized organizations could give incubators better access to favorable lending rates, through the scope-like assembly of larger portfolios of organizations.

Whitaker and Grannemann (2019) have applied ideas of risk pooling to the arts, proposing that artists pool their resale royalties and that performing artists pool their equity shares in order to hold diversified exposure to the proceeds of their work. Whitaker and Kräussl (2020) have proposed fractional equity in art empirically, demonstrating that artists would benefit by holding shares in the art over time. This combined approach of diversified investment and retained equity leads to newer forms of individual investment practice for artists.

2.4 Competing definitions of value

This discussion of risk and financial investment steers close to complex and evergreen debates over questions of value and measurement in the arts. Bourdieu described multiple forms of capital (1993) which Throsby adapts to the arts (1999). Klamer described cultural and social value not only economic (1996). Others including Hutter and Throsby (2008) and Towse and Hernández (2020) have interrogated the overlaps of cultural and economic value. Grampp argued that all value can be converted to economic value (Grampp 1989). Noneconomic forms of value are difficult to measure in any comparable way. A problem shared with contingent valuation methodologies (Noonan 2003, 2013; Sanz et al. 2003), this analysis of value also lacks an available counterfactual. It is difficult to measure the impact of ArtBuilt or REC because we may be measuring them against a baseline that their existence helped to preserve. Even if nothing changed in either organization's environment, they could still have had a strong impact in preserving cultural vibrancy and in slowing a drive toward homogenization. The value of cities depends on creativity and cultural structurally but not in ways that are easily understood or valued economically (Noonan 2003; Johnson and Thomas 1998). The methods of this paper apply these theoretical concerns to a set of interviews with these organizations' founders, to generate hypothetical strategies based on economies of scope.

3 Summary of the case studies

The case studies in this paper are artists' incubators in the broad sense described by Linda Essig (2014). ArtBuilt is a nonprofit organization that is legally structured as a "501(c)3" organization, as named after the corresponding section of the US tax code describing the exemption for charitable purposes. REC is venture-backed and for-profit, and intends to expand beyond its current location. Neither organization is legally a hybrid organization in the sense Michael Rushton (2014) describes. That is, they are not "public benefit corporations" or other newer legal forms that combine aspects of for-profit fiduciary duty and nonprofit drive toward mission. Yet both organizations could be said to have hybrid purpose managerially, if not legally, with both financially and socially engaged structures. The intended beneficiaries are not only the direct members of the organizations but the larger communities as well.

ArtBuilt is a 50,000-square-foot nonprofit (501(c)3) artists' studio space started by Esther Robinson and Guy Buckles and opened in the Brooklyn Army Terminal in 2018.[3] It is the largest artists' studio space to open in New York City in the past twenty years, and the largest studio space before that, the Elizabeth Foundation for the Arts, was co-founded by Buckles. The impetus for ArtBuilt was seeing friends kicked out of artists' studio buildings by developers hoping to make money in redevelopment only to leave the buildings sitting empty for years. Owing to well-meaning city initiatives that were intended to support affordable housing, buildings that would have otherwise been used for artists' studios were now out of price range. The key goal of the organization was not just to provide studio space but to create stability.

ArtBuilt is home to approximately 120 members who share 65 studios ranging from 250 to 2500 square feet (Hamilton 2019). The studios offer 10-year lease terms with a 5-year extension. These are the terms offered to ArtBuilt via the building owner, the New York City Economic Development Corporation (NYC EDC). Per

[3] The Brooklyn Army Terminal is a four-million-square-foot building in Sunset Park, Brooklyn, NY. It was designed by Cass Gilbert, the architect of Manhattan's Woolworth Building, and completed in 1919. Its most famous use was as a supply depot for the army. During World War II, it was the departure point for three million troops (including Elvis Presley) and 37 million tons of supplies.

NYC EDC Mission, the rent is below market rate. Tenants pay \$13–24 per square foot compared to \$28–36 per square foot in comparable commercial buildings.

ArtBuilt is financed by a loan via LISC (the Local Initiatives Support Corporation), the community lender, through a collaboration between Robinson, Buckles, and Anisha Steephen, then the founding director of LISC's economic development lending and policy practice area.[4] Steephen, Robinson, and Buckles structured a deal at a 7% rate.[5] The structure was later replicated in the NYC Inclusive Creative Economy Fund, a partnership between LISC and Upstart Co-Lab (LISC NYC 2018).

REC (Resources for Every Creator) is a music and arts incubator started by Will Toms and David Silver. Having moved its earlier incarnation in an old window factory in north Philadelphia, REC (this location sometimes called REC Philly) opened a 10,000-square-foot space in Fashion District mall in Center City, Philadelphia in 2019. Structured like a gym membership for creatives, REC takes in monthly dues from members who can then use the facilities which include fourteen different technological and maker studios ranging including podcast recording studios, music recording sound rooms, and editing equipment.

The 900 members of REC receive vouchers they can use to book space according to their membership level. Membership levels range from \$49 (8 credits) to \$149 per month (24 credits). Of note, within the REC community, use of resources functions on this barter or credit system, without direct translation to money rents. The mall-front space of REC operates as a store selling goods made by members on consignment. REC to expand to other cities. Their larger aim is to create the conditions that support sustainable economic livelihoods for freelance creatives. They measure their success in members having the financial stability to quit their day jobs. They also aim to be part of a larger social movement for freelance creatives to be able to thrive and be in community. As Toms says, "We've always believed that the role of the artist is to push society forward" (REC, n.d.).

The case studies share that they are founded by creative entrepreneurs—part artist, part community-builder, part activist—that they are sited in physical space, and that they intend to support artists and other creatives in ways that are essentially agnostic to quality. Neither ArtBuilt nor REC curates applicants. Instead, they benefit by word of mouth and reputational awareness.

The sample philanthropic organization is imagined as an artist's foundation such Joan Mitchell Foundation, Rauschenberg Foundation, or the Andy Warhol Foundation that specifically supports artists' programming and direct grants, or foundations such as Mellon Foundation or Ford Foundation that support larger programmatic initiatives in the arts. Because the artists' foundations typically still own substantial collections of artworks that they sell in a controlled fashion, the foundation has a proportionately larger, illiquid balance sheet but could put that more illiquid capital to work in this way with relatively low risk, given that the amount of backstopped debt constitutes a very small proportion of their assets and, in the case of a theoretical default, the funding

[4] LISC is a nonprofit community development financial institution (CDFI) founded in 1979 by managers from the Ford Foundation.

[5] Where not stated otherwise, information on ArtBuilt and REC Philly comes from author interviews.

would generally fall into the scope of the kind of funds that the foundation more typically granted. They have a mission and exemplary track record of supporting individual artists. They are also financially fortunate, through stewardship, discipline, and endowment with the artist's works, to have a strong balance sheet which gives them a stronger loan profile than an artist-run incubator space.[6] They are in a position to take on risk, should they so desire. Grantmaking organizations, such as Springboard for the Arts, Minnesota, and Center for Cultural Innovation, California, could also partner with financial firms to regrant this credit-wrapper as an in-kind donation, given similarities of this work to reinsurance, a common investment of hedge funds. These ideas are speculative, as tax donation policy would theoretically need to recognize and place a valuation on this activity.

4 Analyzing applications of economies of scope

We analyze the key challenges these organizations face from lack of scale and then propose ways of addressing them via operational scope and risk pooling.

4.1 Operational scope

Scope economies in the arts are more common for back-office functions than organizational mission. For example, the firm Artspool allows nonprofit organizations to outsource their bookkeeping. Staff expertise in nonprofit accounting can create cost savings through joint production of bookkeeping across nonstandard organizations. Artspool also has comparative advantage that would not be found in small-scale arts nonprofit organizations (Bernhofen and Brown 2018; Ricardo 1817). They specialize in bookkeeping but because the tasks vary across organization, we would model this as a scope rather than scale economy. The combined managerial skills of the founders in charisma, industry knowledge, and disciplined yet inventive financial modeling are themselves transferrable across distinct yet related projects in a way that constitutes an application of scope.

4.2 Scope risk and the Coasean firm

REC also makes an intervention into risk but in the separate realm of the risk that firms have outsourced onto freelance laborers. Like Uber drivers, freelancers bear the burden of self-investment and do not benefit from the risk management functions of the firm. Yet what REC does is in fact to recreate some benefits of the Coasean firm for a constellation of freelancers. REC has the capacity to serve as a brand umbrella for freelancers. For instance, those looking to hire contract labor might go to REC as a trusted intermediary. Over time, being a REC member could lessen the risk of freelancing by

[6] According to the 2017 Form 990, the most recent available on Guidestar, the Joan Mitchell Foundation holds $130.8 million in net assets. Those figures list art holdings at book value; at fair market value, the foundation's assets are $363.8 million (Joan Mitchell 2017, at 2 and 43). The difference between book and market value of the art collection is from $26.4 million to $257.4 million (Statement 14, p. 43).

creating these network benefits to members. REC also creates economies of scope in the use of its resources for creators. No one could use a podcast studio 24 hours a day, making it an ideal kind of shared resource. Equally, if REC is able to expand, directly or by franchise, to other cities then it starts to benefit from the same economies of scope that are proposed above for ArtBuilt but with a franchise rather than federation model. Both would be operating as part of a cooperative group of artists' incubator spaces with varying degrees of standardization and coordination across them.

4.3 Institutionally backed risk pooling

A key challenge for ArtBuilt was access to capital and the analysis that funders did of ArtBuilt's risk. The founders raised $1.3 million in order to secure a lease and then replaced an investor with the LISC loan, ultimately borrowing 600,000 for the 1.3 million project. Concurrent to ArtBuilt's founding, a one-million-square-foot development in comparable building received a much lower rate, on the order of 3.5%. The higher cost of capital for ArtBuilt stems both from its scale and from its risk profile. ArtBuilt does not have a large balance sheet. If it could access one, via philanthropic guaranteeing by a foundation or in-kind donation from a financial institution or its nonprofit arm, ArtBuilt could access these lower rates.

The financial parallel to economies of scope is risk pooling in access to capital. This paper proposes a kind of balance sheet philanthropy—one that Robinson herself investigated in opening ArtBuilt. A foundation with substantial assets could guarantee the loan, bringing ArtBuilt or a peer institution a lower lending rate. There are two different but related mechanisms at work. First, the consortium of ArtBuilt-like spaces could apply for funding together. In this way, they form a portfolio. Although they do share common risk characteristics, they theoretically benefit from diversification across geographic area and management teams. Their idiosyncratic risk benefits from diversification while their industry-specific risk still exists.

Second, ArtBuilt alone or the entire consortium could receive a third-party guarantee from a foundation. A foundation agrees to repay the loan if ArtBuilt defaults. The foundation becomes the bank that can reclaim assets of the organization, while the bank becomes a cash-flow lender who would, in the event of default, be repaid by the foundation. The bank insures its risk in two ways. First, the foundation has now backstopped the loan. Second, the bank has more information on the loan recipients because the foundation, which is arguably more expert in the field than the bank is, has vetted and vouched for them.[7]

In addition to a foundation backstopping debt as a form of philanthropic support, other financial actors could do the same. The foundation arms of large banks could donate, or the banks themselves could adapt reinsurance structure for hedge funds.

[7] In this specific case, Esther Robinson and Guy Buckles have reputations that precede them. In addition to Buckles' role in founding the Elizabeth Foundation for the Arts, Robinson was a member of the early team at Creative Capital and founder of ArtHome, an advocacy organization for artists' home ownership. She is also a filmmaker by background, a training that helped her with the risk profile of the fundraising ask, given how risky film financing generally is.

The investment firm is putting money to work by assigning to their reserves this reinsurance allocation. If this in-kind donation were credited to the investment firm as a philanthropic contribution, they would have incentive to provide it. There might need to be legislation to give tax credits for this in-kind donation, but many other forms of philanthropy would benefit from this development of in-kind insurance products as part of philanthropy.

Insurance is a generally under-explored area of philanthropy. For example, marathon runners who accept charity slots of large races are often asked to provide a credit card guaranteeing a certain minimum fundraising amount should they be unable to run, including for reasons of injury. Similarly, there is an advantageous match-up of a large insurance provider—or financial entity—and the ability to guarantee relatively low value amounts that have relatively low systemic risk of default. As long as the USA continues to support a tax credit for charitable contributions, it makes sense for there to be an equivalency that helping an organization seek lower lending rates has a charitable benefit that can be quantified.

Critics might say that these proposals replicate the credit wrappers offered inadvisably by ratings agencies precipitating the 2008 financial crisis. What is critical here is the alignment of interest between the funder and the beneficiary. It is not in the interest of a foundation to risk its capital unless it believes in the underlying venture. While the abrupt catastrophe of coronavirus circumstance makes any backstopping of debt look too risky, if we imagine a more typical risk environment, this approach can allow a foundation to support creative ventures without cash outlay.

4.4 Ground up risk pooling and collaborative investment trusts

In addition to risk arbitrage through financial partnership, the artists' incubators may also wish to pool risk from the ground up by taking a financial interest in artists' work or facilitating artists to build risk-sharing investment trusts across their work (Whitaker and Grannemann 2019). The sharing of upside can be formalized and made collective. The logic stems from resale royalties for art, the percentage shared back to the artist when an artwork is resold in the secondary market. Some have proposed fractional equity in art that is managed by contract not, as resale royalties are, by legislation (Whitaker 2018; Whitaker and Kräussl 2020). Here, we can imagine fractional equity in concert with pooled investment trusts for the fellows within organization (Whitaker and Grannemann 2019). Theories of agglomeration may inform the networks within which creative-industry practitioners have enough affinity—or benefits of co-location but differing activities—such that joint investment trusts may share risk collectively in interesting ways.

For a residential incubator, fractional equity could be used in two broad ways: (1) with the incubator as the minority equity holder or (2) with the incubator as a collector of art and a majority holder of equity, with artists retaining minority shares. In the first case, incubator would claim or purchase 10% (for example) shares in the work artists made while fellows there. When that work was sold and resold into markets, the incubator would receive a share. In the second case, the incubator would collect work, paying artists in the residency in order to purchase their work. (The governance and pricing around these purchases would require careful attention.) Here, the incubator would be able to either keep the collection indefinitely or to sell into markets to raise funds for the incubator's projects. These sales would also benefit the artists as minority shareholder. If the incubator chose to keep the artworks indefinitely, it could also hypothetically secure capital by taking art loans against them.

In the case of incubators with a mission, including a mission to revitalize a local community, the institution may share part of the fractional equity with the local community, with a larger group of artists, or with a charitable cause. For example, the retained equity could go 80% to the artist, 10% to the incubator and 10% to the community. This structure—of not just creating value but capturing it—is essentially flexible and generative. It allows artists, organizations, and causes to benefit in lockstep. Each group of residents could buy into a larger investment trust or there could be separate investment trusts for each cohort of an incubator, or a combination of the two, with successive classes buying in at a net asset value (NAV). The fractional equity split could include streams for charity, social justice causes, community development, or anything else the organization and its members decided. Kadist Foundation has created a private resale royalties contract that models this specific aspect of giving a portion of a royalty—here, a proportion of fractional equity—to a charitable cause (del Pesco 2020, Kadist 2019). The values of supporting artists and the community can be inculcated in a fund structure and reinforced with governance design as to who decides the equity split and recipients.

5 Managerial implications

In the case of organizations such as ArtBuilt and REC, the economy of scope for the overall organization can be modeled as a franchise or federation. REC Philly anticipates expanding to other markets, operating as a franchise. ArtBuilt has no such plans but could join a federation or coop of other likeminded spaces, adapting to the challenge of maximum scale by federating with other organizations. This federation could be at a local, state, or national level so that transaction costs of managing regulatory and tax regimes are not onerously high as they might be if operating across national jurisdictions. If following a resource-sharing method exemplified by Springboard for the Arts or Gener8tor, these networks could operate internationally as well.[8] Whether through formal legal alliance or collective advocacy, that consortium can find advantages of scope across a network of standalone art spaces.

The key outcome of economies of scope in the economic sense is capacity building. The key outcome in the risk-pooling sense is both capacity building—through advantageous interest rates, freeing up capital—and also forms of investment that are flexible to the ways in which value in the arts changes substantially

[8] The artist-run, barter economy school Trade School open-sourced the software to set up a Trade School, taking a resource-sharing model that led to fifty chapters and over 22,000 students attending Trade Schools worldwide (Woolard 2020; Tradeschool.coop, n.d.).

over time. With the difficulty of pricing early-stage creative work, these artists' incubator ventures benefit from retaining equity so that their success grows financially alongside the success of their inhabitants. Their inhabitants can also benefit from this risk-pooling effect.

In addition, these financing arrangements offer incubators and co-working spaces novel means by which to measure their outputs. Along with REC and hypothetical financial structures, ArtBuilt has a structurally difficult time modeling its metrics because the change it aims to create is transformational rather than incremental. Community economic development more typically measures jobs per square foot. An incubator does not necessarily bring jobs per square foot because of the complexities of labor classification, for instance, of studio artists with separate full-time teaching positions. ArtBuilt brought a number of jobs per square foot that is comparable to some industrial spaces, but that was not necessarily commensurate with ArtBuilt's activities. A proverbial Bed, Bath, and Beyond store would bring 10 × the jobs of ArtBuilt's tenants, the largest of which is an eight-person video collective called Meerkat, and many of which are solo practitioners, such as Matthew Rubendall, the last classical guitar maker in New York City.

Instead, the measure that ArtBuilt gave to tell its story of risk is that of occupancy. Because ArtBuilt has below-market rent, it is unlikely—outside acute natural disaster or pandemic circumstances—to have vacancies. Although it does not bring set value to the economy through jobs, it does bring value through savings to artists on the below-market rent. ArtBuilt also takes advantage of long-term contracts, which serve the organization and its tenants in minimizing ongoing negotiation and transaction risk. Its tenants reflect Woronkowicz's and Noonan's findings that artists disproportionately freelance compared to other professions (2019) and build portfolio careers. These portfolio careers mirror the nature of the incubator as collaborative and pixelated, a constellation of actors not a monolithic firm. The full value of the organization is in its ability to support creative workers and to contribute to the heterogeneity and vibrancy of its neighborhood. This outcome is difficult to measure, even by contingent valuation (Noonan 2003).

Tools for describing the outputs of social ventures—notably David Grant's method of rubrics from the *Social Profit Handbook*—can be put to work (2015). To design these metrics once must go back to the reason these organizations were founded. In ArtBuilt's case, Robinson sees the organization as a socially engaged artwork itself, an intervention against extractive capitalism and a protection against reduction of the arts to a monoculture. Robinson says, "when I solve a problem the question becomes what medium is the best medium to solve that problem? And sometimes that medium is a film. Sometimes that medium is a non-profit organization…. For me it often feels like a performance art piece called, I'm the executive director of an institution."

Additionally, ArtBuilt aims to preserve New York City's cultural diversity. It is extremely hard to measure this outcome because—in the face of inertia toward a monocultural environment—the preservation of the status quo is a form of change. Robinson says, "As an individual I feel like most of the ills of my society are about strip-mining people and value and culture and place, and placing it in the hands of a group of a few set oligarchs and a system that does not return that value to a community more broadly." ArtBuilt's collaborator Steephen echoes these sentiments when she says, "The purpose of my work is to…, in the absence of a revolution, drive money and resources to the place that doesn't typically get it and to the people who don't typically get it."

The measure of these projects goes beyond their direct and indirect financial impact. Because their ultimate measure is in opportunity cost to culture of real-estate-driven homogenization, their outcomes may best be measured in stories. The economist Akerlof, in his essay "Sins of Omission and the Practice of Economics," observes the tendency of economics as a field to value "hard" skills over "soft" ones, and to favor forms of analysis that can conform to the scientific method and rely on quantitative analysis (Akerlof 2020). Yet he observes that many important questions—from predicting the 2008 credit crisis to working meaningfully on global warming—are poorly addressed because of a lack of interdisciplinarity. Similarly, these incubator projects aim to deal with large, complex problems and to bring about transformational change. Their success proves their own case but in ways that are most visible in hindsight.

What ArtBuilt is trying to preserve and encourage cannot always be seen. It is too amorphous to translate into survey form, too reliant on imagined futures to model that way. It is architected as a nonprofit organization for this reason. We do not need to adjudicate its mission to say that efficient access to capital at its organic scale of operation serves the organization in furtherance of its mission. ArtBuilt's value is in preserving cultural vibrancy in an environment which supports the proliferation of Bed, Bath, and Beyond over the independent guitar maker. Arguably, the best way to support this work is to use financial tools on the support side—in access to capital, in collective risk sharing, in designing for economies of scope—and to ignore financial measures on the delivery side. In the metaphor of soccer, finance gets the ball down the field but it is not the goal.

6 Conclusions

This paper has considered two case studies of ArtBuilt and REC in the context of franchise, federated, and resource-sharing network models of arts incubator. These models show strong cases for economies of scope in the capacity building for artists via organizational supports. Where some of the literature on freelancing or working as an artist has noted socioeconomic privilege (Woronkowicz and Noonan 2019, at 657; Borowiecki and Dahl 2021, at 4), these models of joint production and risk pooling may allow more artists to freelance sustainably by helping them access resources and operating cooperatively both operationally and in their investment in their own works.

Three different experiments would help to test this conceptual framework empirically. First is a study of foundations that might back-stop credit. With a scan of foundation balance sheets and tax returns, one could identify specific potential foundations and attributes of attractive types of foundations. Financial service organizations, including banks, hedge funds, and other reinsurance practitioners, could be included. Survey and interview methods could complement financial statement analysis. Speculatively, researchers would survey existing tax policy for in-kind donation to charity and wrote model legislation.

Second, as REC expands, its data can also serve empirical analysis, alongside surveys of its members, inclusive of detailed study of REC's partnership with Live Nation, the concert organizing firm.

Third, the property rights investment trust can be explored through survey and ethnographic interview of incubator participants and then through design of pilot study. This study could either be based on an actual operating fund or run as a hypothetical portfolio as if works made in a residency program had been collected. Additional studies could apply speculative financial models in practice in contemporary incubators or use archival methods to reconstruct from artists' residencies and grant-making programs of older vintage (e.g., US- and New York-based programs such as Franklin Furnace or Creative Capital) and amass fictionalized investment funds made out of the works created by the residents in each year.

Thematically, this study of economies of scope is emblematic of stability and security—via increased capacity and decreased risk but also stability and reduced precarity and unpredictability for artists. One of the main benefits of ArtBuilt is the stability it brings artists. Robinson says, "If you ask individuals, 'Will you be in New York fifteen years from now?,' they say 'yes.' But if you ask them, 'What are the structures that are in place in your life that insure you will be able to stay here?,'" they are unsure and start to say that they will leave the city at their next lease break. As Robinson notes, a city such as New York—one with creative cluster (Florida 2002, 2014) and agglomeration benefits (Coll-Martínez 2015)—also exerts exceptional real estate pressures both in level of rent and short term lease structure. As Robinson says, "[I]f somebody thinks that they are going to have to be displaced every three years the majority of their innovation is thinking about how not to be displaced." If we measure the output of their work, we can estimate this drag of uncertainty. Or we can reduce this drag of uncertainty via lateral network and shared investment trust.

The solution may require a reversal of methods in arts philanthropy and reconsideration of the artistic pillar of curatorial selection based on perceived artistic merit. It may require becoming, in Robinson's phrasing, "agnostic about quality." The grant-making industrial complex tries to choose and support the best work. But what if instead they chose and supported partners such as Robinson and Buckle in passive credit backstopping, and then let them support artists, no matter one individual's or one institution's ideas about quality? Robinson calls it a social justice issue: "the idea that quality is culturally determined and if we believe in a justice lens or we want to look at equity or imagine supporting culture more broadly in a place, like America or New York city, we have to ask ourselves to adjudicate: How do people get turned down? What are the biases implicit in those systems?" REC has such an agnostic system, a sense of community not of curated entry.

Of course, all of these ventures that have a real estate footprint have started a new world during the COVID pandemic. ArtBuilt has ways of approaching COVID, as a community centric "we" story with its tenants and in partnership with its larger community that encapsulates its potential role as a public good or positive externality. As these organizations build out digital presence, perhaps some of the digitally managed investment trusts are that step closer to entering the realm of possibility. At the same time, perhaps some of the benefits of agglomeration will change as remote working habits learned during the pandemic alter working patterns afterwards.

If that value is hard to measure, it is easier to know over time if represented in property rights. Designing new measures for best use *for whom* allows for the kinds of transformational not only incremental change brought about through creative placemaking and artists' incubators. Perhaps, their value cannot be known through measures of capitalism but these tools allow that value to be established more efficiently, distributed more equitably, and known at least better.

Acknowledgements The author wishes to thank Esther Robinson, Guy Buckles, Will Toms, Titus Kaphar, Jason Price, Will Goetzmann, Roman Kräussl, Angie Kim, Abdiel Lopez, Kay Takeda, Patton Hindle, Hannah Grannemann, Sandy Lee, Neil Alper, students in the Hybrid Practice class at NYU, and participants in the Leveraging Creativity Research Workshop at Indiana University, especially the workshop convenors Joanna Woronkowicz and Doug Noonan. The author also thanks the anonymous reviewers for their comments which greatly strengthened the paper.

Funding Not applicable.

Declarations

Conflict of interest The author declares that she has no conflict of interest statement.

References

Akerlof, G. A. (2020). Sins of omission and the practice of economics. *Journal of Economic Literature, 58*(2), 405–418.

Arts Council England, TBR, a-n The Artists Information Company & Doeser, J. (2018). Livelihoods of visual artists: Literature and data review. Retrieved from https://www.artscouncil.org.uk/sites/default/files/download-file/Livelihoods%20of%20Visual%20Artists%20Literature%20and%20Data%20Review.pdf

Baumol, W. J., & Bowen, W. G. (1966). *Performing arts, the economic dilemma: A Study of problems common to theater, opera, music, and dance*. . Cambridge: MIT Press.

Baumol, W. J., & Braunstein, Y. M. (1977). Empirical study of scale economies and production complementarity: The case of journal publication. *Journal of Political Economy, 85*(5), 1037–1048.

Bernhofen, D. M., & Brown, J. C. (2018). Retrospectives: On the genius behind David Ricardo's 1817 formulation of comparative advantage. *Journal of Economic Perspectives, 32*(4), 227–240.

Besharov, G. (2005). The outbreak of the cost disease: Baumol and Bowen's founding of cultural economics. *History of Political Economy, 37*(3), 413–430.

Blaug, M. (1996). Introduction to the plenary session on the 30th anniversary of the performing arts: An economic Dilemma by Baumol and Bowen-Ninth international conference on cultural economics. *Journal of Cultural Economics*, 20(3): 181–181.

Borowicki, K. J. (2015). Agglomeration economies in classical music. *Papers in Regional Science, 94*(3), 443–468.

Borowiecki, K. J., & Dahl, C. M. (2021). What makes an artist? The evolution and clustering of creative activity in the US since 1850. *Regional Science and Urban Economics, 86*(1), 1–23.

Bourdieu, P. (1993). The field of cultural production, or: the economic world reversed. In R. Johnson (Ed.), *The field of cultural production*. (pp. 29–73). New York: Polity.

Brandenburger, A., & Nalebuff, B. (1997). *Co-opetition*. . New York: Crown.

Brandenburger, A., & Nalebuff, B. (2020). The rules of co-opetition. *Harvard Business Review*. https://hbr.org/2021/01/the-rules-of-co-opetition

Caves, R. E. (2000). *Creative industries: Contracts between art and commerce*. . Cambridge: Harvard University Press.

Chandler Alfred, D. (1994). *Scale and scope: The dynamics of industrial capitalism.* . Cambridge: Harvard University Press.
Cheung, S. N. S. (1973). The fable of the bees: An economic investigation. *The Journal of Law and Economics, 16*(1), 11–33.
Coase, R. H. (1937). The nature of the firm. *Economica, 4*(16), 386–405.
Cohen, T. (1996). Why I do not believe in the cost disease: Comment on Baumol. *Journal of Cultural Economics, 20*(3), 207–214.
Collier, C., & Serota, N. (2015). Plus Tate: Connecting art to people and places. London: Tate. www.tate.org.uk/about-us/national-international-local/plus-tate.
Coll-Martínez, E. (2019). Creativity and the city: Testing the attenuation of agglomeration economies in Barcelona. *Journal of Cultural Economics, 43*(3), 365–395.
Coll-Martínez, E., Moreno-Monroy, A.-I., & Arauzo-Carod, J.-M. (2019). Agglomeration of creative industries: An inter-metropolitan analysis for Barcelona. *Papers in Regional Science, 98*(1), 409–431.
del Pesco, J. (2020). How a new kind of Artist's Contract could provide a simple, effective way to redistribute the art market's wealth. *Artnet News.* https://news.artnet.com/opinion/resale-royalties-contract-kadist-joseph-del-pesco-1897169.
Doyle, F. (2000). The economics of monomedia and cross-media expansion: A study of the case favouring deregulation of TV and newspaper ownership in the UK. *Journal of Cultural Economics, 24*(1), 1–26.
Engelstätter, B., & Ward, M. R. (2018). Strategic timing of entry: Evidence from video games. *Journal of Cultural Economics, 42*(1), 1–22.
Essig, L. (2014). Arts incubators: A typology. *The Journal of Arts Management, Law, and Society, 44*, 169–180.
Fazioli, R., & Filippini, M. (1997). Cost structure and profit mix of local public theatres. *Journal of Cultural Economics, 21*(1), 77–86.
Fernández-Blanco, V., Rodríguez-Álvarez, A., & Wiśniewska, A. (2019). Measuring technical efficiency and marginal costs in the performing arts: The case of the municipal theatres of Warsaw. *Journal of Cultural Economics, 43*(1), 97–119.
Florida, R. (2002). *The rise of the creative class.* . New York: Basic Books.
Florida, R. (2014). The creative class and economic development. *Economic Development Quarterly, 28*(3), 196–205.
Florida, R., Mellander, C., & Stolarick, K. (2012). Geographies of scope: An empirical analysis of entertainment, 1970–2000. *Journal of Economic Geography, 12*(1), 183–204.
Friedman, M. (1980). Power of the market. Free to choose. PBS. https://www.youtube.com/watch?v=R5Gppi-O3a8.
Grampp, W. D. (1989). *Pricing the priceless.* New York: Basic Books.
Grant, D. (2015). *The social profit handbook.* . White River Junction, VT: Chelsea Green.
Hamilton, W. L. (2019). Displaced artists open a new front at the Brooklyn Army Terminal. *New York Times.* https://www.nytimes.com/2019/04/22/arts/design/artbuilt-brooklyn-army-terminal.html.
Hutter, M., & Throsby, D. (Eds.). (2008). *Beyond price: Value in culture, economics, and the arts.* . Cambridge: Cambridge University Press.
Johnson, P., & Thomas, B. (1998). The economics of museums: A research perspective. *Journal of Cultural Economics, 22*(2–3), 75–85.
Kadist.org. (2019). Artist contract. https://kadist.org/program/artist-contract/.
Klamer, A. (1996). *The value of culture: On the relationship between economics and arts.* . Amsterdam: Amsterdam University Press.
Lange, M. D., & Luksetich, W. A. (1993). The cost of producing symphony orchestra services. *Journal of Cultural Economics, 17*(2), 1–15.
Last, A.-K., & Wetzel, H. (2010). The efficiency of German public theaters: A stochastic frontier analysis approach. *Journal of Cultural Economics, 34*(2), 89–110.
LISC NYC. (2018). LISC NYC launches impact investment fund to support NYC's Creative Economy at SOCAP18. *PR Newswire.* https://www.prnewswire.com/news-releases/lisc-nyc-launches-impact-investment-fund-to-support-nycs-creative-economy-at-socap18-300735096.html.
Locher, L. (2005). Public library fees in Germany. *Journal of Cultural Economics, 29*(4), 313–324.
MacKay, R. B., & Costanzo, L. A. (2009). Introduction. In R. B. MacKay & L. A. Costanzo (Eds.), *Handbook of research on strategy and foresight.* (pp. 1–12). Cheltenham: Edward Elgar.
Markowitz, H. (1952). Portfolio selection. *The Journal of Finance, 7*(1), 77–91.

Mellander, C., Florida, R., Rentfrow, P. J., & Potter, J. (2018). The Geography of music preferences. *Journal of Cultural Economics, 42*(4), 593–618.
Montoro-Pons, J. D., & Cuadrado-García, M. (2018). 'Let's make lots of money': The determinants of performance in the recorded music sector. *Journal of Cultural Economics, 42*(2), 287–307.
Noonan, D. (2003). Contingent valuation and cultural resources: A meta-analytic review of the literature. *Journal of Cultural Economics, 27*(3–4), 205–221.
Noonan, D. (2013). How U.S. cultural districts reshape neighborhoods. *Cultural Trends, 22*(3–4), 203–212.
Peacock, A. (1996). The "manifest destiny" of the performing arts. *Journal of Cultural Economics, 20*(3), 215–224.
REC. (n.d.). REC Relief. https://recphilly.com/relief/.
Read, L. E. (1958). I, pencil: My family tree as told to Leonard E. Read. Library of Economics and Liberty. http://www.econlib.org/library/Essays/rdPncl1.html.
Ricardo, D. (1817). *On the principles of political economy and taxation*. . London: John Murray, Albemarle Street.
Rushton, M. (2014). Hybrid organizations in the arts: A cautionary view. *The Journal of Arts Management, Law, and Society, 44*, 145–152.
Sanz, J. A., Herrero, L. C., & Bedate, A. M. (2003). Contingent valuation and semiparametric methods: A case study of the National Museum of Sculpture in Valladolid, Spain. *Journal of Cultural Economics, 27*(3–4), 241–257.
Schulze, G. G. (1999). International trade in art. *Journal of Cultural Economics, 23*(1–2), 109–136.
The Creative Independent. (2018). A study of the financial state of visual artists today. Retrieved from https://thecreativeindependent.com/artist-survey/.
Throsby, D. (1996). Economic circumstances of the performing artist: Baumol and Bowen thirty years on. *Journal of Cultural Economics, 20*(3), 225–240.
Throsby, D. (1999). Cultural capital. *Journal of Cultural Economics, 23*(1), 3–12.
Towse, R. (1997). *Introduction to Baumol's cost disease: The Arts and Other Victims*. . Northampton: Edward Elgar.
Towse, R., & Hernández, T. N. (Eds.). (2020). *Handbook of cultural economics*. (3rd ed.). Cheltenham, Northampton, MA: Edward Elgar.
Tradeschool.coop. (n.d.). Trade School everywhere. https://tradeschool.coop.
Van der Wurff, R. (2005). Competition, concentration and diversity in European television markets. *Journal of Cultural Economics, 29*(4), 249–275.
Whitaker, A. (2018). Artist as owner not guarantor: The art market from the artist's point of view. *Visual Resources, 34*(1–2), 48–64.
Whitaker, A. (2021). *Economics of visual art: Market practice and market resistance*. Cambridge, UK: Cambridge University Press.
Whitaker, A., & Grannemann, H. (2019). Artists' royalties and performers' equity: A ground-up approach to social impact investment in creative fields. *Cultural Management, Science and Education, 3*(2), 33–51.
Whitaker, A., & Kräussl, R. (2020). Fractional equity, blockchain, and the future of creative work. *Management Science, 66*(10), 4594–4611.
Woolard, C. (2020). *Trade School: 2009–2019*. . Caroline Woolard.
Woronkowicz, J., & Noonan, D. S. (2019). Who goes freelance? The determinants of self-employment for artists. *Entrepreneurship Theory and Practice, 43*(4), 651–672.
Yin, R. K. (2009). *Case study research: Design and methods*. (4th ed.). Thousand Oaks: Sage.

Journal of Cultural Economics (2021) 45:633–670
https://doi.org/10.1007/s10824-021-09412-9

ORIGINAL ARTICLE

Direct memberships in foreign copyright collecting societies as an entrepreneurial opportunity for music publishers – needs, challenges, opportunities and solutions

Stephan Klingner[1] · Mihail Miller[1] · Michael Becker[1] · Frank Schumacher[1]

Received: 31 July 2020 / Accepted: 13 March 2021 / Published online: 7 April 2021

Abstract
In the competitive, increasingly international music business, publishers are developing new ways to increase effectiveness and efficiency of the monetization of the copyrights they own or manage. Driven by various needs, publishers become entrepreneurs in new markets by choosing the path of direct memberships in foreign copyright collecting societies, rather than entrusting sub-publishers or taking the detour through their domestic copyright collecting society. Since with great power comes great responsibility, publishers as entrepreneurs are pursuing various economic opportunities, but at the same time are also facing great challenges. This paper aims at studying the motivation, obstacles and potentials and deriving possible solutions for this step and thus improving the understanding of as well as supporting publishers in this entrepreneurial activity.

Keywords Music publishers · Sub-publisher · Copyright collecting societies · Copyright management · Exploitation of music copyrights · Royalties

1 Introduction

Stagnation is regression – this also applies to companies in the music industry, an environment characterized by strong competition, multiple technological developments and disruptive market players. Reinventing business, constantly questioning the traditional approach, responding to new trends and developing and pursuing long-term strategies are the prerequisites for sustainable corporate success. Combining the principles of evolution and entrepreneurial research, various analogies can be found (Nielsen and Lassen 2012), highlighting the application of an entrepreneurial mindset as a viable approach for existing businesses.

✉ Stephan Klingner
stephan.klingner@uni-leipzig.de
https://stephanklingner.de

1 Computer Center at the University of Leipzig, Leipzig, Germany

Thus, not only new market actors and their entrepreneurial activities, but also existing companies are subject to continuous development in order not to be made obsolete by economic evolution. Very few industries are static, but the music industry is particularly creatively challenged because it has clung to established but anachronistic models for too long (Wilde and Schwerzmann 2004). So what are the new needs and challenges that the players in the industry are confronted with, which make them continuously become entrepreneurs within their industry? The paper at hand aims to answer this question from the perspective of music publishers focusing their interaction with copyright collecting societies (CCS) and sub-publishers in the context of the international exploitation of music copyrights.

In contrast to the past, the business model of music publishers today is more extensive and complex, involving the management, promotion and licensing of the use of copyrights of their represented writers. Due to the complexity and volume, the licensing of these rights is not feasible for a single economic entity. Therefore, this task is solved cooperatively: publishers become members of copyright collecting societies, authorizing them to handle the licensing of various types of copyright use on their behalf. If licensing takes place outside the area of operation of the (usually domestic) CCS, royalties are paid via intermediaries such as foreign collecting societies or sub-publishers. Consequences are payment delays, non-transparency and higher transaction costs. Due to increasing technology-driven internationalization, this has also a major impact on smaller publishers, as they generate increasing amounts of royalties in foreign markets. However, there is growing awareness among music publishers regarding a relevant market change: Legal harmonization and technological developments have facilitated the option of direct memberships of publishers in multiple, international CCS.

Due to these trends and challenges, also existing music publishing companies need to evolve constantly by applying entrepreneurial principles. Transferring these principles to the current situation of music publishers in general and the opportunity of direct membership in particular illustrates the analogies. The first aspect is the correct interpretation of market-changes (Kirzner 1973). Applied to the music industry this covers the recognition of an increasing competition for music publishers driven by self-marketing platforms and technology-driven publishing administrators. Second, entrepreneurs need to perceive opportunities to improve the current state (Stevenson et al. 1999). In terms of the music business, publishers, for example, need to identify ways to increase payment speed, reduce transaction costs and transparency which is enabled by direct CCS membership. Third, entrepreneurs must implement proactive decision making and risk taking (Miller 1983). Since applying for direct CCS membership in foreign countries is still in its infancy, music publishers are often faced with technical and organizational challenges and risks. Finally, it can be argued that direct membership of music publishers in foreign CCS is consistent with the emerging consensus that internationalization is an entrepreneurial activity (O'Cass and Weerawardena 2009).

In this paper, we observe this market change and contribute to this topic from multiple perspectives by gathering needs, challenges, opportunities and highlighting solutions for music publishers in the implementation of direct memberships in foreign CCS. The first sections cover a short summary of the mechanics of the music business (Sect. 2) and a detailed explanation of direct memberships as an entrepreneurial opportunity (Sect. 3). In Sect. 4, we give details about the methodology used to gather information about the state of the art of copyright exploitation. Based on these findings, Sects. 5, 6 and 7 present needs, challenges and opportunities from the publishers' perspective. Major outcomes are clearly depicted requirements of the publishers and an aggregated view on the interaction with CCS by deriving harmonized process and data models. Based on these models, software tools supporting a seamless integration of different international CCS can be developed. Corresponding prototypes are introduced in Sect. 8. The economic potential of direct membership is assessed in Sect. 9, whereas a more prospective view including future research steps and necessary development tasks is presented in Sect. 10.

2 Economics of music copyright

Today's music business is characterized by a plethora of different income channels, one of which is copyrights. Copyright holders, for instance composers, authors or publishers, generate the majority of their income based on three different categories (Pitt 2010, p. 16). First, performance rights royalties are generated by licensing the performance of music, such as public performances, performances on radio or television and non-interactive streaming. Second, mechanical rights royalties result from the licensing of recordings and their reproduction as audio files on storage media and through interactive streaming. Finally, synchronization royalties are generated by licensing the syncing of the musical work with another (usually visual) medium, e.g., in movie/TV soundtracks. Besides different income channels, music business is getting more and more global resulting in an increased economic potential – a development underlined by the following financial numbers.

The distribution of royalties by CCS is steadily increasing. Since 2003, collected royalties of CCS increased from 6.15 billion to 9.65 billion Euro per year (CISAC 2014, 2019). With a 53 percent share of global collections, Europe is the largest region in terms of music collections (CISAC 2019). Although the digital sector is constantly growing, the traditional income channels "Live" and "TV and Radio" account for 69 percent of the royalties collected (CISAC 2019). Recent technological, organizational and legal advances are challenging the traditional network of collecting societies and opening the market for direct multi-territorial licensing. However, advances are largely focused on online rights. For example, technology-driven publishing administration companies such as Kobalt Music Group[1] or Songtrust[2] offer a large network of contracts with CCS and digital service providers. In addition, CCS consolidate their repertoire through joint ventures such as ICE.[3] Territorially managed uses of copyright, such as performances at local events or terrestrial radio/TV, however, remain outside the focus. In order to save deductions and to

[1] https://www.kobaltmusic.com.

[2] https://www.songtrust.com.

[3] https://www.iceservices.com.

speed up the exploitation process, publishers are increasingly choosing the option of "direct memberships." While this option is open to all types of copyright holders, publishers are inherently focused on managing the copyright exploitation process and therefore recognize entrepreneurial opportunities herein first. Therefore, we set the research focus specifically on the needs of music publishers. Furthermore, we narrow the scope of our study to small-to-medium-sized music publishers focusing on the live music sector in Europe. Although the applicability of the results can be expected beyond this scope, the variance in economic, institutional or legal factors between different types of copyright holders and markets leads to the necessity of a closer examination of concrete scenarios.

To gain a better understanding of stakeholders and their responsibilities as well as the different ways of exploiting music copyrights internationally, the following paragraphs give a short introduction to the music business' value chain. For the sake of brevity, the variety of stakeholders is reduced to a minimum and iteratively extended. Furthermore, a few simplifications have been applied.

Any exploitation of music copyrights starts with the composition of a musical work by one or more writers. Since the commercialization of the work can be tedious, writers usually entrust a publisher with this task. Even if limited to the national level, the ways of exploitation are so extensive that publishers cannot license every use of the work themselves. Due to this fact, CCS handle this task as intermediaries. A CCS represents a great number of copyright holders and an even greater number of their musical works, thus allowing for applying economies of scale (Handke and Towse 2007). However, since copyright depends on legal frameworks, CCS generally restrict their licensing activities to a specific country (Handke 2013). In order to still receive international royalties, various options with different advantages and disadvantages exist.

The default option is the management of international copyrights by domestic CCS. In this case, international royalties are collected by foreign CCS, transferred to domestic CCS, and later distributed to copyright holders. Though this is a comfortable option for copyright holders, it is likely to result in additional deductions and significantly delayed royalty payments.[4] To accelerate the process, the second option, particularly for publishers, is to transfer the copyrights for a limited territory to another publisher – a so-called sub-publisher (Towse 2017).[5] On behalf of the publisher the sub-publisher deals with the foreign CCS. However, this in turn leads to a decrease in revenue due to administrative costs (Towse 2017). A third option that has recently gained attention are direct memberships with foreign CCS.[6] This

[4] The distribution of international performing rights by the German CCS GEMA can be taken as an example for delayed payments, e.g., Australian performing rights from 07/2018 until 06/2019 are paid off on July 1, 2020 (https://www.gema.de/en/music-authors/royalties/pay-outsdistribution-of-international-income/international-performing-rights-2020/).

[5] For the sake of simplicity, sub-publishing in this context refers to all contractual relationships like co-publishing or administration agreements as well, since the business structure – an additional entity within the process – remains the same.

[6] Although most traditional European CCS support only a membership model in which control over the operation of the CCS is granted to the members, there is increasing support for purely commercially motivated models, in which copyright holders are merely clients or principals of the CCS, e.g., in so-

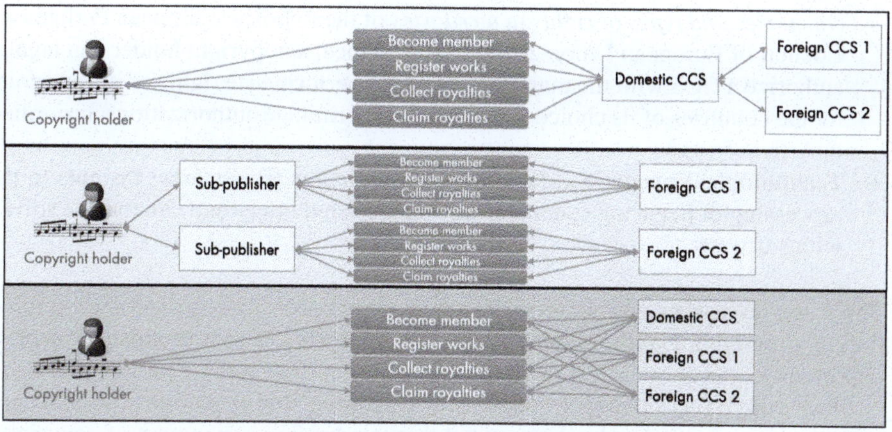

Fig. 1 Three options of the international music copyright exploitation process

option overcomes the necessity to include intermediaries at the expense of increasing efforts for the copyright holders (see Fig. 1).

3 The direct membership – a universal economical remedy?

In order to transform an entrepreneurial opportunity into economic benefits, a number of conditions must be met. In Davidsson (2015), 210 leading journal articles that focused the term "entrepreneurial opportunity" in their research were analyzed. The study proposed a triadic construct: External Enablers (e.g., regulation, technological advances), New Venture Ideas (an entrepreneur's ideas for future businesses) and Opportunity Confidence ("actor's subjective evaluation of the attractiveness" of an opportunity) (Davidsson 2015).

The act of introducing a new type of entrepreneurial action requires the recognition of an entrepreneurial opportunity. While majors have been using the approach of direct memberships for a long time and address international markets via offices in various countries, small-to-medium-sized publishers cannot afford to do so. Likewise, additional experts addressing legal and marketing specifics are beyond the budget. However, the current trend toward direct memberships is supported by two external enablers:

1. **Legal harmonization**: Under Directive 2014/26/EU Article 5 (2) the European Parliament and Council directed its member states to grant that copyright holders shall have the right to authorize collecting societies with the management of

Footnote 6 (continued)
called independent management entities. Because the study focused on traditional CCSs, and to minimize the terminological variety used in this paper, the term "direct membership" includes these options.

categories and types of rights in *territories* of their choice (European Parliament, Council of European Union 2014).[7] For instance, a copyright holder can legally authorize a CCS with the management of the performance rights of its repertoire for the countries of its choice and conversely terminate authorizations, according to Article 5 (4).[8]

2. **Technological progress**: Many potential problems from market insights to the processing of licensing statements are data-related issues and can thus be solved with software.

These are the reasons why an increasing number of publishers consider the exploitation of copyrights via direct memberships in foreign CCS as a promising business opportunity.

Since copyrights relating to territories, categories and types must be managed exclusively by a CCS, it should be noted that overlapping assignment of copyrights to different CCS must be avoided. This is the responsibility of the copyright holder – and is noted on many registration forms. On the other hand, since the three criteria *territory*, *categories* and *types* are independent of each other, direct memberships in several CCSs in the same country are possible or even necessary.

Following the above introduced classification of Davidsson , the motivation of publishers to pursue the option of direct membership will be discussed in Sect. 5, aiming at a better understanding of the business expectations of publishers connected with this rather new approach (opportunity confidence). External conditions disabling the implementation of this option for publishers are discussed in Sect. 6, while Sect. 7 describes new entrepreneurial chances arising from this new state (including new venture ideas). Finally, prototypical technologies that were developed in the research process and can be regarded as additional external enablers will be presented.

4 Methodology

As methodological basis we follow the design science research (DSR) approach as proposed by Peffers et al. (2007). The six steps of the DSR methodology mapped to our research and the content of this paper are as follows:

1. Identify problem and motivate: Global music copyright handling is a complex task. Publishers need support to cope with new developments and demands. The

[7] Prior to this Directive, the European Commission determined in Case COMP/C-2/38.698 the membership and exclusivity clauses of earlier CISAC sample contracts as restrictive of competition. In addition, the "concerted practice" between the CISAC-CCS on "territorial delineation" was called into question. A detailed description of the legislative history leading to the current legal framework can be found in (Guibault and Gompel 2015).

[8] Obviously, this is only possible with those CCS that are capable of the administration of these rights and offer their management.

current situation of global music copyrights was presented in section 2, details from a publishers' point of view and are given in the following chapters.
2. Define objectives of a solution: The objective of our research is to enable new entrepreneurial opportunities for music publishing companies as presented in Sect. 3. Therefore, we develop software tools supporting music publishers to effectively and efficiently work with multiple, international CCS allowing them to generate values from international copyrights.
3. Design and development: The majority of this paper deals with the presentation of the underlying concepts to implement a solution. This covers the presentation of the needs, challenges and opportunities in the following sections.
4. Demonstration: We present a web application for evaluating the performance of European CCS and a prototypical desktop application for a standardized registration process for musical works with CCS. Both software tools were developed by the authors and are described in Sect. 8 of this paper.
5. Evaluation: Several music publishers have already tested prototypical implementations of various software tools and gave feedback as presented in Sect. 8. We have implemented their feedback to improve effectiveness and efficiency of the tools. In addition, we are continuously working together with a software company providing tools for music publishers to gather feedback about needs of the domain.
6. Communication: This paper presents an overview of the insights from a research project. Additional information can be found on the project's website.[9]

To identify needs, challenges and opportunities concerning the management of music copyrights, we followed a threefold approach, addressing publishers and CCS as the most relevant stakeholders within the value chain. First, we conducted semi-structured interviews with representatives of publishers. Second, we gathered key performance indicators of European CCS. Finally, based on the findings we selected six CCS and analyzed processes and data necessary for collaboration with publishers. In the following sections, these three steps are introduced in more detail.

4.1 Interviews

To gain a better understanding of the music publishers' perspective on the status quo, challenges and trends of international copyright management, we conducted a survey. To ensure openness and objectivity within this exploratory context, a qualitative research setup was chosen (Sutton and Austin 2015). To allow for a comparison of the results and to ensure completeness of the interviews, semi-structured questionnaires comprising 26 questions were used. The questions cover basic demographic information, current workflows, the state of the art of international copyright exploitation, experiences in collaborating with CCS, challenges and wishes in that regard.

[9] https://www.soclear.de.

The sample included nine interviews with representatives of German music publishers held between June and September 2019. All interviews were conducted by phone- or Internet-based conference tools by two people and recorded digitally to allow for a comprehensive, comfortable and traceable analysis. The duration of the interviews varied between 17 and 45 minutes with a cumulative duration of almost five hours. Following the approach suggested by Sutton and Austin (2015), the recordings were fully transcribed, coded and evaluated. Transcription and coding was done using the software tool f4.[10]

4.1.1 Demography

Since the music business and the involved companies' roles are diverse, the compilation of survey participants was aimed to cover different segments of the business, like genre, markets or size. To get an impression of the spectrum of interviewees, basic demographic information was surveyed (see Table 1). If a publisher is active in more than one business role or on more than one market, the dominant option is marked bold. Despite the broad spectrum of different publishers, it is important to note that due to the underlying methodology the survey is not representative and, thus, no general conclusions can be drawn (see Sect. 4.1.2). Nevertheless, the demographics should help to evaluate the background of participants. The figures on the market share of independent publishers [42% in 2019, compared to 25% of Sony and 21% of Universal Music Publishing Group, according to Music and Copyright (2020)] as well as Germany being the fourth largest market worldwide (CISAC 2019) show the relevance of the type of companies examined.

Most of the interviewees' companies cover two roles, label and publisher. This is a common practice in the modern music industry (Tschmuck 2016). Regarding the musical focus, all but one company covered popular music. Besides conventional exploitation of musical works for consumers with bands and releases, a few companies were active in niches like production music, illustration music or custom compositions for the TV sector. The companies were all internationally active, i.e., generating revenue on markets other than their home country as well, although the predominant market in many cases was Germany. The role of the interviewees ranged from managers and owners to employees responsible for copyrights ensuring relevant as well as competent feedback. Reflecting the common corporate structures within the music industry, all interviewees worked in micro-, small- and medium-sized enterprises with corresponding revenues.

4.1.2 Limitations

As a result of the study design, a few limitations emerge. Due to the qualitative character of the study, the general applicability of the statements is limited. More generic conclusions in any means cannot be drawn and would require a quantitative study. Hence, the limitation on German publishing companies impairs conclusions for a

[10] https://www.audiotranskription.de/f4.

Table 1 Demographics of survey participants

	P1	P2	P3	P4	P5	P6	P7	P8	P9
Business role	Label, Publisher	Publisher	Label, Publisher	Publisher	Label, Publisher	Label, Publisher	Publisher, Label, Studio	Publisher, Label	Publisher, Label
Genre	Popular music; no specific genre	Classical music	Popular music; Jazz	Popular music; no specific genre	Popular music; Pop	Popular music; Production music TV	Popular music; Pop	Popular music; Illustration music TV	Popular music; Compositions TV
Market	**National/ International**	**International**	**EU/ International**	**EU**	**EU/ International**	**International**	**National/ International**	**National/ International**	**National/ International**
Role of interviewee	Managing-Director	Wide range of tasks	Wide range of tasks	Managing-Director	Contracts, A&R, Copyrights	Managing-Director	International Copyrights	Wide range of tasks	Managing-Director, Royalties, Administration
Number of employees	7 + 4 freelancer	20	9	4	10	2	15	6	9
Sales Revenue (€)	100,00-2 Mio.	10-50 Mio.	100,000-2 Mio.	100,000-2 Mio.	100,000-2 Mio.	2–10 Mio.	100,000–2 Mio.	2–10 Mio.	100,000–2 Mio.

Table 2 List of captured key performance indicators

Total turnover	Total turnover of a collecting society in the reporting year (including royalty income and other forms of income, e.g., balance from derivatives)
Royalty turnover	Domestic and foreign turnover from collected licensing fees in the reporting year
Distribution sum	Total amount for distribution to represented domestic and foreign copyright holders (and social and cultural funds) in the reporting year after deduction of costs from total turnover
Distributed royalties	Internally allocated royalties in the reporting year by a collecting society to domestic and foreign copyright holders; independent of minimum amounts to be paid out
Paid royalties	Paid out royalties to domestic and foreign beneficiaries; may include outstanding payments from previous years; payable only if minimum amounts are reached
Number of employees	Number of employees of a collecting society, if available full-time equivalents
Cost rate	$1 - \frac{distribution\_sum}{total\_turnover}$; while the distribution sum also benefits social and cultural purposes, in a purely microeconomically motivated consideration, the deduction of this allocation would be of interest to the publisher. In the database shown, however, the sums for social and cultural purposes were not collected. Thus, the KPI "cost rate" is also affected by this side effect
Number of copyright holders	Number of copyright holders represented by the CCS (including publishers and writers, full members and clients without voting rights)
Number of employees	Number of employees (FTE if available) working for the respective CCS
Membership costs for authors	Costs of membership/ contractual relationship for an author
Membership costs for publishers	Costs of membership/ contractual relationship for a publisher
Population	Number of citizens in the country where the headquarter of the respective CCS is located

more global perspective. Additionally, the focus on independent music companies prevents transferring the findings to the majors of the music business.

Furthermore, the interviews were conducted in German. In order to be able to illustrate the findings by citations, the statements were translated. Rather colloquial descriptions were interpreted with the aim of achieving the best possible compromise between authenticity and comprehensibility.

4.2 Key performance indicators

For the effective and efficient exploitation of music copyrights, CCS play a crucial role. To capture the general economic performance of these stakeholders, a quantitative analysis of European CCS was conducted.

Therefore, annual business and transparency reports were analyzed. To create a standardized basis for comparing and deriving insights from commonly reported financial data, KPIs were collected, normalized and analyzed.[11] Altogether, ten different KPIs were extracted (see Table 2). The results of the data collection and harmonization steps described were compiled in a semi-structured format (CSV) providing the basis for a quantitative analysis of the data.[12]

4.2.1 Data preparation

To prepare the data for quantitative analysis, it first had to be extracted. For this purpose, the publicly available data of 40 CCS (for musical performing rights, mechanical reproduction rights and both) of 35 European countries were extracted and consolidated from their annual business and transparency reports. The data collection took place between September and November 2019. In order to capture the current situation as closely as possible, the most recent report available was chosen. For the majority of the CCS ($\approx$ 84%), the most recent reporting year was 2018 while the oldest report was from 2016. Manual extraction was necessary, since the annual reports were published as non-standardized PDF documents.

It was noticeable that most CCS report similar KPIs, although partly under different names. However, due to differences in data quality and scope, semantic mappings were not applicable to every CCS-specific KPI. In case of semantic deviations preventing a mapping, some KPIs had to be calculated, e.g., the total turnover, which was not always explicitly stated. As an additional remedy, missing figures were supplemented from other sources (e.g., the official website of the respective CCS or the CISAC members directory.[13]) Sources differing from the annual reports as well as data transformations were assigned to the corresponding data set. Additionally to the CCS-national currency, a uniform currency was chosen (EUR) to ensure comparability. For this purpose, exchange rates[14] at the end of the reporting year were used to convert the national currency of the respective collecting society into EUR. However, even taking these aspects into account, relevant KPIs could not be found for every CCS. Due to this fact, the sample size of individual KPIs may vary.

4.2.2 Limitations

The methodology presented is subject to several limitations. First, the data collected represent only a snapshot not capturing annual fluctuations. Second, the mapping of CCS-individual KPIs to standardized KPIs is lossy, considering varying monetary information, price levels and conversion rates. Finally, the statistical analysis of the data is also subject to the limitation that only a small sample could be collected.

[11] Rochelandet (2003) had introduced a similar approach to allow comparison of economic features of European CCS. However, this study was limited to three CCS and conducted decades ago. Since then, the environment has changed and so have the financial characteristics of the CCS. With regard to the collection of characteristics and comparison, we also made some alternative choices.

[12] https://creativeartefact.org/static/vgstats/vgstats.js.

[13] https://members.cisac.org/CisacPortal/annuaire.do?method=membersDirectoryList&by=society.

[14] retrieved from OANDA: https://www.oanda.com/currency/converter/.

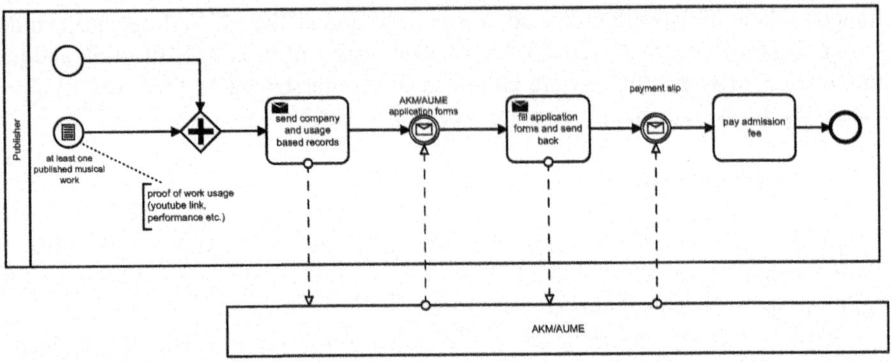

Fig. 2 Process model for registering with the Austrian CCS AKM/AUME

Other limitations may result from translation errors or generally from the manual nature of data extraction.

4.3 Process and data modeling

While the previously described method draws a coarse-grained and generic picture of the economics of CCS, a more detailed analysis of CCS was conducted in a supplementary study. The aim was to investigate technological and organizational requirements for interaction between CCS and publishers. Furthermore, based on the findings of this methodological approach, possible software solutions for managing the complex interactions with CCS can be developed.

We focused our work on the societies that were considered relevant by the interviewees: GEMA (Germany), AKM/AUME (Austria), SUISA (Switzerland), BUMA/STEMRA (The Netherlands), SACEM (France), and SIAE (Italy). To reconstruct processes and data models, we took publicly available membership application forms into account.

4.3.1 Process modeling

Modeling took place in a workshop-based format consisting of three authors of this article. We collaboratively analyzed available registration information and simultaneously extracted the underlying processes.

Based on the textual descriptions, we defined structured process models using the Business Process Model and Notation (BPMN) – a widespread notation for graphically capturing and structuring processes (Chinosi and Trombetta 2012). With these process models, we are able to identify the chronological order of activities publishing companies have to perform. Figures 2 and 3 depict the registration processes for the Austrian CCS AKM/AUME and the German CCS GEMA, respectively. For the sake of brevity and comprehensibility, the process models do not display exceptional situations but only the idealized registration process. As can already be seen without any prior knowledge of reading BPMN,

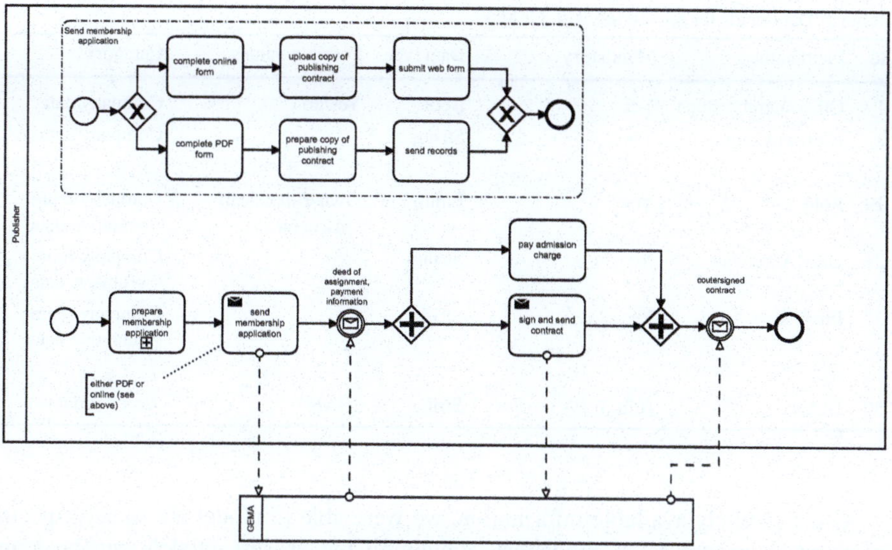

Fig. 3 Process model for registering with the German CCS GEMA

there are differences in both, structure and content of the process models. In the following, we present the GEMA registration process (Fig. 3) in more detail.

Each BPMN process consists of a sequence of so-called activities. An activity represents a precisely defined piece of work performed by a specific actor. As can be seen from Fig. 3, the registration process consists of the two actors *publisher* and *GEMA*. As we are only interested in the activities of the publisher, the GEMA activities are undisclosed. In the lower part of Fig. 3, the registration process is depicted beginning with the preparation of the membership application. Using BPMN, it is possible to outline activities on different levels of detail. This is shown with the second activity, *send membership application*, which is detailed in the upper part of Fig. 3. Depending on the reader of the process model, a more coarse-grained view, i.e., *send membership application,* might be sufficient or a more fine-grained view (using the detailed sub-process) is necessary.

For synchronizing various process participants, BPMN provides messages and events. For example, in the GEMA registration process, the publishing company waits for receiving the deed of assignment and payment information – this reflects the textual description of the process as shown above. As the internal GEMA process is not relevant, we do not outline how and when GEMA sends these information. Instead, the event element pauses the process until the documents arrive. After arrival of the deed and payment information, the publishing company has to pay the admission charge, sign and send the contract back to GEMA. Since the order of these activities is not of particular relevance, they are encapsulated in a so-called AND-gateway. This gateway splits up the process into two parallel sequences. After both activities were performed, the process is merged and waits for receiving the countersigned contract.

Table 3 Data fields for registering with GEMA

Id	Field name	Mandatory	Data type	Possible values	Category
1	Other memberships	Yes	Bool	Yes/no	Company data
2	Company name	Yes	String		Company data
.					
19	Role	Yes	Enum	Owner/manager/ associate	Company representative data
21	GEMA number	No	String		Company representative data
22	First name	Yes	String		Company representative data
.					
30	IBAN	If in SEPA territory	String	IBAN	Account data

Using publicly available information, we were able to model six society-specific registration processes. A repository containing the process models can be found online.[15] Based on these models, we were able to identify commonalities and differences in registering with the various collecting societies. These findings are a starting point for unifying and allow for multi-society registration.

4.3.2 Data modeling

Using the above-mentioned sources, we identified data necessary for registering with CCS. Since every CCS follows its own naming convention and has distinct requirements on mandatory data fields, we had to harmonize the data. In addition, CCS from different countries use different languages resulting in even more transformation efforts. Table 3 shows an example record of data required when registering with the German CCS GEMA.

As a result of the harmonization, we established a categorized list of data fields used by different CCS as presented in Table 4. The entire data model containing mappings of data fields between different CCS and the result of the data harmonization can be found online.[16]

4.3.3 Limitations

With the help of publicly available information, we were able to reconstruct registration processes and data requirements. However, using this method, a few limitations need to be considered. First and foremost, it is not possible to deduce thorough process models from the given information due to missing and ambiguous information in the textual description or PDF/web forms. In addition, for some CCS we cannot

[15] https://creativeartefact.org/articles/2020-07-14-ccs-models/#registration-processes.

[16] http://www.creativeartefact.org/articles/2020-07-14-ccs-models/index/index.html#data-modelling.

Table 4 Categories of registration data

Category	Description	Example fields
Company data	Data about the publishing company intending to register with a CCS	Company name, legal form, address, commercial registration number
Company representative data	Data about a contact person from the publishing company	Name, address, CCS membership status
Account data	Data for CCS membership fees and for paying royalties.	Bank account number, payment mode
Tax data	Data for tax payment	Company subject to turnover tax, tax ID
Receipts	Proof of statements concerning the legal embodiment of a publishing company	Trade register excerpt, trade certificate, shareholder agreement
Exploit. data	Restrictions and permissions concerning the exploitation of musical works	Included rights, included territories
Other data	Uncategorized data fields	Privacy agreement, payment confirmation

Table 5 Application of various exploitation options by the interviewed publishers

International exploitation via	Domestic CCS	Sub-publisher	Publishing administrator	Direct membership in foreign CCS
P1	–	X	X	X
P2	X	X	–	–
P3	X	X	–	X
P4	X	X	–	X
P5	X	–	X	–
P6	X	X	–	X
P7	X	X	–	–
P8	X	X	–	–
P9	X	X	–	–

infer the whole process. For example, the AKM/AUME registration form is only available on demand. Since information are not available beforehand, it is not possible to identify necessary registration data.

It is important to mention that process and data models only represent a snapshot in time. As various CCS currently shift from offline application processes to online processes using webforms, processes may decrease in size and become more homogeneous, since the entered data need to be processed automatically.

5 Needs

After introducing the methodological elements applied, the following sections merge the findings to draw a comprehensive figure of the needs, challenges and opportunities in the international management of music copyright.

In the following, quotations from the interviews are listed according to the scheme (P5:42). The first part represents the interviewee (P5) and the second part (42) the paragraph in which the quoted statement was made.

As mentioned above, there are various options for publishers to exploit their copyrights internationally. For a long time, the predominant way was via sub-publishers (Towse 2017) or via domestic CCS and their reciprocal agreements (as the default option). This is also reflected in the interviews – almost all interviewees used these two constructs (see Table 5). In the recent past, the option of direct memberships gained practical relevance, which, however, still has a much lower market penetration. This section covers the needs of the publishers by analyzing advantages and disadvantages of the different options and thus examining the motivation of the publishers for direct memberships at multiple CCS.

As can be seen in Table 5, the different options are not mutually exclusive – a decision has only to be made per territory and type of rights. It should be noted that the table only shows the paths of international exploitation – on national level, the exploitation of copyrights for all the publishers was done via their domestic CCS (in this case the GEMA).

According to which criteria and with which motives do publishers decide for or against a certain exploitation channel? A first decisive factor is the importance of the respective market for the publisher. However, two different interpretative approaches prevail here. First, there is the strategy of reaching important markets via sub-publishing partners.

> "We have sub-publishing partners in the core markets, so to speak, and otherwise we administer the rights through GEMA. (P3:30)"

Second, it is also argued that direct membership of the respective CCS would provide better access to the market and data.

> "Yeah, Switzerland. Switzerland for example, simply because of transparency and of course also because of its value. (P6:52)"

How can this apparent contradiction be resolved? The answer lies in the role of the sub-publisher. The expectation is that the sub-publisher will actively take care of the marketing and exploitation of the catalog transferred to it or cover communication with the foreign CCS. If it does so, it can become a valuable partner in the addressed market.

> "So France is a bit of an exception for me personally because it is a very important market for us and because we need local partners there who actively exploit our repertoire. [...] But as I said, Spain, Portugal, Poland, England, I can think of a whole series of countries or territories where it [a direct membership] would make absolute sense. (P3:50)"

If this expectation remains unfulfilled, the option of a direct membership becomes more appealing, since expenses for services with questionable effects can be avoided. Even without comprehensive expertise in the relevant market, the publisher can provide basic services itself. If the publisher can already draw on market knowledge, it is all the easier to choose the path of taking more responsibility but also to develop more economic opportunities through a direct membership.

> "But I have for example a sub-publisher in Spain/Portugal, who of course takes a pretty good percentage for managing our rights, but even though it is a really well known publisher it is not really active exploiting our repertoire. And the fact that they just manage our rights there and take their fee without taking care about sync rights or anything else, that I would of course like to replace it by simply becoming a member in the country and then just pay the usual fees of the collecting society. (P3:45)"

In addition to the sub-publisher's lack of marketing and exploitation activities, shortcomings regarding controlling (checking of statements, complaints) were also mentioned. All in all, it can be stated that publishers increasingly critically assess the value for money of their publishing partners and are therefore beginning to replace partners with direct memberships.

"Because you can see what kind of turnover is coming in and you think about it, you always give something away and if you have the possibility and the resources or you do it yourself...We have the monitoring system and we can see for ourselves what has to be reported, what can be complained and of course we always had to tell our sub-publisher that. We can then almost do the work ourselves. (P9:32)"

In addition to partner-induced and strategic considerations, financial needs also provide arguments for direct membership. The processing steps by additional stakeholders between the foreign CCS and the publisher require additional time, regardless of whether the route via a sub-publisher or domestic CCS is chosen.

"That is one reason, the second reason which of course is absolutely an argument in favor is simply the time factor. It doesn't matter if you have a sub-publisher or if you let [domestic CCS] take care of your international rights, it just takes a long time. It's quicker via sub-publishers than via [domestic CCS], but money that comes from a foreign collecting society via [domestic CCS] needs often two years for transit. And if you could accelerate that, that's a bad performance, of course. (P3:46)"

Thus, the choice of a particular exploitation option for a country is an issue with several criteria to be considered. In addition to the economic relevance of the targeted market, the performance of the sub-publisher is crucial. Furthermore, driven by their heterogeneity (see also Sect. 6.2) various characteristics of the CCS are also relevant factors in the decision-making process.

"The criteria ...collecting society: communication, efficiency, friendliness, language. Although language doesn't matter, really. Sub-publisher: the decisive criterion is: can they really do something for us. (P4:33 - 34)"

It can be concluded that dissatisfaction is often the driving force for developing new ways of exploiting copyrights. This aligns with antecedents of entrepreneurship which can be found in the context of employees (Serviere 2010). The potential of sub-publishers compared to exploitation via domestic CCS is a limited acceleration of financial transactions and potential improvements regarding the marketing of the repertoire. As with any form of cooperation, expectations are linked to such partnerships. If the publisher's expectations are not met or financial conditions seem not rewarding, direct membership offers an additional option. The increased responsibility and workload of the publisher is matched by greater freedom of action and greater efficiency in terms of time and money. This again aligns with the paradigm of an entrepreneurial return based on lowering transaction costs by establishing new improved organization structures (Foss and Foss 2008).

It also becomes apparent that the decision for or against an exploitation option cannot be made in a globally uniform manner. Similarly to other entrepreneurial decisions, various criteria such as possible partners, addressed territories and own competences have to be taken into account. The choice of a direct membership is of increasing importance in the variety of options, but comes with a variety of challenges discussed in the next chapter.

Table 6 Organizational challenges

Id	Challenge
OC1	Additional effort when registering with foreign CCS
	"It is always a matter of effort and up to now we did well having partners that represent us" (P7:31)
	"[...] global administrative publishing should include work registration, income tracking, usage registration, clearing control, complaints [...]" (P1:98)
	CCS evaluation: immense research effort in determining which CCS objectively represents the best strategic fit for the publisher (see Sect. 4.2.2)
	Process modeling: different registration processes
	Data modeling: inconsistent field names
OC2	Language barriers
	"France adds to the fact that, even in the business, people do not speak English very good" (P3:50)
OC3	Legal barriers and company guidelines
	"Basically, all CCS operate according to the same principles. The exact formulation of single regularities and constitutions, of course, differs in details that are relevant for work." (P1:116)
	Process models: different requirements concerning proof of work usage during registration processes
OC4	Heterogeneity of CCS performance
	"[…] it must also be said that a collecting society is actually in a position to collect and distribute a large proportion of the licenses that arise. That is, of course, also its task, but some do it well and some do it badly." (P4:76)
	KPI: Wide range of various KPI between different CCS

6 Challenges

In this section, we present an overview of challenges for publishers when registering with foreign CCS. Based on the interviews, process and data modeling, and capturing of KPIs, three categories of challenges were identified. *Organizational challenges* cover communication with CCS. *Technological challenges* occur due to heterogeneities in the technological basis of the interaction with different CCS. *Subjective challenges* result from a lack of knowledge and thus lead to a situation where dealing with foreign CCS is avoided.

6.1 Organizational challenges

Organizational challenges for direct membership in foreign CCS are triggered by both, the publisher and the specific CCS (see Table 6). While the first indicates weaknesses of the publisher hindering it to become a direct member, the latter indicates the lack of external enablers needed for direct memberships to be perceived as an entrepreneurial opportunity (Davidsson 2015). The majority of challenges result from the fact that publishers must adhere to heterogeneous registration processes and might have to put additional effort into legal adaptions of existing documents.

Organizational challenges hampering entrepreneurial opportunities occur, in particular, in fragmented markets like Europe with different languages, regulations and customer preferences (van Weele et al. 2018).

OC1: Additional effort when registering with foreign CCS is induced by the different organizational structures of CCS. First and foremost, registering with foreign CCS is associated with additional costs. Publishing companies need to gather information about specific registration requirements. Adding to this fact, during process and data modeling, we were able to identify a vast amount of deviations in the registration process. These deviations can be categorized as follows:

- Different order of mandatory steps: While most CCS allow for registration using a web-based form, subtle differences in the process models occur. For example, when registering with the German CCS GEMA, publishers have to pay the registration fees before they receive a signed copy of their membership contract. Contrary, the French CCS SACEM sends signed contracts before membership fees are to be paid.
- Additionally required steps: Publishers registering with a foreign CCS have to fulfill different requirements including presentation of statements concerning aspects of the company. For example, the Italian CCS SIAE and the French SACEM additionally require publishers to validate the name of their company. This step is not necessary for registering with the other analyzed CCS.
- Non-transparent registration processes: Some CCS do not make their registration process completely transparent. For example, when registering with the Austrian CCS AKM, publishing companies first have to complete a minimal membership application. After processing of this application by AKM, publishing companies receive an online link to the complete application. Without further information gathering, publishers do not have knowledge about necessary registration data.

Besides deviations in the registration process, publishers are faced with the fact that different CCS do not comply with a standardized data model. Thus, differences in data field names and semantics of data fields occur or additional data is required. While naming ambiguities are usually easy to solve (e.g., GEMA calls the data field company name *entire publishing company name*, SACEM calls this field *company name*), semantic differences are often more subtle but hamper automated registration with different CCS. For example, the meaning of the legal type of a publisher varies between the different CCS.

Challenge OC2: Language barriers are related to data field naming inconsistencies. Since registration with foreign CCS is a relatively new phenomenon, most European CCS only provide application forms in their national language. This may result in ambiguous interpretations due to poorly or not at all translated forms. In addition, communication with representatives of a CCS might get even more complicated in a multilingual context.

Publishers wanting to register with foreign CCS have to adhere to different restrictions, resulting from OC3: Legal barriers and corporate guidelines. Although the national legal frameworks are transpositions of the Directive 2014/26/EU within the European Economic Area (EEA), the rather abstract definitions of the Directive

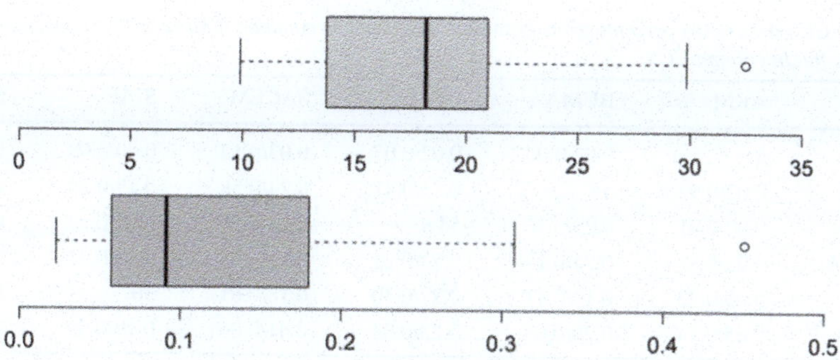

Fig. 4 Boxplots for *cost_rate* (top) and $|1 - \frac{distribution\_sum}{distributed\_sum}|$ (bottom)

Table 7 Technological challenges

Id	Challenge
TC1	Lack of unified data standards
	"One thing is for sure compatibility with our software. How data are being migrated and exported. What seems to make a huge effort is to receive verified data that you can pass on. Foreign publishers frequently tell us, the data are not compatible" (P7:63)
	"The main challenge lies in different data locations and data formats." (P1:130)
	Heterogeneous data models
	Inconsistent mandatory/optional fields
	Heterogeneity of CCS performance
TC2	Lack of methods and tools for automated data processing
	"Currently, we manually process data from both CCS. Since, there is not much data volume as of yet, this is possible. But this is no permanent solution" (P1:128)
	"I really cannot comprehend why this is still problematic as of today. That there are still thing you have to by hand is pretty exhausting" (P7:65)
	Varying order of registration process steps

leave national legislators and individual CCS room for interpretation – for further discussion on this see Matanovac Vučković (2016). According to specific legal requirements or the policies defined by the CCS, publishers might have to consider different possibilities and restrictions of work registrations or have to supply different verification and supporting documents. For example, for registering with the SIAE, publishers need to provide proof of work usage during registration process.

Challenge OC4: Heterogeneity of CCS performance is again induced by the different organizational structures of CCS and different designs of business processes, which in turn can derive from legal specifics [cf. OC3 and Rochelandet (2003)], the lack of unified data standards (TC1) and methods/tools for automated data processing (TC2) (see Table 7). Among the music publishers, consciousness about the variance of CCS performance already exists, as the quote in Table 6 emphasizes. This thesis is supported by a quantitative analysis of the KPIs of the CCS in the sample as shown in Fig. 4. The upper boxplot shows the dispersion of the cost rate (n = 32).

Table 8 CCS data fields percentages in common: cells read as *common data fields/data fields only in row CCS but not in column CCS*

	AKM	BUMA	GEMA	SACEM	SIAE	SUISA
AKM	5	0.02/0.06	0.02/0.07	0.03/0.12	0.00/0.08	0.05/0.21
BUMA	0.02/0.92	58	0.23/0.41	0.24/0.58	0.19/0.39	0.20/0.75
GEMA	0.02/0.91	0.23/0.36	54	0.24/0.56	0.27/0.33	0.23/0.73
SACEM	0.03/0.85	0.24/0.18	0.24/0.21	60	0.18/0.21	0.41/0.53
SIAE	0.00/0.92	0.19/0.41	0.27/0.40	0.18/0.61	30	0.19/0.76
SUISA	0.05/0.74	0.20/0.05	0.23/0.04	0.41/0.06	0.19/0.05	15

With a range of 20% between the min and max value (not including the outlier), it becomes visible to what extend cost rates of individual CCS may vary (see also Sect. 8.1). The boxplot below shows the dispersion of the deviation of the distribution sum from the distributed royalties in the same year by each CCS (n = 24). This metric was introduced to approximate the tendency toward delays in the distribution of royalties. While a small difference between the two metrics does not necessarily indicate a nearly synchronous distribution, a larger difference between the two metrics indicates that the distribution was not carried out on an accrual basis. Here, the range between the minimum and maximum values indicates the variance in aspects of time efficiency among CCS.

6.2 Technological challenges

Technological challenges in registering with foreign CCS result from different registration processes and diverse data requirements and are indicating the lack of external enablers for direct memberships to be perceived as an entrepreneurial opportunity. Due to this situation, publishers have to transform data into different formats. Transformation is faced with two difficulties. On the one hand, data mappings might not be possible, since data formats are not equivalent. On the other hand, every transformation has the potential of mistakes resulting in erroneous data. An overview about identified technological challenges is presented in Table 7.

One of the major challenges for direct membership in foreign CCS is *TC1: Lack of unified data standards*. Due to this fact, communication with different CCS is cumbersome. Since different CCS use different data models, publishers have to keep in mind how to map data fields between the CCS. In addition, data might be represented differently, e.g., normalized to different degrees. To give a simple but illustrative example, the street address of a publisher is a single field in the SACEM data model, where GEMA splits it up to the fields street and number. Adding to this situation is the fact that CCS use different names for identical data fields, be it due to language reasons or to varying regional habits.

Table 8 shows an aggregated view of data heterogeneities by depicting the matching of data fields of different CCS. First, the total amount of data fields per CCS is shown, e.g., five fields for AKM/AUME. In addition, the coverage between two CCS data is displayed. For example, two percent of the data fields of AKM and

Table 9 Subjective challenges

Id	Challenge
SC1	Lack of knowledge about the possibility for direct membership
	"Quite the contrary. With me now knowing that this is possible there are plenty reasons for becoming member." (P3:43-44)
	"To be honest, we did not think about whether it would be more reasonable for individual territories" (P8:32)
SC2	Lack of knowledge about costs and benefits from direct membership
	"Indeed, we did not calculate this [...]. I understand that every intermediary causes costs and I assume you get a larger share when eliminating GEMA as intermediary." (P5:37)
SC3	Lack of knowledge about future developments concerning European CCS
	"In Europe, we first have to watch out for restructurings due to ICE" (P5:39-40)

BUMA correspond with each other. In addition, six percent of AKM data fields are not present as BUMA data fields and 92 percent of BUMA data fields are not available as AKM data fields. As indicated in Table 8, the majority of data fields does not match and, thus, publishers need to adhere to different data models.

In conclusion, it can be stated that there is a *lack of methods and tools for automated data processing (TC2)* due to heterogeneous data and process models. Data heterogeneities increase the effort required when communicating with CCS because publishers cannot automatically parse requests and responses. In addition, process deviations result in the need for systems tailored to a specific CCS. While this might be feasible when interacting with a small number of CCS, it is a limiting factor when managing a great number of musical works globally.

6.3 Subjective challenges

Subjective challenges hinder the evaluation of the attractiveness of direct memberships as entrepreneurial opportunities due to a lack of awareness or opportunity confidence (Davidsson 2015). In fact, the main reason for subjective challenges is lack of knowledge, as Table 9 indicates.

The first subjective challenge results from the fact that not all publishers were aware of the fact they can become direct members of foreign CCS (*C1: Lack of knowledge about the possibility for direct membership*). Thus, these publishers did not consider direct membership until now and did not estimate the costs and benefits of doing so. This lack of knowledge results from the territorial characteristics of CCS (Harrison 2011). Due to this fact, most CCS do not actively present themselves as partners for foreign publishing companies. (This is also indicated by *OC2: Language barriers*, since a majority of CCS membership applications are only available in the national language but not in English.)

Several publishers are reluctant about direct memberships because costs and benefits are not completely transparent (*SC2: Lack of knowledge about costs and benefits from direct membership*). Depending on the previously chosen exploitation options, various aspects have to be weighed up. Compared to the way via domestic

CCS, direct memberships can in particular increase the transparency and reduce the latency of royalty payments – advantages that are difficult to quantify financially. If a cooperation with a sub-publisher is replaced by a direct membership, the financial advantages are clear (avoiding the sub-publisher's fee), but the value of the services provided by the sub-publisher, such as administration or marketing activities, might be hard to quantify as well. As a result, publishers often cannot reliably calculate the revenue differences between direct and indirect international copyright exploitation options.

As the music market is constantly evolving, publishers cannot be sure about future developments resulting in uncertainties (*SC3: Lack of knowledge about future developments concerning European CCS*). As these future developments may have the potential to restructure existing markets, cautious publishers might be reluctant to put additional effort into direct memberships but rather wait for European-wide harmonized solutions, like ICE. However, the focus of such joint ventures to date has been exclusively on online rights. While these represent a key source of revenue, they are only a fraction of all the copyright-types that a CCS can represent. A more objective alternative would therefore be to examine which territories are covered by the already authorized CCS and which types of rights are already represented in these territories, and then to optimize in terms of costs and time-efficiency.

7 Opportunities

Direct memberships with foreign CCS can contribute to a better copyright exploitation process in various ways. As being potentially lucrative it is an entrepreneurial opportunity for publishers, following the definition of Short et al. (2010). This section will first discuss improvements derived from a direct membership which are immediately beneficial to a publisher after joining a foreign CCS and subsequently the opportunities which a publisher may develop and exploit in the long-term view.

7.1 Short-term view

Before the positive effects of a direct membership can be taken advantage of by a music publisher, an economic analysis of the target market should precede, evaluating the currently chosen way for exploitation. Only if the published works already enjoy great popularity in the target market due to their characteristics or promotional work, migrating from the current exploitation option to a direct membership will make sense from an economical point of view (see also Sect. 5).

> "Sure, I would say you have to look at each country individually, see what kind of sales you are doing or have done in the past and then evaluate the revenue in that country, if it's worth the effort to become a member of that country and register everything yourself and so on or if the revenue is simply too small, so that you say, then [the domestic CCS] should continue to collect it. (P3:54)"

The first advantage of direct memberships for music publishers is increased transparency, which is supported by various developments: First, transparency is increased by disintermediation as the direct relationship to a single CCS makes data transfers of royalties less complex and easier to document. Second, as with any outsourcing solution, there is an encapsulation of tasks resulting in less transparency, which would be counteracted through insourcing. Furthermore, statements of domestic CCS concerning foreign royalties are less transparent, while statements received directly from a CCS may list royalties in direct allocation to uses. The interviewees describe this situation as follows:

> "Unfortunately, [the domestic CCS] is not transparent about the payments as we expect it to be and with direct membership in the [foreign CCS] it is simply more transparent. We get an amount X and details on what took place and where. (P6:48)"

> "It's just that if we hadn't done this now, we would get an amount X which we can't even assign [...] and if we are a direct member, we get a detailed statement [...] (P6:54)"

Due to the greater transparency, there is also greater certainty about the correctness of royalty statements, which could reduce complex communication chains.

> "But it is of course already so, if I have the feeling that, for example, a sub-publisher delivers a statement of account that does not seem plausible to me and does not come round the corner with a proper explanation, then I naturally contact the respective collecting societies and make sure that I get the information from them that I did not get otherwise. (P3:64)"

In summary, direct memberships can improve copyright exploitation for music publishers regarding transparency, time and costs of transactions. Based on this factors, music publishers can focus on an improved service quality.

7.2 Long-term view

As a direct member the publisher neither depends on the service of sub-publishers nor on the domestic CCS with representation agreements. This comes with increased responsibility, but also gives the chance to offer a better service to clients. Successfully addressing additional challenges like language barriers and market specifics (cf. Sect. 6) makes publishers more attractive for authors located in the region of the foreign society. In addition to economic advantages and increased transparency, as a member of a CCS publishers can influence decision making processes and thus advance a needs-based development of the CCS.

Some services, such as usage reports, complaints, cessions and inquiry-lists are only available for direct members and cannot be implemented through a reciprocal representation agreement with another CCS. For publishers, direct memberships simplify access to these services, leading to an extension or increased efficiency of services for its represented writers in return.

> "At PRS – I think that's very nice – they have these inquiry lists that GEMA has for sync and TV, PRS even has to live. These are things that I find very attractive. (P5:61)"

> "It is limited to asking whether they accept assignments granted to non-members. So when we sign Dutch or Australian authors, we ask the collecting societies if they accept cessions – so if there is an advance – cessions from a GEMA member and that is an interesting process. (P5:77)"

For example, data available in a less aggregated form allows for deeper analysis, which can serve as a starting point for improving the publisher's strategic decisions, for optimizing marketing activities or for a simpler and fairer distribution of royalties. Moreover, the review of statements and the possible necessary creation of complaints can be done in a more effective and efficient way.

In addition, music publishers can increase their competitiveness by expanding their core business by becoming sub-publishers in foreign territories themselves – a trend already evident in the interviews.

> "We were progressive enough to say that we are now a direct member of SUISA, so we also offer sub-publishing services for Switzerland. (P1:156)"

To make use of the opportunities, publishers need to address the challenges and overcome the obstacles described in Sect. 6. This is certainly not an easy task and requires corresponding economic strength as well as other resource advantages. If these conditions are met, publishers can use direct memberships to expand and improve their core competencies, create new service offerings and thus gain competitive advantages. To facilitate the exploitation of these opportunities, the necessary external enablers must be available, such as technological advances addressing these challenges.

8 Technology as a solution

In order to support the exploitation of the above-mentioned opportunities, the identified challenges must be addressed appropriately. In the following, two use cases illustrate possibilities of technological support.

As a first technological prototype, we present a tool to compare the commonly reported financial characteristics of European CCS. As Sect. 5 exemplifies, choosing between the different exploitation options is a necessary task. As explained in Sect. 7, in the future such tasks could become even more relevant. The tool addresses *organizational challenge 4* (heterogeneity of CCS performance, cf. Sect. 6.1) and supports the decision making process of publishers for direct memberships.

A second prototype focuses on the registration of works as a specific task of particular interest for publishers in collaboration with CCS. This software addresses various challenges introduced in Sect. 6. First, it reduces the additional effort connected with direct memberships with foreign CCS, as it is a scalable solution for registering works (*organizational challenge 1*). Second, although a data standard

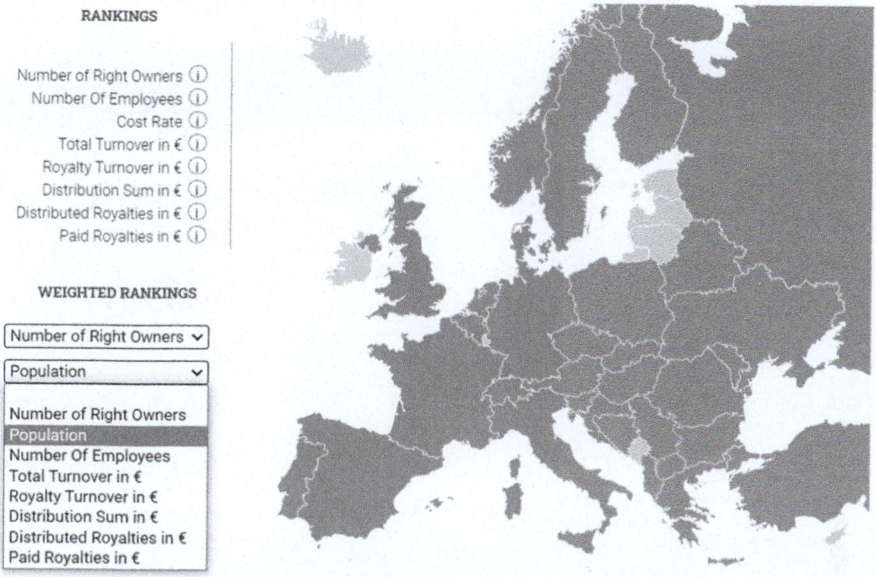

Fig. 5 User interface of the CCS-statistics web-application

for registering works exists,[17] it is not followed consequently (*technological challenge 1*). Third, the creation and verification of files is supported by this tool (*technological challenge 2*).

8.1 Use case "Evaluating CCS"

As described in Sect. 5, various selection criteria are relevant for the decision to become a direct member of a CCS. Music publishers are supported by comparing the introduced KPIs (see Sect. 4.2.1). To simplify this process, a web-application[18] was developed (see Fig. 5), providing three analysis options. The first option allows for a comprehensive view of relevant KPIs of a specific CCS. This view is suitable for evaluating a CCS of an already targeted market, driven by the idea of joining the CCS as a direct member. It provides a summarizing alternative to viewing the annual report of the CCS, focusing on key facts.

As a second option, the tool provides an evaluation of CCS performance by sorting and ranking CCS with respect to a specific KPI. For example, the KPI *cost rate* can serve as an indicator of the efficiency of CCS processes. Figure 6 shows both the three lowest and the three highest cost rates of the investigated sample, detailing the analysis in Sect. 6.1.

[17] *Common Work Registration* (CWR) https://members.cisac.org/CisacPortal/openDocumentPackDP.do?item=item5&docPackId=16.

[18] https://www.soclear.de/statistics/.

Name	Cost Rate	Name	Cost Rate
Stemra Netherlands	**2018: 9,88 %**	SAZAS Slovenia	**2018: 32,47 %**
Koda Denmark	**2018: 10,78 %**	AMUS Bosnia and Herzegovina	**2016: 29,82 %**
Tono Norway	**2018: 11,29 %**	ZAMP Northern Macedonia	**2018: 25,55 %**

Fig. 6 Cost rate ranking

Name	Royalty Turnover in €/ Population	Royalty Turnover in €	Population	Name	Royalty Turnover in €/ Population	Royalty Turnover in €	Population
Koda Denmark	**23,00**	2018: 135.975.000 €	2019: 5.911.019 *	autodia Greece	**0,165806**	2018: 1.778.712,29 €	2018: 10.727.668
Sacem France	**21,13**	2017: 1.415.300.000 €	2019: 66.993.000	MESAM Turkey	**0,129602**	2017: 10.627.900 €	2018: 82.003.882
SUISA Switzerland	**15,66**	2018: 133.843.000 €	2018: 8.544.527	NGO-UACRR Ukraine	**0,015905**	2018: 669.643 €	2019: 42.101.650

Fig. 7 Ranking: royalty turnover per capita

As a third option, weighted rankings of CCS allow for identifying possible correlation between two selected KPIs. As an example, an analysis of the licensed music use per capita can support the decision of a publisher to tap into a new market. This question is targeted by analyzing the royalty turnover of the respective CCS weighted against the population of its country (see Fig. 7).[19] By combining further KPIs, various additional analysis is feasible (e.g., "number of copyright holders per employee" or "paid royalties per copyright holder") allowing further comparative conclusions.

This section presented a tool to support a publisher's strategic decision to become a direct member of a CCS by making CCS economic performance transparent (*organizational challenge 4*). The tool is subject to various limitations which are described in Sect. 4.2.2. Continuously updating the database with current CCS KPIs would allow music publishers to assess the continuity of CCS performance. Also, differentiating between different copyright categories and types would support publishers to strategically align CCS with their business goals.

[19] It is important to note that these figures are distorted by the fact that the stated sum includes royalties from reciprocal contracts with foreign societies. To put this into perspective, foreign collections accounted for, e.g., 6,92% of KODA's royalty turnover and 8,54% of SUISA's total turnover in 2018.

These features would greatly objectify the decision process of whether to invest time, effort and money in a direct membership with a CCS or to retain the current intermediary exploitation option.

8.2 Use case "Registering Works"

According to the common expectation of digitalization, IT-tools can foster efficiency and effectiveness of various work tasks in many aspects. Furthermore, supporting technology is positively influencing the likeliness of exploitation of entrepreneurial opportunities (Choi and Shepherd 2004). Nevertheless, technological solutions must fulfill some conditions to achieve optimal results:

- To provide a basic understanding between various actors, transferred data should adhere to a generally accepted format.
- In order to avoid media discontinuity, all actors involved must offer digitally accessible interfaces.
- To allow for an extensive automation, the addressed processes should ensure a minimum degree of uniformity and frequency of execution.

As not all examined processes meet these requirements to an equal extent (e.g., becoming member in a foreign CCS is usually a one-time task), it can be assumed that software is not an equally effective approach for all identified challenges. The following characteristics illustrate why we chose the *registration of works* process as a case study to be supported by a software prototype:

- Scaling: Whereas it is possible to register new works using e-mail or online forms, it becomes a tedious and error-prone process when registering hundreds or thousands of works. Since the repertoire managed by a publisher is typically on a larger scale, a manual process is not feasible.
- Repetition: The composition of new works is predominantly an ongoing process. New works have to be registered at collecting societies or transferred to sub-publishers on a regular basis. Improvements in this area are therefore not limited to a single, concluding action.
- Standardization: Driven by the previous two arguments and a rather long history of transferring work data between publishers, the CISAC developed CWR (Common Work Registration), a standardized data format describing various aspects relevant for musical works (Zetterlund 2011). Since a broad variety of stakeholders accept this data format for describing work-relevant metadata, a rather uniform way of data exchange could be expected.
- Interfaces: An initial, basic investigation found widespread use of e-mail or FTP servers for exchanging CWR data. Although newer, more advanced technological options exist, this path meets the minimum technological requirements, as it at least prevents media breaks.

Thus, this example serves as a good starting point with manageable technological complexity, while at the same time offering great benefits and a wide application potential. Furthermore, the market offers only a few alternatives.[20]

Various aspects of the CWR file format played a role in the interviews. On the one hand, the relevance of this format not only for the exchange between publishing partners or CCS, but also for the exchange with other platforms and service providers was emphasized.

> "Also many other platforms and service providers, for example Lyricfind, can also be supplied with CWR. And of course, large catalogs have to be delivered in the adapted formats to collecting societies in case of direct memberships. (P1:96)"

On the other hand, various statements indicate challenges to be expected when dealing with the CWR format. First, this is a repeatedly mentioned lack of compatibility of CWR-files exchanged between different stakeholders, which often results in the necessity of manual corrections.

> "And the problem is simple with this CWR story – although it's called Common Work Registration it's not common at all. Because no matter where you do it, it's never right for the country in question. You still have to manually add or remove things. (P4:113)"

It is irrelevant whether the partners of the data exchange are publishers or CCS, the challenges remain the same in both cases. As there is actually a maintained, published and documented standard, the problem is initially surprising from a technological perspective, since it is precisely these problems that standardization is intended to solve – a surprise that the publishers share.

> "What seems to be a huge effort is to get data from GEMA, i.e., verified data that can be used. We hear again and again from foreign publishers that the data is not quite compatible, although there is this CWR format. I always don't understand why this is so problematic. (P7:63)"

A further challenge is the lack of tool support for tasks following the pure exchange of data. According to the standard, the registration of new works is also confirmed with a CWR summarizing information about success or failure of the registration. Due to a lack of IT support, it is not possible for publishers to analyze this feedback, which in turn makes any corrective action that may be required impossible.

> "And now we get registration confirmations via CWR back, we can't read that at all. Yes, we can't check if this is really correct (P1:134)"

In summary, the use case of registering or transferring work data has great potential and practical relevance, but also presents numerous technological and

[20] Example for a not longer maintained tool with limited functionality: https://matijakolaric.com/free/cwr-syntax-highlighter/.

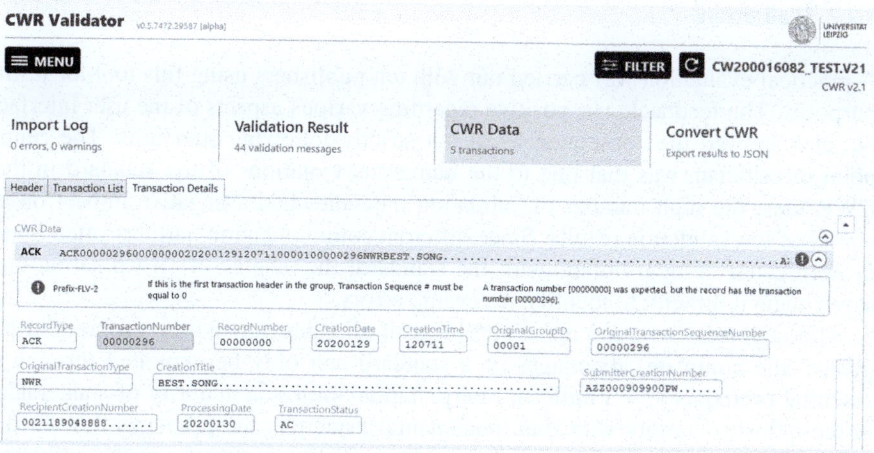

Fig. 8 CWR validator – display CWR data

organizational challenges, which exemplify the difficulties that new ways of exploiting copyrights raise for publishers.

8.2.1 CWR-Validator

Driven by the interview statements we developed a tool for validating CWR files. Based on the described needs and challenges, the functional goals were:

- A strict and comprehensive validation against the published standard to assess the correctness and completeness of CWR files,
- A structured and clear representation of the file contents including registration feedback, as the readability of extensive, fixed-length text-based files is limited,
- And an understandable and detailed description of occurred validation messages to support the creation of valid CWR files.

The prototype was implemented as a desktop application for Windows. The user interface is divided into four parts (see upper part of Fig. 8). First, the *Import Log* lists information, errors and warnings regarding the process of reading the file. Second, the results of the actual check of the CWR file is shown in the *Validation Result* tab, including some metadata such as the violated rule. It is also possible to get a listing of the violation causing works with line numbers and description to support manual corrections. The third tab displays the data of the CWR file in a structured manner along with the validation messages (see lower part of Fig. 8). Finally, the fourth tab allows for an export of the CWR data along with the validation messages to a JSON formatted file.

8.2.2 Evaluation

A practical evaluation was carried out with ten publishers using this tool for testing purposes. The feedback was positive regarding various aspects of the user interface, but also showed the consequences of not strictly following standards. The central point of criticism was that due to the numerous violations of the standard in their CWR files, the high number of validation messages had a negative impact on the clarity of the validation results. Since different communication partners often ignore or even cause certain violations of the standard, the display of all validation messages made it difficult to identify "relevant" errors.

Although relevance and meaningfulness of all rules may not be apparent at first glance, the complete advantages of a standard can only be exploited through its essential prerequisite – a uniform interpretation. Unless a majority of stakeholders in the industry comply with this fundamental principle, the problems described in the interviews cannot be avoided. Since addressing the root cause of the problem is a challenge beyond the scope of a research project, a technological workaround was developed. According to the feedback of the evaluating publishers and assuming the freedom of interpretation of the standard as given, the feature to filter certain types of validation messages was implemented. Additionally, reasonable presets covering known individualized interpretations of the standards were included.

The evaluation revealed that strict conformity to the standard is not the main objective of the music industry. Instead, the pragmatic approach of the publishers is: 100% validity is not necessary, it is sufficient to be as valid as needed so that further processing by partners is possible. Although at first sight this seems to be a valid tactic, a more holistic perspective shows the connection between this approach and the above-mentioned problems. A standard is only useful as long as all stakeholders comply with it.

As the use cases illustrate, software has the potential to address these problems. However, fundamental solutions require changes on an organizational, political level, which are difficult to achieve in a heterogeneous environment consisting of numerous independent actors. The fact that publishers are taking the direct membership route despite these difficulties shows its potential as well as the needs of the industry. In the future, additional case studies may expand the scope of our research by implementing software that supports other processes, including importing, reviewing, and correcting music usage information.

9 Economic potential of technological solutions

In the previous chapters, technological solutions were presented which aim to support small-to medium-sized publishers in taking the entrepreneurial step toward direct memberships in foreign CCS. Table 10 presents three technological approaches for implementing this entrepreneurial opportunity.

Using approach A, the publisher authorizes the CCS directly, saves the costs for sub-publishers and reduces the latency between licensing and royalty payment at the same time. Negative effects occur at the interorganizational interface – insufficient

Table 10 Approaches for direct membership

	Characteristics	Speed	Efficiency	Transparency	Software support
A	Direct membership in a limited number of important markets, no significant technical support	Medium-fast	No costs for sub-publishing (usually something between 10 and 50%), but extensive efficiency reducing manual work may be necessary	High	Low
B	Direct membership in important markets, individual tools to support a limited number of tasks	Fast	Possible costs for software to support particularly complex steps, otherwise no further costs for sub-publisher or service provider	High	Medium
C	Direct membership via technology service providers	Fast	Costs for technology service providers, high efficiency due to applicable economies of scale	Medium–high	High

integration of processes and an increase in manual work lead to higher error-proneness and lower process efficiency. The majority of the publishers surveyed follow this approach.

Approach B is characterized by a software supported reduction of manual tasks which in turn increases process accuracy and efficiency. No comprehensive software solution has been implemented yet; rather single, particularly complex tasks are supported by software tools. There are costs for developing and maintaining the software, and publishers would increase their dependence on software suppliers or developers.

In approach C, technology service providers deliver software that enables the management of the entire interorganizational process, starting with the initial membership application, the management of rights assigned to the CCS, work registrations, and all other processes at the interface to the CCS (cf. Fig. 1). These providers act as a hub to the various CCS, so that the exchange of data can be carried out efficiently by applying economies of scale, supported by technological solutions. On the other hand, there is limited independence, since the publisher may now receive more favorable conditions than with a sub-publisher, but at the expense of the individual support of its artists. Furthermore, the dependence on the sub-publisher is substituted with the dependence on the service provider. In contrast to technology-centered publishing administrators such as *Songtrust* or *Kobalt*, this approach would allow the publisher to establish direct contractual relationships with CCS of their choice to build their own network based on their needs (cf. Sect. 5). While potentially saving administrative costs, the publisher is also closer to the CCS and can take advantage of the opportunities identified in Sect. 7. As of today, no such solution exists according to the best knowledge of the authors.

As noted above, publishers' freedom of choice to authorize CCS directly applies equally to writers and any other eligible copyright holder within the EEA.[21] However, they are facing similar challenges as the publishers (cf. Sect. 6). Due to the conflicting nature of administrative and artistic activities, it can be assumed that writers will tend to focus on the latter, even if the availability of technological support lowers the barriers of direct memberships (approach B). However, a more widespread use of convenient technological services that act as a hub between CCS and copyright holders would have the potential to cause a shift in this respect (approach C).

10 Conclusion and future perspectives

The aim of this paper was to outline the entrepreneurial opportunity of direct memberships of publishers in multiple international copyright societies along with its challenges, opportunities and possible technological solutions. We focused on the

[21] If writers seek to maximize profits by skipping all intermediaries such as publishers and domestic CCS, the legal framework of the addressed market should be thoroughly examined, since national rules on whether or not publishers' shares are paid to writers may differ.

underlying economic motivation and requirements of publishers, highlighted the heterogeneity of economic performance of CCS, differences and commonalities in processes and data and proposed technological solutions supporting the alignment of publishers' needs with current CCS practices.

With our findings, we aim to draw a comprehensive picture of the trend toward direct international copyright management. Despite the extra work involved, a growing number of small- and medium-sized publishers took advantage of this opportunity, motivated mainly by the expectation of economic improvements and driven by the urgency to find international compatibility, especially due to a changing, more international market.

Since this study only marks the outset, a few fundamental questions are yet to be answered. First, in a follow-up study, the qualitative findings are to be translated into quantitative backed statements to allow for more general conclusions to be drawn. Second, since most of the publishers interviewed choose to become members of CCS based more or less on subjective estimates rather than on concrete objective measures, a thorough economic assessment is necessary, examining the conditions and best practices necessary to make this step profitable.

As the study shows, organizational and administrative barriers for direct memberships nowadays are quite high due to heterogeneous processes and data formats as well as varying organizational rules and legal frameworks. As a consequence, publishers focus only on their most important markets. Technological solutions might support further developments. The findings regarding process models and data formats support the deduction of abstract processes and formats, which in turn can contribute to the implementation of generic tools supporting multiple CCS. Software that simplifies interaction with multiple CCS supports a more widespread adoption of direct memberships, extending it to smaller markets as well. Likewise, it could also become an option for small publishers or other copyright holders like composers or authors. In order to lay the theoretical foundation for the implementation of software solutions, the technological requirements needed for a fully integrated solution have to be further detailed in follow-up studies.

One starting point might be to examine existing solutions from technology-driven publishing administration companies; the life cycle of publishers' interaction with CCS outlined in Fig. 1 could also be used as a structuring basis.

A further factor of uncertainty is the ongoing, but very slowly progressing organizational changes in the market of CCS. Partnerships or joint ventures such as ICE may indicate movement in a long time predominantly very static sector, although the implications for the day-to-day business are yet to be determined. Nevertheless, aggregation tendencies on the CCS side may render the construct of multiple direct memberships obsolete. So far, however, these aggregations have focused only on online rights, and current practice demonstrates the urgent need on the part of publishers for more rapid development.

If the focus is on competition rather than consolidation, an interesting point for future research is to evaluate which factors are beneficial in terms of the efficiency and effectiveness to better understand the reasons for heterogeneity of CCS. To what extent do CCS implement efficiency-oriented strategies? What are success factors and best practices?

Although technology is not the driving factor for the rise of direct memberships yet, it is an enabler to support, spread and intensify this trend among publishers. An obstacle to wider acceptance of the direct membership model is in many cases the increased administrative effort required, which publishers are currently prepared to bear in only a few core markets. As the proposed prototypes show, technology can address this challenge and, thus, support this trend. Likewise, reducing transaction costs enables an entrepreneurial return. New organizational structures or technological systems will support that development (Foss and Foss 2008). In addition, even if publishers are currently primarily concerned with improving copyright management for their repertoire, an increased offering of exploitation services for other publishers can be expected in the future – cross-national sub-publishing provided by one publisher. This service can be considered as a further entrepreneurial opportunity, compensating the increased effort of direct memberships by new exploitation options.

We hope that the results presented will help to gain an initial understanding of this trend, as well as draw attention to this growing field, thereby encouraging technological and organizational developments that support publishers in their role as international entrepreneurs.

Funding Open Access funding enabled and organized by Projekt DEAL. Parts of the work were funded by grants of the German Ministry of Education and Research in the context of the joint research project "SO/CLEAR" (01IS18083B) under the supervision of the PT-DLR.

Data availability The tools and many raw data such as process models can be found on the research group's webpage https://creativeartefact.org and on the project's webpage https://soclear.de.

Code availability The tools and further information can be found on the research group's webpage https://creativeartefact.org and on the project's webpage https://soclear.de.

Declarations

Conflict of interest The authors declare that they have no competing interest.

References

Chinosi, M., & Trombetta, A. (2012). Bpmn: An introduction to the standard. *Computer Standards & Interfaces, 34*(1), 124–134. https://doi.org/10.1016/j.csi.2011.06.002.

Choi, Y. R., & Shepherd, D. A. (2004). Entrepreneurs' decisions to exploit opportunities. *Journal of Management, 30*(3), 377–395. https://doi.org/10.1016/j.jm.2003.04.002.

CISAC (2014). Cisac global collections report 2014. Tech. rep., CISAC, https://www.cisac.org/CISAC-University/Library/Global-Collections-Reports/Global-Collections-Report-2014.

CISAC (2019). Cisac global collections report 2019. Tech. rep., CISAC, https://www.cisac.org/CISAC-University/Library/Global-Collections-Reports/Global-Collections-Report-2019.

Davidsson, P. (2015). Entrepreneurial opportunities and the entrepreneurship nexus: A re-conceptualization. *Journal of Business Venturing, 30*(5), 674–695. https://doi.org/10.1016/j.jbusvent.2015.01.002.

European Parliament, Council of European Union (2014). Directive 2014/26/ec of feb. 26, 2014 of the european parliament and of the council on collective management of copyright and related rights and multi-territorial licensing of rights in musical works for online uses in the internal market. https://eur-lex.europa.eu/legal-content/EN/ALL/?uri=CELEX:32014L0026.

Foss, K., & Foss, N. J. (2008). Understanding opportunity discovery and sustainable advantage: The role of transaction costs and property rights. *Strategic Entrepreneurship Journal, 2*(3), 191–207. https://doi.org/10.1002/sej.49.

Guibault, L., & Gompel, S. (2015). Collective Management in the European Union, Kluwer Law International B.V., Zuidpoolsingel 2, 2408 ZE Alphen aan den Rijn, The Netherlands, (pp. 141–143).

Handke, C. (2013). The economics of collective copyright management. resreport, Erasmus University Rotterdam (EUR), https://doi.org/10.2139/ssrn.2256178.

Handke, C., & Towse, R. (2007). Economics of copyright collecting societies. *International Review of Intellectual Property and Competition Law, 38*(8), 937–957. https://doi.org/10.2139/ssrn.1159085.

Harrison, A. (2011). *Music: The Business* (5th ed.). London: Virgin Books.

Kirzner, I.M. (1973). Competition and entrepreneurship. University of Illinois at Urbana-Champaign's Academy for Entrepreneurial Leadership Historical Research Reference in Entrepreneurship.

Matanovac Vučković, R. (2016). Implementation of directive 2014/26/eu on collective management and multi-territorial licensing of musical rights in regulating the tariff-setting systems in central and eastern europe. *IIC - International Review of Intellectual Property and Competition Law, 47*(1), 28–59. https://doi.org/10.1007/s40319-015-0438-5.

Miller, D. (1983). The correlates of entrepreneurship in three types of firms. *Management Science, 29*(7), 770–791.

Music and Copyright (2020). UMG increases recorded-music market share lead, indies enhance publishing dominance. https://musicandcopyright.wordpress.com/2020/05/20/umg-increases-recorded-music-market-share-lead-indies-enhance-publishing-dominance/.

Nielsen, S. L., & Lassen, A. H. (2012). Images of entrepreneurship: towards a new categorization of entrepreneurship. *International Entrepreneurship and Management Journal, 8*(1), 35–53. https://doi.org/10.1007/s11365-010-0159-7.

O'Cass, A., & Weerawardena, J. (2009). Examining the role of international entrepreneurship, innovation and international market performance in sme internationalisation. *European Journal of Marketing, 43*(11/12), 1325–1348. https://doi.org/10.1108/03090560910989911.

Peffers, K., Tuunanen, T., Rothenberger, M., & Chatterjee, S. (2007). A design science research methodology for information systems research. *Journal of Management Information Systems., 24*(3), 45–77.

Pitt, I. L. (2010). Economic analysis of music copyright. *Springer, NY.*https://doi.org/10.1007/978-1-4419-6318-5.

Rochelandet, F. (2003). Are copyright collecting societies efficient organisations? an evaluation of collective administration of copyright in Europe. In W. J. Gordon & R. Watt (Eds.), *The economics of copyright* (pp. 176–191). Cheltenham: Elgar.

Serviere, L. (2010). Forced to entrepreneurship: Modeling the factors behind necessity entrepreneurship. *Journal of Business and Entrepreneurship., 22*(1), 37–53.

Short, J. C., Ketchen, D. J., Shook, C. L., & Ireland, R. D. (2010). The concept of opportunity in entrepreneurship research past accomplishments and future challenges. *Journal of Management, 36*(1), 40–65. https://doi.org/10.1177/0149206309342746.

Stevenson, H. H., Roberts, M. J., & Grousbeck, H. I. (1999). *New business ventures and the entrepreneur.* New York: McGraw-Hill/Irwin.

Sutton, J., & Austin, Z. (2015). Qualitative research: Data collection, analysis, and management. *The Canadian journal of hospital pharmacy, 68*(3), 226–231. https://doi.org/10.4212/cjhp.v68i3.1456.

Towse, R. (2017). Economics of music publishing: Copyright and the market. *Journal of Cultural Economics, 41*(4), 403–420. https://doi.org/10.1007/s10824-016-9268-7.

Tschmuck, P. (2016). From record selling to cultural entrepreneurship: The music economy in the digital paradigm shift. In P. Wikström & B. DeFillippi (Eds.), *Business innovation and disruption in the music industry* (pp. 13–23). Cheltenham, UK: Edward Elgar Publishing.

van Weele, M., van Rijnsoever, F. J., Eveleens, C. P., Steinz, H., van Stijn, N., & Groen, M. (2018). Start-eu-up! lessons from international incubation practices to address the challenges faced by Western

European start-ups. *The Journal of Technology Transfer, 43*(5), 1161–1189. https://doi.org/10.1007/s10961-016-9538-8.

Wilde, E., & Schwerzmann, J. (2004). When business models go bad: The music industry's future. In 1st International Conference on E-Business and Telecommunication Networks. pp. 48–54.

Zetterlund, A. (2011). Common works registration user manual. https://members.cisac.org/CisacPortal/consulterDocument.do?id=22272.

Journal of Cultural Economics (2021) 45:671–704
https://doi.org/10.1007/s10824-021-09418-3

ORIGINAL ARTICLE

Do museums foster innovation through engagement with the cultural and creative industries?

Chiara Dalle Nogare[1] · **Monika Murzyn-Kupisz**[2]

Received: 11 July 2020 / Accepted: 16 April 2021 / Published online: 1 May 2021

Abstract

The recent narrative on museums as catalysts of innovation and growth considers their relations with other cultural and creative industries (CCIs) to be very important. We argue that most relations museums establish with CCI firms and institutions are unlikely to produce strong positive externalities that make the latter more innovative. To prove this claim, we propose a conceptual framework qualifying project-based and supply chain relations between museums and CCIs as either strong, moderate, or weak links, according to their potential in terms of knowledge spillovers from museums to CCIs. We apply this taxonomy to data collected from 261 Polish museums. Our findings indicate that strong links are outnumbered by moderate and weak ones. We then suggest that the traditional missions of museums, in particular education and conservation, need to be more thoroughly assessed in terms of their direct and indirect contributions in order to fully capture the impact of museums on innovation in the wider economy.

Keywords Museums · Cultural and creative industries · Innovation · Knowledge spillovers

JEL Classification Z11 · 030 · D62

1 Introduction

The role of innovation in fostering economic growth is well established in macroeconomics (Barro and Sala-i-Martin 2003; Romer 1996), and recent contributions highlight that creative professions may play a role in making a nation or a region

✉ Chiara Dalle Nogare
chiara.dallenogare@unibs.it

1 Department of Economics and Mangement, University of Brescia, Via S. Faustino 74/B, Brescia, Italy

2 Institute of Geography and Spatial Management, Jagiellonian University, ul. Gronostajowa 7, 30-387 Kraków, Poland

more innovative (Cerisola 2019; Rodriguez-Pose and Lee 2020). This is different from saying that the creative sector (the cultural and creative industries, CCIs hereafter) plays a special role in the innovation ecosystem, yet policymakers often translate scholarly evidence into agendas focusing on (variously defined) CCIs (Sternberg 2017). However, while support for CCIs by governments makes sense in many respects (positive effects on well-being and on the attractiveness of local contexts for individuals and firms), it is not to be taken for granted that this is an effective innovation policy. In fact, there is still a lack of robust evidence on both the relative innovativeness of CCIs compared to other industries and the extent to which CCIs foster innovation in the wider economy.

Museums are included in most recent definitions of CCIs (see Sect. 2), and so policy documents have begun including them in agendas for innovation, highlighting the need for them to closely interact with other CCIs. The very presence of interactions is considered as evidence of their being part of the cultural and creative sector, as well as a positive element in terms of the enhancement of the overall impact of CCIs on innovativeness. This has put pressure on museum directors. Traditionally, contributing to innovation has not been part of museums' goals. Their core missions have long been collection, conservation, research, exhibition, and education.[1] In this article, we aim to highlight that museums do produce positive externalities for the local and regional economy in terms of a higher level of innovativeness, but probably not primarily through their relations with the CCIs.

The claim that museums foster innovation by making the CCIs more creative rests upon the assumption that the links between museums and the CCIs generate strong knowledge spillovers that benefit the latter. In fact, this is how infra-industry relations can spread innovation (Bakhshi and McVittie 2009). A direct way to assess whether this condition is met is to estimate a model where some measure of innovation for the CCI is the dependent variable and the presence of a CCI–museum relation is a covariate. To our knowledge, however, there have been no surveys investigating the innovative products and processes of CCIs in the context of their cooperation with museums. We therefore use an *indirect* way of verifying whether there are strong knowledge spillovers from museums to CCIs, through the analysis of a unique dataset collected from 261 Polish museums regarding their activities and relations with CCI firms and institutions in the 2017–2018 reporting period.

We first elaborate a taxonomy of museum–CCI cooperation modes, distinguishing between those potentially rich and those likely to be poor in knowledge spillovers. For example, designers who access and get direct inspiration from a museum's collection may be considered an instance of a rich relation (which we define as a *strong link*). Space rentals are an example of a much poorer relation in terms of the likelihood of knowledge spillovers (*weak link*). We then apply this taxonomy to the data on Polish museums and conclude that although most museums have relatively frequent exchanges with CCI firms and institutions, weak links greatly outnumber strong ones. This does not conclusively prove, but

[1] These missions are core in the ICOM definition of a museum. This definition is the subject of an ongoing debate (Sandahl 2019).

certainly suggests that the contribution of museums to innovation through their relations with CCIs is not particularly strong in the Polish context.

More generally, our evidence points to the fact that networking with CCI firms may be overrated for museums because often only the quantitative—rather than the qualitative—dimension of the relation is considered (quality is understood here as a strong potential in terms of knowledge spillovers). Such findings may have direct policy implications and may also help inform future quantitative and qualitative investigations of museum–CCI relations and their impact on CCI innovativeness.

On the other hand, what appears to be an underrated phenomenon is that the traditional core missions of museums may have important consequences in terms of enhancement of innovation in a given national or local context, with positive impacts on economic performance. For instance, the knowledge spillover effects when conservation activities are shared with other institutions (firms, universities) in backward supply linkages are often important. Museums' contributions to innovation through their education mission may be even more significant.

This paper is organised as follows. Section 2 introduces to the literature on the definitions of CCIs and the inclusion of museums into these, as well as innovation and innovation spreading mechanisms. Section 3 clarifies how our contribution relates to this literature and outlines the model we refer to. Section 4 lays out the conceptual framework we propose for classifying the relationships between museums and other CCIs. In Sect. 5, we apply this framework to the Polish case and illustrate the core of our evidence. The subsequent section suggests how the education mission of museums (sometimes implemented in cooperation with CCI firms) may impact innovation, while Sect. 7 presents our conclusions.

2 CCIs, museums, and innovation

The last three decades have witnessed an increased interest in the links between culture and creativity on one hand and economic growth and development on the other. Cultural and creative industries (CCIs) is one of the concepts that has been elaborated and often discussed in analyses of these connections, in what has been defined as an industry-based approach to the topic (Cerisola 2019).

2.1 CCI definitions and museums as a CCI

Despite the interest in the topic, there is no agreement among scholars and politicians on the very definition of a CCI and which industries should be included. CCIs generally comprise the 'cultural industries', a term with a long tradition and

Table 1 Museums in CCI definitions

References	CCI sub-sector	Item
KEA (2006)	Core arts field-heritage	Museums, libraries, archaeological sites, archives
Throsby (2008)	Other core cultural industries	Museums, galleries, libraries
UNCTAD (2010)	Heritage	Cultural sites: archaeological sites, museums, libraries, exhibitions
EC (2010)	Cultural heritage	Cultural heritage
Power (2011)	Libraries, museums, heritage	Museums
EC (2016)	Archives, museums, cultural heritage	Museums activities
DCMS (2016)	Museums, galleries and libraries	Museum activities
Statistics Poland (2018)	Cultural heritage	Museum activities
KEA (2019a)	Core cultural subsector	Museums
KEA (2019b)	Heritage, archives and libraries	Museum activities

evolving usage that dates from the 1940s and was redefined in the late 1980s, and the 'creative industries', a term coined in the 1990s in Australia and initially mainly used in the UK context (DCMS 1998; Hartley et al. 2013).[2] Although the initial DCMS (1998) definition included mainly commercially-oriented sectors such as advertising, architecture, art and antiques, crafts, leisure software, design, film and video, music, the performing arts, publishing, radio, and TV, with time it was broadened to incorporate less profit-oriented subsectors and activities—hence the inclusion of the heritage sector, comprising museums, archives, libraries, and heritage sites (DCMS 2016), in line with the more comprehensive approach to the creative economy proposed by Bakhshi et al. (2015). Such a broad definition of CCIs is also used by the European Commission in its green paper 'Unlocking the potential of cultural and creative industries' (EC 2010: 5–6).

According to Throsby (2015: 59; see also UNCTAD 2010), CCI outputs should share three key characteristics: human imagination and creativity as core inputs; some form of symbolic or cultural content and meaning; connection to intellectual property rights (i.e. potential for copyright). They therefore convey or embody (though to a different extent) both cultural (symbolic) and economic (utilitarian) value (Throsby 2008, 2010). The conceptualisation of the creative industries proposed by Throsby is one of the most cited ones, also because many other studies simply list CCIs and do not properly justify the inclusion/exclusion of any given industry. His 'concentric circles model' (Throsby 2008) comprises 'core creative arts' generating original creative ideas; 'other core cultural industries', which include museums and galleries; 'wider cultural industries' and 'related industries'. A similar approach is adopted by other researchers and institutions who place the creation of original content (i.e. generation of artistic ideas) or drawing on existing

[2] It is usually expected either that the two concepts are used as synonyms (Towse, 2003) or that creative industries include cultural industries as a subset (UNCTAD 2010).

creative content (i.e. heritage) at the heart of CCIs (The Work Foundation 2007, 2007; KEA 2019b). According to them, a distinctive feature with respect to creative processes in other industries is the symbolic element embodied in the final output (Galloway and Dunlop 2007).

Although museums were not initially included in studies of either cultural or creative industries, as the definitions broadened they have been incorporated into them (Hartley et al. 2013; Mikić 2012; Throsby 2008). Nowadays, they are generally included as such or under the broader heading of 'cultural heritage'. Table 1 lists a number of scholarly contributions and policy papers doing so.

A summary of potential relations between museums and the other CCIs is presented in the 'Museums and Creative Industries Toolkit' developed by the Northern Ireland Museums Council (2020). For CCI firms, museums can be places of display, dissemination (sale, performance), or production (e.g. filming), as well as sources of creative content and providers of inspiration for such content. In addition, museum employees can be seen as sources of expert knowledge. In other publications, museums are also referred to as potential 'hubs' for creative activities or CCI clusters (OECD-ICOM 2019) or providers of infrastructure for the CCIs (Rectanus 2020). Interactions between museums and CCIs can occur at different stages of the CCI value chain: generation of original creative content, publication, and delivery or distribution of goods and services (KEA 2019b). They can also be discussed from the point of view of the role of museums as aesthetic gatekeepers (Hartley et al. 2013) or gatekeepers in general (Towse 2003), and considering that museums are often public institutions or are heavily subsidised by governments, as a channel through which public policy impacts the CCIs (Hartley et al. 2013).

Even though the links between museums and CCIs have been increasingly mentioned and advocated for recently (OECD-ICOM 2019), they are rarely explored conceptually. Despite general recognition (Simasone et al. 2015; NEMO 2018; OECD-ICOM 2019; Northern Ireland Museums Council 2020) and the establishment of a working group on Museums and Creative Industries within the Network of European Museum Organisations (NEMO) in 2014, both theoretical reflection and empirical evidence is still very limited (Simasone et al. 2015). In particular, the NEMO project provides only limited evidence based on a qualitative study of 24 museums in Latvia.

2.2 Innovation: its definition and transmission channels involving the CCIs

For the purpose of this paper, we will stick to a strictly economic definition of innovation, disregarding social innovation. It is the very narrative about CCIs that tends to state (but often not prove, see Sect. 2.3) that they are an element that makes an economy more competitive. The Oslo Manual (OECD-Eurostat 2005, 2019) broadens the notion of economic innovation by including not just scientific and technological changes but also organisational, financial, and commercial changes that make firms more competitive through novel approaches to production and markets. The broadening of the definition serves the purpose of better covering process innovation and considering not just manufacturing but also the service sector.

The hypothesis that CCIs make a place more innovation-prone is often put forward in relation to either their role as soft location factors, i.e. attractions that the so-called creative class appreciates (Florida 2002), or the fact that CCIs are more innovative than other industries and tend to spread innovation to the rest of the economy.

With reference to CCIs fostering the spread of innovation, Bakhshi and McVittie (2009) argue that the relation between CCIs and other industries must be understood in terms of knowledge spillovers. In particular, they list a number of transmission channels for these spillovers: imitation, worker mobility across industries, project-based cooperation, and supply chain linkages in which prices do not fully reflect the value of the exchanged good or service. They focus on supply chain linkages and claim that what makes CCIs special is the allegedly important knowledge spillovers they produce specifically through this channel. When CCIs play the role of buyers, knowledge spillovers may stem from the *specific* requirements they ask of their providers. When they play the role of suppliers, it is the specificity of their services, coming from a very high degree of product differentiation, that matters. The implicit transmission of knowledge accompanying market exchanges with CCIs may help all sorts of firms be more creative in the development of products and processes. Whether this is the case or not is a matter of empirical investigation: firms establishing relations with CCIs should be more innovative.

The detailed account of transmission channels suggested by Bakhshi and McVittie (2009) can also be adopted in the analysis of the positive externalities emerging when CCIs interact with each other. In the concentric model of CCIs (Throsby 2008), positive externalities emanate from the core circle to the others and especially the outer ones (for instance, cultural industries such as publishing and music industries and creative industries such as design and fashion). These positive externalities, justifying the very notion of CCIs as a whole, may be conceived of as knowledge spillovers. To our knowledge, however, they have not as yet been the object of specific empirical analyses.

2.3 CCIs in the literature on innovation and development

The CCIs allegedly play a special role in the economy, one of the most important reasons being that they are highly innovative (they create new goods and services, hence markets, or organisational solutions) and spread innovation (Petruzzelli and Lerro 2020). They are therefore expected to act as 'conduits for knowledge, innovation and new ideas' (EC 2010: 17) and to be important drivers of technological, economic, and social innovation (KEA 2019a). Moreover, CCIs are said to contribute to the process of adaptation to novelty and the facilitation of change (Potts and Cunningham 2008). Cunningham et al. (2010) suggest this is due to the fact that on the supply side of the market there is complementarity with the ITC sector, while on the demand side of the market CCIs' development is interconnected with the transition to the experience economy (EC 2010). Moreover, recent technological developments have forced some CCI branches to innovate in order to survive in the market.

For instance, the digital disruption inspired various changes in the music and film industries, including the development of new distribution and business models (Tschmuck 2006; Cunningham et al. 2010; Wikström and DeFillippi 2016).

However, the empirical evidence for the CCI–innovation nexus is at best inconclusive. Sometimes CCIs are found to have an impact on outputs such as employment or growth (Innocenti and Lazzeretti 2019), but this is not evidence, per se, of a relation between CCIs and innovation. In fact, CCIs may also have a role as local attractions for tourists and for creative and non-creative professionals (CCIs as soft location factors: see Florida 2002).[3] The links between CCIs and innovation require specific empirical assessment using *measures of innovativeness* as dependent variables. We report here some of the scholarly contributions adopting this approach.

Both Müller et al. (2009) and Lee and Rodríguez-Pose (2014), using survey data from Austria and small and medium-sized enterprises (SMEs) in the UK, respectively, find no evidence that CCIs are themselves particularly innovative. In particular, Müller et al. (2009) use self-reported innovation as their dependent variable, which bypasses the measurement problem affecting many contributions in the innovation literature. This evidence on the whole of CCIs does not exclude that *some* CCIs are innovative: indeed, there is literature on selected CCI sectors such as the music industry (Tschmuck 2006; Wikström and DeFillippi 2016) and the film industry (Cunningham et al. 2010) indicating that they are highly innovative. A possible reconciliation of these contrasting findings may come from the analysis of innovation in other CCI subsectors that may underperform in this respect.

As for the tests of whether CCI interaction with other economic sectors induces the latter to be more innovation-prone, Bakhshi and McVittie (2009) find a positive conditional correlation between CCIs and innovation in an economy: firms that innovate more are in economic sectors that purchase more goods and services from the CCIs. Yet, the direction of causality in this relationship cannot be detected through their empirical strategy. It may be that CCI inputs drive innovation, but it is equally possible that the firms requiring more CCI inputs use those goods/services to promote their innovation, the primary determinants of which lie elsewhere (think of advertising services, for instance). Bakhshi et al. (2015) deal with causality in a more appropriate way. The authors analyse a British business-to-business (B2B) voucher scheme meant to stimulate creative partnerships as a natural experiment. Their dependent variables are SMEs' self-reported introduction of an innovation 6 and 12 months after they received a voucher, and in a second model, the intention to introduce an innovation in the future. Treated firms did show some different behaviour (but not intentions) in the very short run, but after 12 months treated and untreated firms were not statistically different. This evidence on causal effects is especially modest if one considers that the authors refer to the UK definition of CCIs, which also includes software and computer services. Müller et al. (2009) use survey data to identify the determinants of the probability of a CCI contributing

[3] This is especially true for CCIs that qualify as amenities. However, recent empirical evidence shows that cultural amenities are not very effective as soft location factors for professionals (Cerisola 2018; Van Heerden and Bontje 2013).

to innovation in other firms, and they include dummies for the different CCI categories.[4] Arts-related CCIs and architecture have a significantly negative sign (the reference category is engineering). Apparently, the overall positive effect of CCIs masks very different levels of performance, with software and advertising having the most prominent role in fostering innovation in other sectors. Considering data from 187 Italian firms, Santoro et al. (2020) find that the share of sales derived from new products and services, a proxy for innovation performance, depends on a variable capturing the importance attributed by firm CEOs to informal relations with the CCIs (here including software). However, it is not to be taken for granted that the value of this variable actually captures the frequency and quality (or even the existence) of such relations. Using data on Italian provinces, Cerisola (2018, 2019) investigates the determinants of economic, artistic, and scientific creativity, which she measures respectively as the percentage of trademarks, highly specialised employees in arts and highly specialised employees in science over the population. The relative impact of CCIs on the economy (here not including museums and measured 10 years earlier) is not a significant driver of creativity when spatial autocorrelation is accounted for.

In spite of little evidence in favour of the idea that CCIs as a whole are more innovative and spread innovation more than other industries, many still find the narrative about the CCI–innovation nexus convincing and interest in the topic is not diminishing. Making reference to the innovation literature of the Schumpeterian tradition, some argue that the special role of CCIs could derive from their being part of the innovation system that drives the growth of the knowledge process underpinning economic evolution. In other words, they are a higher-order system operating not *within* but *on* the economic system, and it is hard to operationalise this issue (Potts and Cunningham 2008). Alternatively, it may well be that the extant empirical evidence considers highly imprecise measures of innovativeness.

3 Outline of the present investigation

The focus of this article is on the role museums play in fostering innovation in CCI firms and institutions they have ties with. It is their potential in terms of knowledge spillovers we want to investigate. Throsby (2010: 95) himself suggests that there is a need to pay more attention to within-CCI cooperation:

> *'ways in which firms in the cultural industries interact with other businesses... via the supply and demand for goods and services that are exchanged between them (...) Similar interactions occur amongst the cultural industries themselves. Such interrelationships are of course characteristic of all industries in the contemporary economy; interest in the cultural industries might focus on*

[4] Their definition of CCIs is peculiar as they only consider for-profit companies and they include engineering and consulting.

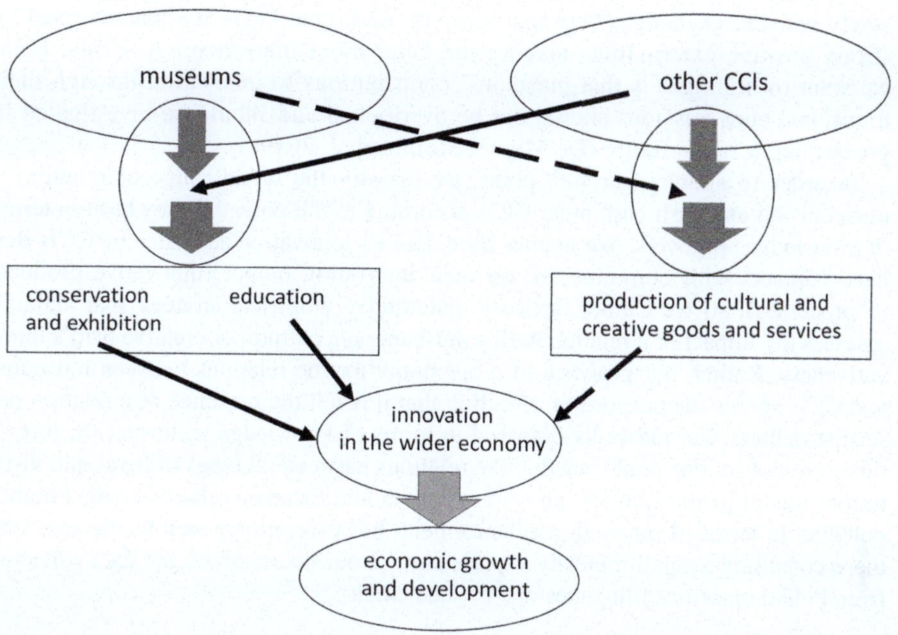

Fig. 1 Positive production externalities between museums and the other CCIs. Source: authors' own elaboration

how far-reaching and how significant these interdependencies are' (Throsby 2010: 95).

We follow Throsby's (2008) conceptualisation of CCIs, and we therefore define the CCIs as comprising the following industries: contemporary visual arts and photography; performing arts; music (both artists and the industry); the book and publishing industry; the radio, TV and film industries; internet portals and the press; the advertising industry; design and architecture; fashion. We also include artistic crafts and toys as part of design.

We consider the cooperation between museums and CCIs from the point of view of the innovation processes generated or enhanced as a consequence of this. Figure 1 illustrates our conceptual framework.

The vertical ovals represent museums and CCI production functions. The dashed arrow represents the potential knowledge spillovers from museums to the other CCIs, making the latter more innovative and hence producing more added value and a competitive advantage. The solid arrow refers to the positive externalities generated by the other CCIs and benefitting museums.

Most of the narrative on the relations between museums and CCIs has been focusing on the dashed arrows. It often tends to overlook the circumstance that what makes the associated interactions relevant is not their existence per se but the associated spillovers, if present. Accordingly, our first aim in this paper is to verify whether exchanges between museums and other CCIs are characterised by strong positive externalities making the latter more innovative. A second point we want to highlight is that museums' contributions to innovation through their traditional core missions should not be overlooked and should be investigated in greater depth in the future (De Miguel Molina et al. 2019a).

In order to address our first point, we classify the broad range of relations a museum can establish with other CCIs according to the potential they have in terms of knowledge spillovers. We neither have data on innovation activities by CCIs that have contacts with museums nor on their innovation output (innovative products or processes), so we cannot devise a quantitative empirical strategy that actually assesses the impact of a relation with a museum on a cultural or creative firm's innovativeness. Rather, our proposal of a taxonomy for the relations between museums and CCIs serves the purpose of revealing that it is not the presence of a relation per se that matters, but rather its potential in terms of knowledge spillovers. In fact, if this were not so, one could say that the relations between all types of firms and institutions would be relevant for innovation. We should focus on relations with a higher potential in terms of innovation enhancement; however, it may well be the case that these constitute a small minority. Application of our taxonomy to the data collected from Polish museums illustrates one of such cases.

4 Assessing museum relations with CCIs: a conceptual framework

Given the essential role knowledge spillovers play in making the relationship between museums and CCIs fruitful in terms of innovativeness, it is important to assess the actual existence of such spillovers. We focus on two of the transmission channels identified by Bakhshi and McVittie (2009): project-based cooperation and supply chain linkages, as imitation and qualified worker mobility between museums and other CCI firms and institutions are not strong, given the high specialisation characterising museum operations.

As stressed earlier, the very presence of project-based cooperation or a supply chain link is not in itself proof of knowledge spillovers. Rather, it is the quality of links that makes them more likely. Quality is understood here in terms of the type or characteristics of such relations that make them likely to generate innovations. We hence consider two aspects of the links between museums and other CCIs that indicate a greater potential for such positive externalities to occur, namely the frequency and nature of interactions.

First of all, museums may interact with designers, theatres, TV producers, advertising companies, and other CCIs occasionally or on a permanent basis, and a permanent relation is often more likely to entail the transmission of ideas and competences. Frequency is a rough indicator, however, because it is a (perhaps) necessary but not sufficient condition for positive externalities to occur.

Secondly, if information on the *nature* of the contacts between a museum and a CCI firm or institution is available, it is possible to categorise them according to their likelihood of entailing knowledge spillovers fostering innovation. Whether or not a museum is, for a CCI firm, just another supplier/client counterpart or a unique and irreplaceable partner making it more innovation-prone depends on the exchanged service. This is what we want our taxonomy to capture.

Symbolic meanings are among the discriminatory elements many authors cite as essential in defining creative goods and hence creative industries (Galloway and Dunlop 2007; Throsby 2015). The transmission of symbolic meanings (conducive to new creation) may then be exactly what makes it impossible for other counterparts to deliver the same as a specific museum in the context of infra-industry relations. The knowledge spillovers stem from access to museum collections and/or from the knowledge possessed and passed on by museum staff.

On the other hand, if a CCI company can easily exchange with an alternative partner to obtain the same type of goods/services it gets from a museum, the relationship between it and the museum is likely to be poor in knowledge spillovers. In this case, in fact, the object of the exchange does not have anything to do with what makes a museum unique, i.e. its collection.

We therefore propose the following definition:

Definition 1 (*Strong museum–other CCI firm link*) A relation between a museum and a CCI firm or institution is defined as a strong link if there are important knowledge spillovers from the former to the latter. These spillovers are generated by the transmission of symbolic meanings, more often than not stemming from expertise and knowledge about the particular museum collection. The knowledge spillovers increase the probability for a cooperating firm or institution to innovate, i.e. to generate either of the following: (a) new creative content; (b) an innovative reinterpretation of existing creative content; c) new ways of conveying creative content.

An example of forward supply chain linkages rich in potential spillovers is the case of museums making their collections available as inspiration for designers or artists (for instance, through an artist-in-residence programme). An example of a strong link in the backward supply chain is the case of museums asking an architect to design an extension of its premises. The architect will probably have a chance to access the museums' archives and deepen their knowledge of the collection the extension will host, as well as of museum functions in general. These are cases in which the contact with a museum entails a potential increase in creativity for a CCI firm and/or the addition of unique content to the goods/services it produces now and in the future.

Our definition of a moderate museum–other CCI firm link is as follows:

Definition 2 (*Moderate museum–other CCI firm link*) A relation between a museum and a CCI firm or institution is defined as a moderate link if there are some knowledge spillovers of the type described in Definition 1 from the former to the latter, but they are less likely and not as relevant for the improvement of the firm's innovativeness.

The definition of a weak link thus follows:

Table 2 Classification of museums' relations with CCI firms and institutions according to the strength of knowledge spillovers

CCI branch	Weak link	Moderate link	Strong link
Contemporary visual arts and photography			
	Original artworks or their copies sold in the museum shop	*Purchasing artworks for the collection directly from artists*	Providing information and access to the museum collection as artistic inspiration (e.g. artists' residences organised by the museum, organisation of creative sessions for artists)
	Renting or free of charge provision of museum space for visual arts ateliers	*Works of art of living artists borrowed from them and displayed at exhibitions*	Artists engaged as exhibition curators
			Artists design exhibition interiors, areas and layouts
			Artists design graphic layouts for exhibitions (prints, posters, catalogues, etc.)
			Long-term cooperation with artists on the development of museum visual identification systems
Performing arts			
	Renting space to theatre institutions for their performances, recordings, rehearsals	Exhibitions of objects from the museum collection in theatres	Using knowledge of museum staff to develop performances' content
	Renting museum objects and costumes for theatre activities	Co-organisation of events, festivals	Joint theatre productions
			Joint historical reconstructions
Music			
	Renting museum premises to music rehearsals, productions, concerts or recordings	Exhibition of objects from the museum collection in music institutions	Providing information and access to the museum collection to contemporary musicians

Table 2 (continued)

CCI branch	Weak link	Moderate link	Strong link
	Promotion of creative work in the field of music (e.g. specific music genres and artists)	Co-organisation of events, festivals	Music compositions and recordings for the museum (for instance, an audio drama as an element of an audio-visual installation)
Books and publishing industry			
	Renting of museum space for a bookshop	Use of museum images and archival materials in publications	Joint publishing projects
	Sale of publications in the museum shop or bookshop	Co-organisation of events, festivals	Consultations on publishing content with museums
	Book promotions and meetings with authors in the museum		
TV and film industry, radio, the press, internet portals, advertising			
	Media partnerships focused on the provision of information on the museum events and offer	Artefacts from museum collection or their images used in the preparation of creative content	Joint film projects, TV productions, radio programmes, web pages
	Museums as purchasers of advertising spaces	Using museum images and texts on-line	Participation of museum staff in the preparation of cultural contents
	Provision of film/TV/advertising locations	Commissioning films or commercials on the museum	
	Live-streaming of museum events	Inclusion of information on museums, their collections and offer in TV programmes	
	Purchasing licences to use films in exhibitions		

Table 2 (continued)

CCI branch	Weak link	Moderate link	Strong link
Architecture and design, fashion, artistic craft, toys			
	Original design items sold in the museum shop	*Purchasing design items for the museum collection*	Provision of information and training for the use of collection as design inspiration
	Providing opportunities for direct sales of design and artistic craft items in museum venues and at museum events	*Exhibitions of design items*	Organisation of design competitions
		Commissioning production and/or design of original museum souvenirs for the museum	Commissions for design of museum interiors, exhibition areas and layouts
			Commissions for architectural extensions and new buildings
			Commissions for replicas of museum objects/historic objects used in research, exhibitions or as educational materials

In moderate links, items in italics refer to the role of museums as art markets' gatekeepers

Definition 3 (*Weak museum–other CCI firm link*) Cooperation between a museum and a CCI firm or institution may be considered as a weak link if there are very few or no knowledge spillovers from the former to the latter, and hence no or very little effect on the CCI firm's behaviour and choices.

An example of forward supply chain linkages likely to be poor in spillovers is, for instance, museum space rentals—provision of museum space that does not involve other closer forms of cooperation between a museum and its tenant. Indeed, a CCI company may rent prestigious historic locations from a number of other providers (e.g. private owners of historic buildings and sites). An example of backward supply chain linkages poor in knowledge spillovers is a contract for the provision of advertising space, or the function of museums as places of sale for artworks, design, and artistic craft items produced regardless of cooperation with the museum and with no reference to the museum collection.

Table 2 presents a tentative classification of relations between museums and other CCIs according to their potential in terms of the enhancement of the latter's creativity, hence distinguishing between strong, moderate, and weak links.[5] The list of exchanges in each category is not exhaustive: the types of museums are so numerous and some of them are so specialised that it is impossible to take account of all idiosyncratic relations they engage in. Rather, this is a grid classifying the (potential) partnerships with CCIs that a standard museum is likely to set up.

In line with the above, weak links are very unlikely to inspire the transmission of symbolic meanings. Most of the weak links involve hosting (either for free or for money),[6] purchasing already produced goods and services for the museum, and buying advertising space. This is unlike most of the strong links, which involve the co-production of creative content and circumstances in which artists and/or CCI staff have long and deep exposure to the collection and interact closely with the museum staff.

In the moderate category, we place a miscellany of activities such as lending items from the museum collection to other cultural institutions and the co-organisation of events such as festivals, assuming that there are some positive externalities stemming from the contact between museum staff and the employees of CCI firms and institutions. The category also includes relations in which a museum plays a role as an art market gatekeeper. We explain the choice of categorising these specific exchanges as moderate links in the Appendix. In general, these types of cooperation are likely to produce knowledge spillovers entailing transmission of symbolic meanings with some probability, but not a very high one.

Table 2 may be interpreted in two different ways. On the one hand, it offers a reading of museum relations with the other CCIs in terms of their potential for increasing CCI innovativeness. It is a positive analysis and may be useful to scholars who wish

[5] Some museums are not just institutions focused on conservation and exhibition but enlarge their scope of action by including in their operations activities such publishing books and producing content. However, this is not the rule, and we abstract here from these non-core activities.

[6] Dalle Nogare and Scuderi (2020) find that, in Italy, renting spaces is a museum policy aimed at generating revenue more than anything else, and in fact private museums, which rely less on public subsidies, adopt this strategy more often.

to assess the contribution of museums to the innovativeness of the CCI firms engaging with them. In fact, it invites them to consider the right explanatory variable: what matters is not how many relations the investigated CCIs have with museums, but the number of strong links. On the other hand, the table may also be referred to by museum directors in normative terms. A contribution to CCI innovativeness may be a feasible museum mission, but only if certain types of cooperation are established.

5 Evaluating museum relations with CCIs in terms of the potential for CCI innovation: the Polish case

Despite the growing interest in the economic impact of museums and their links with the CCIs (NEMO 2018), to the best of our knowledge there are very few publications dealing with this issue comprehensively and in depth. This may be due to a lack of detailed statistical data—a Latvian qualitative pilot study of a small number of museums may be regarded as an exception (Sīmansone et al. 2015). This is why the data from the museum survey conducted by the Polish National Institute for Museums and Public Collections (NIMOZ) that we use here, which is based on a much larger sample of museums, is of particular importance.[7] The survey was inspired by recent recommendations on the analysis of the impact and economic relevance of museums (OECD-ICOM 2019).[8] The information provided to NIMOZ by 261 museums in Poland with respect to the 2017–2018 reporting period includes responses to detailed questions on cooperation between museums and the CCIs.[9]

[7] For several years, NIMOZ has recognised the need for more detailed and comprehensive statistical data on museums in Poland. In 2013, it started its 'Museum Statistics' programme, parallel to standard surveys conducted by Statistics Poland (the National Statistical Office).

[8] In Poland, there are case studies of selected museums and analyses of general data on museum employment, income, and spending (Murzyn-Kupisz 2017) but a dearth of deep analyses of processes, structures, or relations between museums and other institutions and firms (Murzyn-Kupisz et al. 2019). As for the CCIs, there are standard statistical data on value added, employment, and the number of firms (e.g. Kasprzak 2017; Statistics Poland 2018), and on selected locations and CCI subsectors (Chapain and Stryjakiewicz 2017).

[9] The 261 museums include 203 single-site institutions and 58 multi-site ones. Some (20%) are located in the five Polish metropolitan areas (over 500,000 inhabitants), 20% are in large cities (100,000–500,000 residents), 44% (two in five) are in towns and small municipalities (10,000–100,000 residents), and 16% in very small municipalities (up to 10,000 residents). Thus, both urban and non-urban contexts are covered. This makes the sample representative of the entire population of Polish museums. This representativeness also holds for ownership type. The museums in the survey are mainly public institutions: about 8% are owned and managed by the central government, 70% are local, county, or regional government institutions, 9% are run jointly by different governments, and 7% are museums owned and run by NGOs. Our sample also covers a vast range of collection types. History museums represent 15%, ethno-anthropological museums 7%, specialised collections 6%, and science and technology museums 5% of the sample. The majority (60%), however, declare having an interdisciplinary profile, including the arts. In the Polish context, in fact, it is common to assign to a single institution the management of different types of collections.

Table 3 Cooperation between Polish museums and firms in other CCI branches

CCI branch/sector	Number of responding museums which indicated cooperation	Share of museums cooperating with a given CCI branch in the whole sample (N=261)	Type of cooperation	
			Long-term, regular (%)	Occasional (%)
Contemporary visual arts and photography	136	52.1	11.5	42.5
Performing arts	93	35.6	3.8	32.2
Music	174	66.7	12.3	57.5
Books and publishing industry	155	59.4	12.3	51.0
Advertising, TV and film	183	70.1	20.3	54.8
Radio, the press, internet portals	207	79.3	42.9	44.1
Design and artistic crafts including fashion and toys*	111	42.5	10.7	34.1

*Does not include architecture and video games

Source: authors' own elaboration of NIMOZ data, 2019

Polish museums that participated in the above-mentioned survey report a variety of engagements with different branches of the CCIs (Table 3).[10]

The most frequent partners of museum institutions are firms representing the advertising, film, and TV industries and radio, the press, and internet portals. Cooperation with such firms was indicated by over 70% of museums that took part in the survey. Two-thirds of museums pointed to cooperation with the music industry and three out of five with the book and publishing industry. Slightly over half of institutions cooperate with the contemporary visual arts sector. Two in five museums report cooperation with the design and artistic crafts sector and over one-third with the performing arts sector.

However, these relatively high shares must be read with caution. Indeed, Table 3 also illustrates the distinction between regular and occasional cooperation.[11] In all cases, occasional cooperation with both local and non-local firms and creative professionals dominated. The only relation with a relatively high percentage of regular cooperation is that between museums and radio stations, the press, and internet portals, yet here occasional exchanges dominate too.

Even more importantly, the fact that Polish museums cooperate with the CCIs does not necessarily mean that their links are complex and conducive to innovation through knowledge spillovers. Hereafter, we illustrate evidence confirming this, derived by applying the taxonomy in Table 2 to our dataset. Each of the following figures refers to the relation between museums and a different CCI subsector, and percentages are shares over the whole sample.

Before illustrating these figures, it is necessary to clarify that in many instances, a museum–CCI firm relation has many facets that can be classified in different ways. Think, for instance, of an artist-in-residence programme: it often entails both exposure to the museum collection (possibly mediated by the expertise of museum staff) and the use of workspaces within the museum. The first instance is a strong link, and the second is a weak one. In the survey, museums were asked to choose out of a menu of relations, and an 'other' category was also present in which museums could write unmentioned items. We believe that reputational incentives led museums to classify their relations with the different CCI subsectors so as to draw attention to their cultural programmes. Therefore, it is highly unlikely that, say, a museum with an artist-in-residence programme classified it as rental of spaces. Similarly, any relation with advertising companies involving the transmission of symbolic meanings is not likely to have been classified as the mere purchasing of advertising space, even if a commercial aim was present. In other words, we consider it unlikely that weak links are inflated by the misallocation of items by the respondents to the survey.

[10] The survey does not include questions on cooperation with companies in the architecture and computer games subsectors.

[11] The survey asked museums to categorise their relations with each CCI subsector as either occasional or regular. It may well be that a museum cooperated with the press regularly and with internet portals occasionally, for example—this is counted as 1 in the nominator of *both* columns 4 and 5 in the row corresponding to 'radio, press, and internet portals'. That is why the percentages in the last two columns do not sum up to give the percentage in column 3 in the same row.

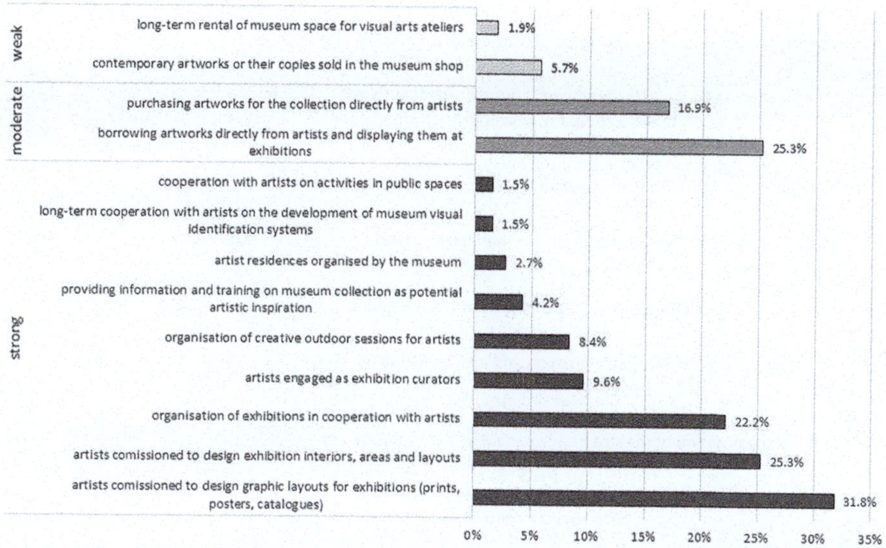

Fig. 2 Main forms of cooperation between Polish museums and the photography and visual arts sector. Source: authors' own elaboration of NIMOZ data, 2019

5.1 Contemporary visual arts and photography

We start with the visual arts, for which—taking into account that most museums in the sample have an arts collection—we expect relatively higher engagement (i.e. more diverse and more complex forms of exchanges, mainly with visual artists, who in our conceptual framework can be considered as SMEs) (Fig. 2).

Contrary to expectations, the share of museums involved in this type of interaction is, in general, not very high. However, in line with our expectations, strong links dominate, though the strongest ones among them are not so common. There are very few weak links. The role of museums as intermediaries in the sale of artworks or providers of space is rare (only 5.7% of museums offer opportunities to purchase contemporary artworks in the museum shop, and only 1.9% of museums rent space for artist ateliers). Exchanges connected with the gatekeeping role of museums, classified as moderate links, are present but not so important. Only one in six museums admits to purchasing artwork for their collections directly from artists, and one-fourth borrows artworks directly from artists and display them in exhibitions. The two most frequent forms of strong links are possibly the least rich in the category in terms of knowledge spillovers: about one-third of museums report that they commission artists to design graphic materials for exhibitions; one-fourth of museums commission artists to design museum and exhibition interiors, areas, and layouts. We then find joint exhibition projects (one in five museums) and inviting artists to act as exhibition curators (one in ten museums). This cooperation is beneficial to artists in terms of a broader knowledge of museum collections, possibly a source of artistic inspiration. Other strong links between museums and the visual arts sector are rarer. These include the organisation of creative sessions, workshops,

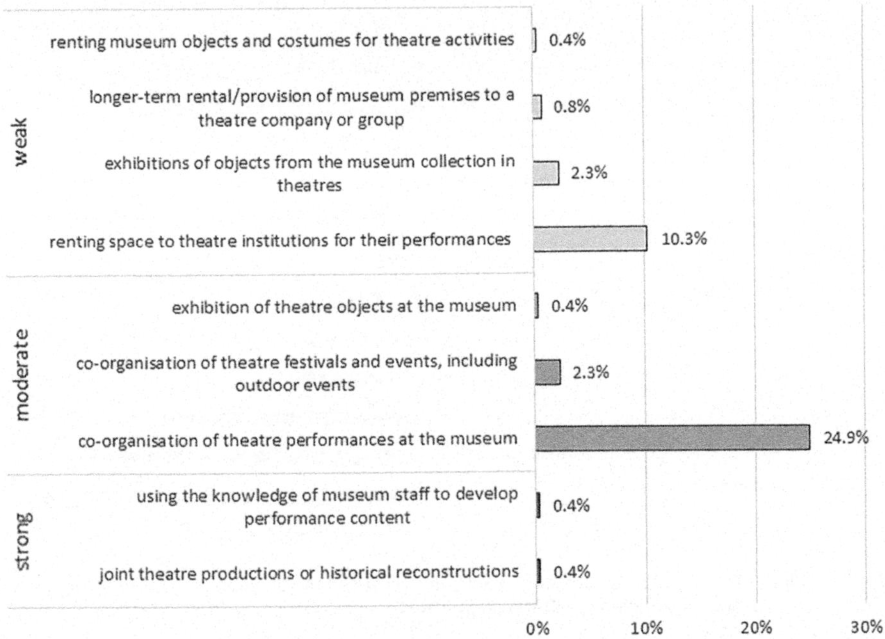

Fig. 3 Main forms of cooperation between Polish museums and the performing arts sector. Source: authors' own elaboration of NIMOZ data, 2019

or competitions for artists (8.4% museums), direct encouragement given to artists to get inspired by museum collections or venues by providing specialist training and organising workshops and information sessions on museum collections (4.2% museums), or organising artist residences at museums (2.7% museums).

5.2 Performing arts

Cooperation between museums and the performing arts sector in Poland is neither frequent, strong, nor complex (Fig. 3).

The most frequent forms of cooperation are the co-organisation of performances at museums (one-fourth of respondents) and renting museum space for theatre performances, shows, and recordings (one in ten museums) or rehearsals (two museum institutions that participated in the survey). These forms of cooperation are meant for the promotion and delivery of existing performing arts content and for making the museum more attractive to diverse audiences rather than for the exchange of knowledge or provision of inspiration for the performing arts sector. Other forms of cooperation are extremely rare, in particular those which could enable interesting knowledge spillovers such as joint theatre productions or specialist consultations with museum staff. We conclude that if Polish museums engage with the performing arts sector, they most often have aims other than offering opportunities for innovation to the institutions working in the field.

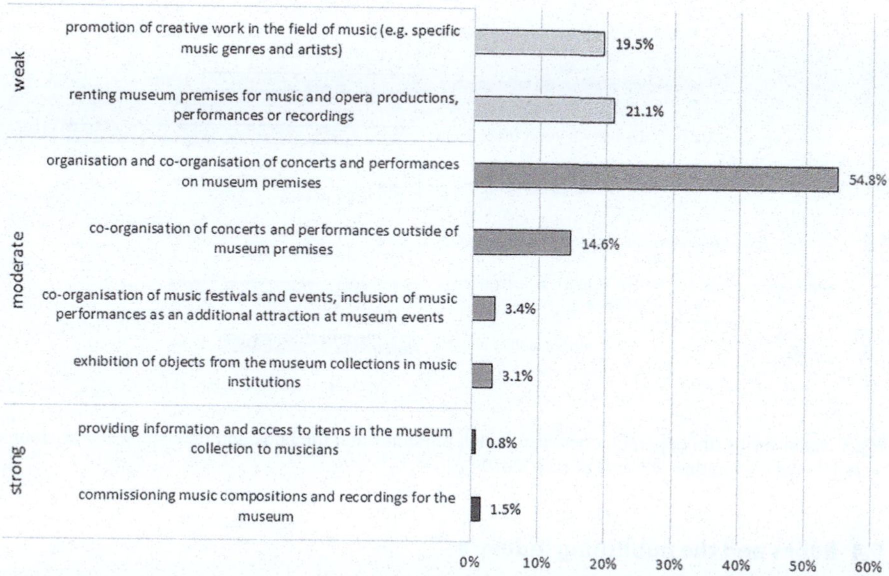

Fig. 4 Main forms of cooperation between Polish museums and the music sector. Source: authors' own elaboration of NIMOZ data, 2019

5.3 Music

The music sector (musicians, music institutions, and companies) appears to be a relatively frequent partner of museum institutions in Poland: two-thirds of museums report cooperation with this CCI branch. This cooperation, however, is often linked with the dissemination of existing creative content in the field of music and providing opportunities for promotion and additional earnings to the sector rather than inspiring new artistic creations and influencing their creative content (Fig. 4).

Museums in Poland host music events (concerts, performances, and festivals) on museum premises relatively often. Over half of surveyed museums organise and co-organise concerts at the museum, one in five rent museum spaces for such events, and one in seven co-organise such events outside of the museum premises. Music performances sometimes accompany major museum events (e.g. open-door days, exhibition openings). Occasionally, museums also organise or host music festivals. Depending on the museum profile and type, a relatively large number of museums engage in the promotion of creative work in the field of music, for example, for specific music genres or artists (one in five museums). Strong links are very rare, however. Very few museums (1.5%) commissioned unique music compositions and recordings for the museum (e.g. an audio-drama as an element of a museum installation or a unique music recording commissioned as part of the museum's promotion activities). Rarely (0.8%) do they specifically promote and provide information and access to interesting items in the museum collection that could inspire contemporary music endeavours (e.g. the possibility to perform on historic instruments or providing access to historic music recordings).

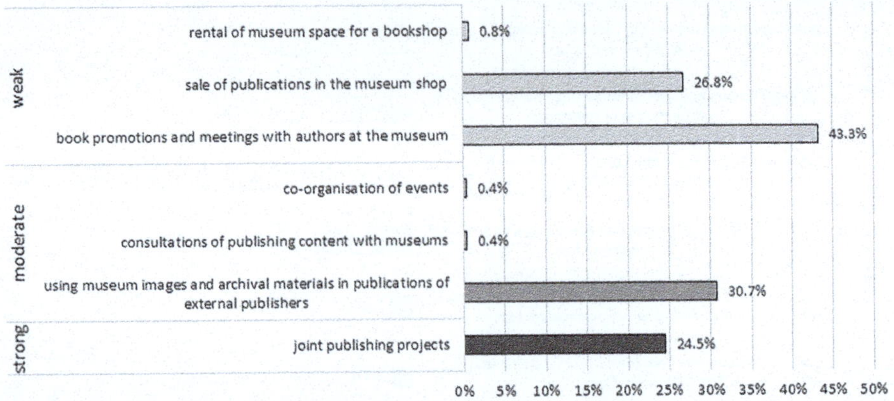

Fig. 5 Main forms of cooperation between Polish museums and the book and publishing sector. Source: authors' own elaboration of NIMOZ data, 2019

5.4 Books and the publishing industry

Museums in Poland rather frequently cooperate with firms and professionals in the book and publishing industry (Fig. 5).

Some of these links are weak. Two in five museums are venues or co-organisers of book promotions and meetings with book authors at the museum. One in four offer the possibility to purchase books in the museum shop. In rare instances, museums also rent space for a bookshop. Such cooperation enriches what museums have to offer their visitors, but again, this is mainly linked with the promotion, dissemination, and sale of already-produced publications ('ready'/ 'final' products of the book industry). Moderate links with the publishing sector in terms of potential knowledge spillovers are also present: almost one-third of museums report providing opportunities to use images and archival materials from the museum in publications by external publishers. One-fourth of museums, a non-negligible number, report joint publishing projects with commercial publishers, potentially a strong link. This may be due to a particular circumstance: most Polish museums are themselves part of the industry, acting as publishers of books and journals. In 2018, 62.8% of Polish museums issued their own publications, and although the average number of books published in a year was small (5), the maximum number was as high as 45 (NIMOZ 2019).[12] Moreover, three museums reported having their own printing units (printing of books, posters, and promotional materials). Whether the interactions reported are just between the staff of commercial publishing companies and the staff of museum publishing units or whether they involve exchanges of information and the development of content in direct cooperation with curators and other specialist staff makes a difference in terms of knowledge spillovers. As such fine distinctions

[12] Sales of books published by museums are relatively limited because apart from guidebooks and illustrated books on major museums, they usually publish specialist scientific publications.

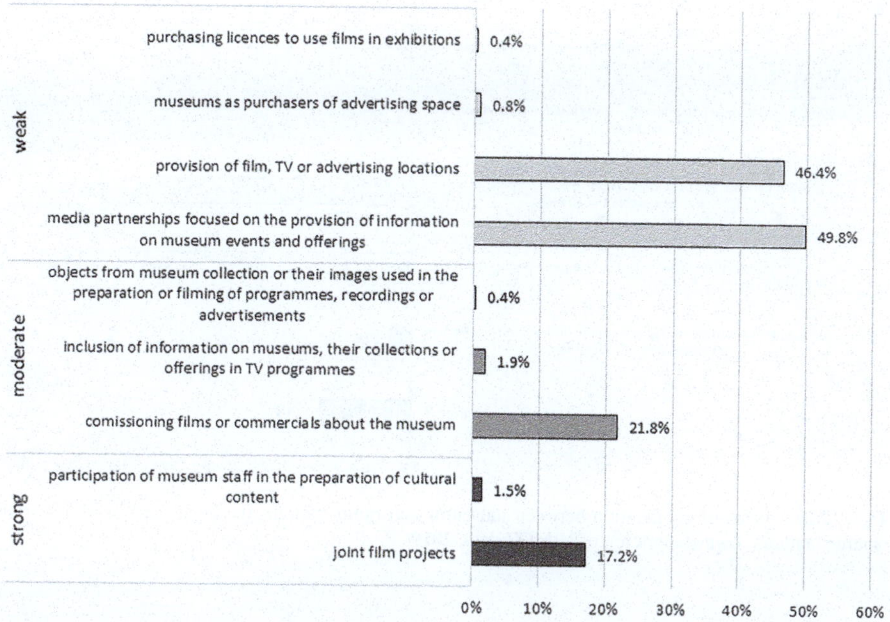

Fig. 6 Main forms of cooperation between museums and advertising, TV, and film sectors. Source: authors' own elaboration of NIMOZ data, 2019

were not included in the survey question, joint publishing projects might merely be collaborations focused on the distribution of creative content already produced by museums, which would not entail significant knowledge spillovers. More insight into the nature of these projects is therefore necessary to understand whether those reported are all strong links.

5.5 Film, TV, and advertising companies

Most Polish museums cooperate in some way with firms and institutions in the advertising, TV, and film industries. Moreover, one-fifth of museums report long-term, regular cooperation with this CCI branch (Fig. 6).

However, the dominant links are either media partnerships focused on the provision of information on museum activities, whereby these industries use creative content supplied by museums for promotion among potential visitors (49.8% of institutions that participated in the survey), or pertain to the use of museum spaces as TV, film, and advertising locations (46.4% of museums). This second type of connection may impact the creative content produced, but it is not usually encouraged by museums due to conservation concerns. In a few cases, museums act as direct buyers of creative content already produced by the sector (e.g. purchasing licences to use films in exhibitions) or purchase advertising spaces. Moderate links occur when museums commission films or commercials about the museum or cooperate with TV stations in the production of TV programmes including museum venues, information on museum collections, or objects

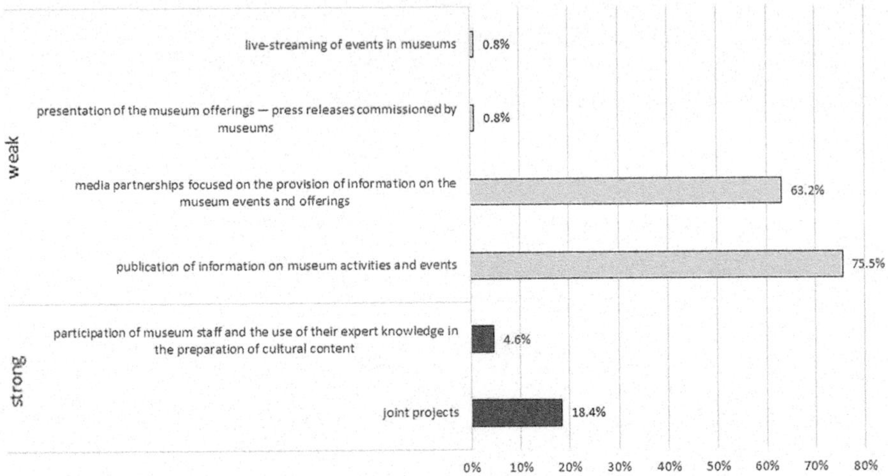

Fig. 7 Main forms of cooperation between museums and radio stations, the press, and internet portals. Source: authors' own elaboration of NIMOZ data, 2019

from the museum collections, but this type of cooperation is rarer than weak links (one in four respondents). Among the strong links, the share of museums having joint film projects with these CCIs is 17.2%, while drawing on the expert knowledge and participation of museum staff in the preparation or filming of TV programmes is rarely reported (1.5%).

5.6 Radio stations, the press, and internet portals

Four in five museums cooperate with radio stations, the press, and internet portals. Most of this cooperation is again focused on making information on museum activities and events available to the general public (75.5% of museum institutions reported this type of cooperation) or media partnerships similar in scope (almost two-thirds of institutions). In selected cases (only two in the analysed sample), the cooperation involves the live streaming of events (e.g. concerts) at the museum (Fig. 7).

Forms of cooperation that are likely to generate knowledge spillovers and involve stronger collaboration in the development of creative content are not as common. Joint projects such as radio programmes, regular newspaper articles on selected topics, or the co-organisation of competitions for radio, press, and internet portals involve 18.4% of the sample. The participation of museum staff in the generation of creative content (expert commentary and scientific consultations for programmes and the press, or for internet pages) is reported by very few museums (4.6%).

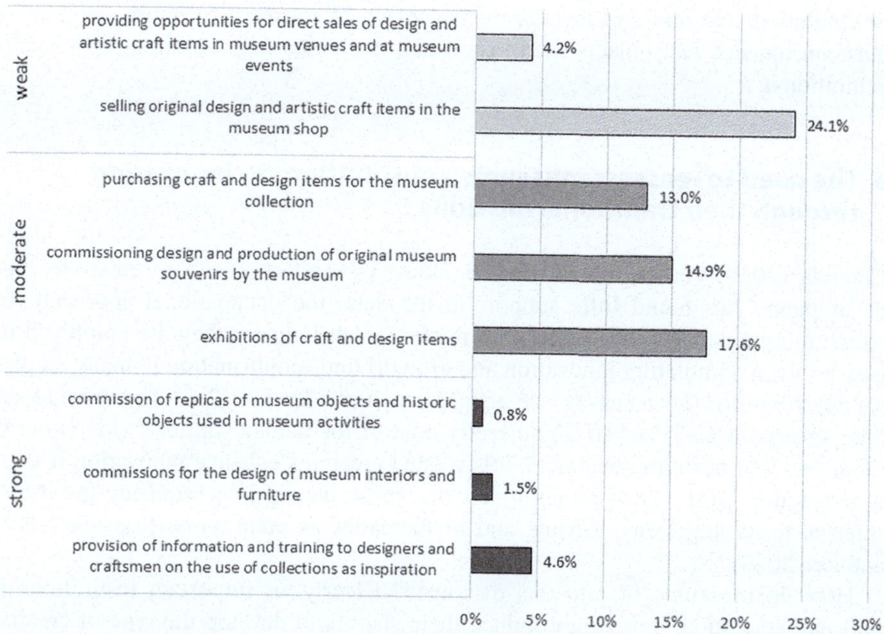

Fig. 8 Main forms of cooperation between Polish museums and the design, fashion, toy and artistic crafts sectors. Source: authors' own elaboration of NIMOZ data, 2019

5.7 Design, fashion, artistic craft, and toy companies

Cooperation between museums and the design and artistic crafts sector most frequently pertains to forms of interaction focused on the dissemination and promotion of already designed and produced artistic crafts and designer items (Fig. 8).

Museums may provide opportunities for the direct sale of such items either in the museum shop (almost one-fourth of museums), directly in museum venues (e.g. seasonal stalls), or during museum events, in particular fairs and outdoor events (4.2% of museums participating in the survey). Museums also act as gatekeepers for the crafts and design sector, as organisers of exhibitions of craft and design items (one in six museums) or as buyers of items for the museum collection (one in eight museums). Among other moderate links, the commissioning of products such as souvenirs designed specifically for the museum (one in seven museums) should be mentioned. Strong links are not so common. The provision of information and training on the potential of museum collections as inspiration for design and contemporary artistic crafts was reported by only 4.6% of Polish museums.[13] According to the survey, designers and craftsmen are also rarely involved in the development

[13] Design competitions organised or co-organised by some more innovative museums in Poland, especially those connected with contemporary designers drawing inspiration from museum collections or venues, though not reported in the survey, could be understood as a part of the same trend.

of exhibition interiors and layouts or the design of museum furniture, replicas of museum objects, and objects used in museum activities (e.g. clothing for museum exhibitions).

6 The need to reassess museums' contributions to innovation through their traditional missions

Cerisola (2019) claims that while the industry-based approach to creativity and development has found little support in the data, the occupational approach (by which more creative professionals, no matter which industry they are employed in, play a role in stimulating innovation and growth) finds confirmation in many empirical contributions (for a survey, see also Marrocu and Paci 2012).[14] The more recent ones (Marrocu and Paci 2012) correctly control for human capital,[15] and some of them find that even non-technical, arts-related creatives enhance innovation if there is interaction with STEM professionals, i.e. those having jobs requiring the use of science, technology, engineering, and mathematics as main tools (Rodríguez-Pose and Lee 2020).

How do museums fit into this discourse? Clearly, as important institutions in *informal* education, they might induce their visitors to develop the type of creative attitude (problem creation and solving) characterising both STEM and artistic professionals. Cerisola (2019) finds that heritage has a positive impact on both artistic and scientific creativity. Through this impact, heritage also qualifies as a driver of local growth—probably because highly creative minds are associated with a greater ability to innovate. Though museums are not considered in the analysis, they often act as mediators of cultural heritage through their education mission. The statistical significance of the heritage variable may then be read as indirect evidence of some importance of the educational role of museums for innovation, through the mediating role of diffuse creativity. Finally, a recent contribution to the literature on cultural participation has found that consuming the services of museums and archaeological sites impacts the very formation of human capital, one of the fundamental drivers of growth and development. Using data on Italian regions and sound econometric methodologies, Crociata et al. (2020) show that exposure to heritage induces a higher probability of achieving tertiary education and attending lifelong learning programmes.

It is therefore likely that a museum can contribute to making its community more innovative mainly through its role as an education agency. The strength of this contribution depends on the character and contents conveyed by its educational programmes. Museums can also contribute to innovation in education, and their close relationship with schools may help spread innovative educational strategies.

[14] The idea that the allocation of talents is relevant for growth was first proposed by Baumol (1990) and Murphy et al. (1991).

[15] The earlier version of this literature (Florida 2002) was heavily criticised because of the lack of this fundamental control (Glaeser 2005).

Table 4 Examples of Polish museums' educational services enhancing creativity in cooperation with other CCI

Museum	Educational activity	CCI branch involved
POLIN. Museum of the History of Polish Jews in Warsaw	*Memory in a comic book*, workshop on the development and making of comic books	Visual arts and photography
Museum of Folk Music Instruments in Szydłowiec	*From grey to black*, a photography competition on noctural photography of local heritage sites	Visual arts and photography
Museum of King Jan III's Palace at Wilanów, Warsaw	*Wilanów Academy*, theatre group based at the museum teaching performing arts skills to children and youths	Performing arts
National Museum in Warsaw	*Theatre workshops in the Królikarnia Sculpture gallery*, workshops on using performing arts skills to interpret artworks (sculpture, paintings) in the museum collection	Performing arts
Etnographic Museum in Krakow	*Music at home*, creative music workshops	Music
Museum of Folk Music Instruments in Szydłowiec	Workshops for youths on playing traditional folk music instruments or interpreting traditional music	Music
National Museum in Krakow	*Tales of objects*, creative storytelling sessions for children based on objects from the museum collection	Book and publishing industry
POLIN. Museum of the History of Polish Jews in Warsaw	*Leśmian Field*, poetry slam session with the audience acting as the jury	Book and publishing industry
Emmigration Museum in Gdynia	Creative writing workshops	Book and publishing industry
National Museum in Warsaw	*Summer Film Workshop*, workshop on film production inspired by the museum collection	TV and film industry
Gdynia City Museum, Gdynia	*Ha!Dwa!O!*, design thinking workshops focused on design skills and implementation of ideas for a souvenir from the Polish sea coast	Architecture and design
National Museum in Krakow	*Design Bomb*, workshops on the principles of design using the museum collection as inspiration (for pre-school children)	Architecture and design

If innovation in education makes education more effective, this may be a powerful indirect way to support innovation in a community and hence its economic success and resilience, provided that the content conveyed and attitudes encouraged help innovative products and processes emerge. While science museums are at the forefront in this human capital enhancement agenda, art museums do not lag behind, as numerous case studies have shown.

Clearly, CCIs may play a role in making museum education strategies more effective. In the last two decades, the digital revolution and cooperation with firms in the IT sector has impacted museums profoundly (Bautista 2014; Borowiecki and Navarrete 2017), especially in terms of the way they function and communicate with their audiences, and this has often implied relations with CCI firms as well. Using videos, augmented reality, or videogames may make museum education better (although there are also cases of museum Disneyfication that go in the opposite direction). In this sense, focusing on the solid arrow of Fig. 1 probably makes more sense than looking at the dashed one. Table 4 illustrates some examples referring to Poland (see also Murzyn-Kupisz and Działek 2015):

As for museums' conservation activities, the knowledge spillover effects that occur when these are shared with other institutions (firms, universities) in backward supply linkages may be important (De Miguel Molina et al. 2019a, b), as the numerous scientific projects on innovative techniques originating from challenging restoration works testify. Moreover, the exhibition mission may drive innovation when associated with positive externalities in backward supply linkages. Technical sponsorships are often motivated not just by visibility (association with a well-known museum brand) but also by the fact that museum demand often poses new, interesting challenges and problems for the provider, inducing firms to improve their products (e.g. lighting, showcases, alarm systems).

7 Conclusions

In this paper, we propose a re-discussion and re-valuation of the role museums can play in fostering innovation. By doing so, we add to the growing body of literature on the diverse aspects of the museum–innovation nexus. We argue that the mediating role of other CCIs in channelling museums' stimulation of innovation is likely to be overrated. To illustrate our point, we propose a categorisation of relations between museums and the other CCIs according to their potential in terms of knowledge spillovers from the former to the latter. We then test this conceptual framework by applying it to Poland, a national context where the role of museums in regional and local development has been increasingly recognised in recent years and for which a unique dataset on the types of relations formed between museums and the other CCIs is available. We discover that despite their diversity, relations between museums and other CCI firms and institutions that qualify as poor in terms of their potential for innovation enhancement (weak links) greatly outnumber those rich in knowledge spillovers.

The fact that in recent years museums have often been encouraged by policymakers to foster relations with the other CCIs in hopes of both innovation- and economic-related outcomes (OECD-ICOM 2019) has put a lot of stress on museums (Selwood 2009). Considering their limited human and financial resources, these demands often leave them less time and opportunities to properly rethink and develop their core activities such as conservation, research, and education. Based on our analysis, we argue that inducing museums to focus on relations with the CCIs is not necessarily desirable or effective. Considering museums as actors of innovation may make sense, but perhaps more for their traditional missions—and especially education—than for inspiring firms and institutions in the cultural and creative industries. Generally, incentivising collaboration between the CCIs and museums is not an appropriate innovation policy in itself and may even result in museums mainly engaging in relationships that are poor in positive externalities. The distinction we propose between weak, moderate, and strong links between museums and CCIs calls for a selective consideration of these exchanges and may help policymakers single out the types of interactions with some real potential in this respect.

The conclusions presented in this study are based on data that pertains to a specific post-socialist context: a country in Central Europe. While in Poland we do not find frequent strong links between museums and CCIs, it is possible that in some other countries this is indeed the case. The taxonomy of links between museums and CCIs that we propose should therefore be further tested and applied in other cultural and national contexts. It may be that the potential for innovation stemming from cooperation between museums and the CCIs is greater in some countries than others, depending on core–periphery relations, a given country's overall level of development, and the importance of CCIs in its economy. It would also be interesting to take into account potential differences in the quantity and quality of links between museums and CCIs according to museum reputation (superstar and major museums versus other), the size of their collections, ownership and organisational model, location (major cities versus more peripheral locations), or museum type (e.g. open-air museums, historic houses and palaces, technology and science museums).

Some other important limitations of the dataset used for the present analysis and which could be addressed in future research should also be mentioned. First, the Polish museum survey did not include explicit questions regarding cooperation between museums and the architecture and computer games sectors, while some CCI branches were considered jointly (e.g. under the broad heading of 'design'). Second, the survey provides the perspective of museums, reflecting museum managers' opinions on the existence and frequency of links and does not provide direct information on the precise nature of such links and their assessment from the point of view of CCI firms. Such information could be obtained if a similar survey was performed among CCI firms and supplemented with qualitative research (e.g. interviews on innovation with particular CCI firms and museum employees).

Nonetheless, our findings have two important policy implications. First, public support for cooperation between museums and other CCIs (e.g. via manuals, technical and organisational assistance, incentives, or grants) should be selective and based on a more in-depth consideration and assessment of the quality of links established and strengthened thanks to such support. Partnerships and relations that are more likely to generate stronger knowledge spillovers should be encouraged if the aim is to foster innovation in the CCIs: for instance, cooperation involving museum collections as a source of inspiration and basis for new creative content or new aesthetic, organisational, and technological solutions. While this cooperation might help CCI firms innovate more, policymakers must also be aware that their support is not guaranteed to have an impact on the innovation rate in the wider economy. In fact, the evidence on the exportability of innovation from the CCIs to other industries is inconclusive.

Secondly, core museum activities such as conservation, research, and especially education should be included in the analysis of museum impacts on innovation. These traditional missions are worthy of a more in-depth investigation from the point of view of the positive externalities they produce and consequent increases in innovativeness. Museum educational activities and services are a particularly underrated transmission channel, and other CCIs may sometimes help museums contribute to innovation through these. As a matter of fact, one could also consider the different interactions between museums and CCIs from the point of view of the knowledge spillovers produced by CCIs and impacting museum educational services.

In this perspective, the analysis presented here, distinguishing between various types of links between museums and CCIs in terms of the frequency and strength of knowledge spillovers, could be extended to relations between other cultural institutions (for instance, performing arts institutions) and the CCIs. Rather than assessing just their *quantity*, it would be interesting to take into account their *quality*—intensity (occasional, long-term) and innovation potential (weak, moderate, or strong). In fact, the benefits of infra-CCIs relations are too often taken for granted, whereas their presence should be investigated, both conceptually and empirically, in a more rigorous way.

Appendix: Do museums foster innovation in their role as art market gatekeepers?

An important aspect of museum management of collections is acquisitions, and museums often exhibit artworks not pertaining to their collections. These activities may see museums interact with artists, who can be conceived as SMEs within the CCIs. There is a specificity in these relations pertaining to the gatekeeping role museums play in the art world. A question to consider is whether museums foster innovation in art through the effect of their selection of artists and artworks.

As the value of artworks is unknown both to buyers and to sellers, the role of experts as gatekeepers of the art market serves the purpose of reducing market uncertainty (Powell 1990; Yogev 2010). Museums are part of the gatekeepers community. In fact, when museums buy or exhibit art, living artists may be involved. Musealisation is, for a contemporary artist, the ultimate recognition of the cultural and economic value of her or his work.

Do museums, in their role as gatekeepers, foster innovation in contemporary art? A positive answer must not be taken for granted. First of all, a network of experts acting as gatekeepers to a market usually agree on the selection criteria to adopt, and innovativeness *may not* be one of these, as history shows. For instance, in Eastern

Europe an icon used to be judged to have more artistic value the more adherent it was to predefined models, rather than for its innovative features.

Yet it is true that since the end of the Middle Ages innovativeness *has* been considered a positive aspect of new art in Western civilisation. In today's globalised world, the idea that we should value art primarily for its ability to give *new* insights into human understandings of the world and for its use of *new* languages in doing so has spread from Western countries to almost everywhere. The ecosystem of a gatekeepers' community may make mistakes in judgement at times, and since path dependence is an important aspect of value creation in art markets (Bonus and Ronte 1997), this is indeed a problem—unlike in science, sudden and stark reversals of an artist's fortunes are not to be excluded. Yet these reversals are not the rule, and this comes from the very expertise of gatekeepers: exactly because they know a great deal about already existing artistic expressions, they can tell whether some artwork is new in conception or not.

Nowadays, it is often the most innovative artist who survives the scrutiny of art gallerists, curators, and museums,but is it this scrutiny per se that stimulates innovation or is it the competition for art lovers' attention, while gatekeepers simply act as *certifiers* of innovation? In this second hypothesis, clearly their role in stimulating innovativeness is, so to speak, of a second order of relevance.

To understand if this is the case, it is essential to understand that gatekeepers are not all the same and they interact with artists in different ways and with different degrees of intensity. As Yogev (2010) clearly illustrates, art supply is subject to a first screening by art gallerists and curators. These act as talent scouts, and their closeness to the artists they select allows them to stimulate their inspiration in a selective way, i.e. privileging those aspects of it that are most innovative, and respondent to the requirements of the gatekeepers' networks. Museums are the protagonists of a second-round selection taking place sometime later. They mostly interact with art galleries; their interactions with artists are often limited, especially in the case of the purchase or exhibition of previously created artworks. Within the ecosystem of gatekeepers, museums then act mostly as providers of credibility for art galleries and artists. Even in a context such as today's art market, where innovation is considered an important selection criterion, their stimulus to innovation in art is of a second-order magnitude: vis-à-vis innovation, they mostly act as certifiers, not as catalysts. Given these considerations, and also taking into account that we are not able to differentiate between the purchase/exhibition of previously created artworks and commissioned ones, we propose categorising relations in which a museum plays a role as a market gatekeeper as moderate links.

Acknowledgement None.

Funding Open access funding provided by Università degli Studi di Brescia within the CRUI-CARE Agreement. Research funding was provided by Narodowe Centrum Nauki (Grant No. UMO-2018/31/B/HS4/02961).

Availability of data and materials The datasets analysed for the current study are not publicly available due to restrictions imposed by its originator, the Polish National Institute for Museums and Public Collections.

Code availability NA.

Declarations

Conflict of interest The authors declare no conflict of interest.

References

Bakhshi, H., & McVittie, E. (2009). Creative supply-chain linkages and innovation: Do the creative industries stimulate business innovation in the wider economy? *Innovation, 11*(2), 169–189

Bakhshi, H., Edwards, J. S., Roper, S., Scully, J., Shaw, D., Morley, L., & Rathbone, N. (2015). Assessing an experimental approach to industrial policy evaluation: Applying RCT+ to the case of Creative Credits. *Research Policy, 44*(8), 1462–1472

Barro, R. & Sala-i-Martin, X. (2003). *Economic growth.* Cambridge, MA and London: MIT Press.

Baumol, W. J. (1990). Entrepreneurship: Productive, unproductive and destructive. *Journal of Political Economy, 43*, 893–921

Bautista, S. S. (2014). *Museums in the digital age*. Plymouth: Altamira Press.

Bonus, H., & Ronte, D. (1997). Credibility and economic value in the visual arts. *Journal of Cultural Economics, 21*, 103–118

Borowiecki, K., & Navarette, T. (2017). Digitization of heritage collections as an indicator of innovation. *Economics of Innovation and New Technology*, *26*(3), 227–246.

Cerisola, S. (2018). Multiple creative talents and their determinants at the local level. *Journal of Cultural Economics, 42*, 243–269

Cerisola, S. (2019). *Cultural heritage, creativity and economic development.* Cheltenham-Northampton: Edward Elgar Publishing.

Chapain, C. & Stryjakiewicz, T. (2017). Introduction – Creative industries in Europe: Drivers of (new) sectoral and spatial dynamics. In C. Chapain, T. Stryjakiewicz (Eds.), *Creative industries in Europe. Drivers of new sectoral and spatial dynamics* (pp. 1–15). Cham: Springer.

Crociata, A., Isoardi, I., Agovino, M., & Sacco, P. L. (2020). A missing link? Cultural capital as a source of human capital: Evidence from Italian regional data. *The Annals of Regional Science, 64*, 79–109

Cunningham, S., Silver, J., & McDonnell, J. (2010). Rates of change: Online distribution as disruptive technology in the film industry. *Media International Australia, 136*(1), 119–132

Dalle Nogare, C., & Scuderi, R. (2020). Branching out beyond the core: Museums hosting events. *Annals of Tourism Research, 82*, 102773

DCMS - Department for Culture, Media & Sport (1998). *Creative industries mapping document.* London: DCMS.

DCMS - Department for Culture, Media & Sport (2016). *Creative industries economic estimates methodology.* London: DCMS.

De Miguel Molina, B., Hervás-Oliver, J.-L., & Boix Domenech, R. (2019a). Understanding innovation in creative industries: Knowledge bases and innovation performance in art restoration organisations. *Innovation, 21*(3), 421–442.

De Miguel Molina, B., Boix Domenech, R., & de Miguel Molina, M. (2019b). Analysing innovation in museums through qualitative comparative analysis. *Knowledge Management Research & Practice*, *17*(2), 213–226.

European Commission (EC) (2010). *Unlocking the potential of cultural and creative industries. Green paper*, Brussels, COM(2010) 183 final, https://op.europa.eu/en/publication-detail/-/publication/1cb6f484-074b-4913-87b3-344ccf020eef/language-en. Accessed 19 June 2020.
European Commission (EC) (2016). *Boosting the competitiveness of the cultural and creative industries for growth and jobs*. Brussels, EASME/COSME/2015/003. https://ec.europa.eu/growth/content/boosting-competitiveness-cultural-and-creative-industries-growth-and-jobs-0_en. Accessed 19 June 2020.
Florida, R. (2002). *The rise of the creative class... and how it's transforming work, leisure, community and everyday life*. New York: Basic Books.
Galloway, S., & Dunlop, S. (2007). A critique of definitions of the cultural and creative industries in public policy. *International Journal of Cultural Policy, 13*(1), 17–31
Glaeser, E. (2005). Review of Richard Florida's the rise of the creative class. *Regional Science and Urban Economics, 35*, 593–596
Hartley, J., Potts, J., Cunningham, S., Flew, T., Keane, M., & Banks, J. (2013). *Key concepts in creative industries*. London: Sage.
Kasprzak, R. (2017). Creative industries in the Polish economy: Growth and operating conditions. In C. Chapain, T. Stryjakiewicz (Eds.), *Creative industries in Europe. Drivers of new sectoral and spatial dynamics* (pp. 151–176). Cham: Springer.
Innocenti, N., & Lazzeretti, L. (2019). Do the creative industries support growth and innovation in the wider economy? Industry relatedness and employment growth in Italy. *Industry and Innovation, 26*(10), 1152–1173
KEA European Affairs (2006). *The economy of culture in Europe*. Brussels: European Commission, Directorate-General for Education and Culture.
KEA European Affairs (2019a). *Impulse paper on the role of cultural and creative sectors in innovating European industry*. Brussels: European Commission.
KEA European Affairs (2019b). *Market analysis of the cultural and creative sectors in Europe. A sector to invest in*. Brussels: European Investment Fund, KEA, European Affairs.
Lee, N., & Rodríguez-Pose, A. (2014). Creativity, cities and innovation. *Environment and Planning A, 46*, 1139–1159
Marrocu, E., & Paci, R. (2012). Education or creativity: What matters most for economic performance? *Geography, 88*(4), 369–401
Mikić, H. (2012). *Measuring the economic contribution of cultural industries. A review and assessment of current methodological approaches*. Montreal: UNESCO Institute of Statistics.
Müller, K., Rammer, C., & Trüby, J. (2009). The role of creative industries in industrial innovation. *Innovation, 11*(2), 148–168
Murphy, K. M., Shleifer, A., & Vishny, R. W. (1991). The allocation of talent: Implications for growth. *The Quarterly Journal of Economics, 106*(2), 503–530
Murzyn-Kupisz, M. & Działek, J. (2015). Libraries and museums as breeding grounds of social capital and creativity: potential and challenges in the post-socialist context. In S. Warren, P. Jones (Eds.), *Creative economies, creative communities. Rethinking place, policy and practice* (pp. 145–169). Farnham: Ashgate.
Murzyn-Kupisz, M. (2017). Socio-economic aspects of museum operations: Employment, income and expenditure in museums. In *Museums in Poland. Reports based on data from the Museum Statistics project (2013–2015)* (pp. 79–112). Warsaw: NIMOZ.
Murzyn-Kupisz, M., Hołuj, D., Działek, J., & Gorczyca, K. (2019). Museums and local governments in Poland: Partners in local development? *Museum International, 71*, 28–45
Northern Ireland Museums Council (2020). *Museums and creative industries toolkit*. Holywood: Northern Ireland Museums Council, https://www.nimc.co.uk/what-we-do/guidance-and-information/museum-and-creative-industries-toolkit. Accessed 19 June 2020.
NEMO (2018). *Museums and creative industries. Caste studies from across Europe*. Berlin: NEMO.
NIMOZ (2019). *Museums in 2018*. Warsaw: NIMOZ.
OECD. (2019). *Museums and local development in Poland*. OECD Publishing.
OECD/Eurostat (2005). *Oslo manual: Guidelines for collecting and interpreting innovation data, 3rd Edition*. Paris-Luxembourg: OECD Publishing, Eurostat.
OECD-ICOM (2019). *Culture and local development: Maximising the impact*. Paris: OECD Publishing.
OECD-Eurostat (2019). *Oslo manual 2018: Guidelines for collecting, reporting and using data on innovation, 4th Edition, The Measurement of Scientific, Technological and Innovation Activities*. Paris-Luxembourg: OECD Publishing, Eurostat.

Petruzzelli, A., & Lerro, A. (2020). Editorial. *Technovation, 92*, 102132
Potts, J., & Cunningham, S. (2008). Four models of the creative industries. *International Journal of Cultural Policy, 14*(3), 233–247
Powell, W. W. (1990). Neither market nor hierarchy: Network forms of organization. *Research in Organizational Behavior, 12*, 295–336
Power, D. (2011). *The European Cluster Observatory priority sector report: Creative and cultural industries*. Luxembourg: Publications Office of the European Union.
Rectanus, M. W. (2020). *Museums inside out. Artist collaborations and new exhibition ecologies*. Minneapolis: University of Minnesota Press.
Rodríguez-Pose, A., & Lee, N. (2020). Hipsters vs geeks? Creative workers, STEM and innovation in US cities. *Cities, 100*, 102653
Romer, D. (1996). *Advanced macroeconomics*. New York: McGraw-Hill.
Santoro, G., Bresciani, S., & Papa, A. (2020). Collaborative modes with cultural and creative industries and innovation performance: The moderating role of heterogeneous sources of knowledge and absorptive capacity. *Technovation, 92*, 102040
Sandahl, J. (2019). The museum definition as the backbone of ICOM. *Museum International, 71*(1–2), 1–9
Selwood, S. (2009). Museums, galleries and the visual arts. In A. C. Pratt, P. Jeffcutt (Eds), *Creativity, innovation and the cultural economy* (pp. 219–240). Routledge: London, New York.
Sīmansone, I. Z., Sīmansons, R., Spuriņš, U., & Klāsons, G. (2015). *Museums and creative industries: Mapping cooperation creative toolkit*. Riga: Creative Museum Riga, https://www.ne-mo.org/fileadmin/Dateien/public/Working_Group_1/Working_Group_MCI/Museums_and_Creative_Industries_MappingCooperation_NEMO_MCIWG.pdf. Accessed June 20 2020.
Statistics Poland (2018). *Cultural and creative industries in 2014–2018*. Warsaw: Statistics Poland.
Sternberg, R. (2017) Creativity support policies as a means of development policy for the global South? A critical appraisal of the UNESCO Creative Economy Report 2013. *Regional Studies, 51*(2), 336–345.
The Work Foundation (2007). *Staying ahead: The economic performance of the UK's creative industries*. London: DCMS.
Throsby, D. (2008). The concentric circle model of the cultural industries. *Cultural Trends, 17*(3), 147–164
Throsby, D. (2010). *The economics of cultural policy*. Cambridge: Cambridge University Press.
Throsby, D. (2015). The cultural industries as a sector of the economy. In K. Oakley, J. O'Connor (Eds.), *The Routledge companion to the cultural industries* (pp. 56–69). London: Routledge.
Towse, R. (2003). Cultural industries. In R. Towse (Ed.), *A handbook of cultural economics* (pp. 170–176). Cheltenham: Edward Elgar.
Tschmuck, P. (2006). *Creativity and innovation in the music industry*. Dordrecht: Springer.
UNCAD (2010). *Creative economy report 2010*. Geneva: UNCTAD.
van Heerden, S., & Bontje, M. (2013). What about culture for the ordinary workforce? A study on the locational preferences of the creative class in Prenzlauer Berg, Berlin. *Journal of Urban Affairs, 36*(3), 465–481.
Wikström, P. & DeFillippi, R. (Eds.) (2016). *Business innovation and disruption in the music industry*. Cheltenham: Edward Elgar.
Work Foundation. (2007). *Staying ahead: The economic performance of the UK's creative industries*. London: DCMS.
Yogev, T. (2010). The social construction of quality: Status dynamics in the market of contemporary art. *Socio-Economic Review, 8*, 511–536.

Publisher's Note Springer Nature remains neutral with regard to jurisdictional claims in published maps and institutional affiliations.

Journal of Cultural Economics (2021) 45:705–733
https://doi.org/10.1007/s10824-021-09420-9

ORIGINAL ARTICLE

Innovation and diversity in the digital cultural and creative industries

Jen Snowball[1] · Delon Tarentaal[2] · Jonathan Sapsed[3]

Received: 27 September 2020 / Accepted: 30 April 2021 / Published online: 22 May 2021

Abstract

The cultural and creative industries (CCIs) are increasingly being recognised in South Africa, as in other countries, as wealth-creating, given appropriate investment, rather than primarily a non-market subsidized sector. However, national innovation policy is still predominantly focused on STEM (science, technology, engineering and mathematics) skillsets and related product markets. This paper analyses how the CCIs in the Cape Town cluster innovate by combining digital technology, creative inputs, and workforce diversity. Based on a similar study conducted in Brighton, UK, a cluster of innovative CCI firms was identified that are to varying degrees "fused", defined as combining digital technology and creative design in production. Fused firms have higher levels of innovation in business processes, goods and services. Fused firms were also more likely to employ demographically diverse people, adding insights from the South African mix to the UK studies on disciplinary diversity. While fused creative-digital firms employ greater diversity, a qualitative analysis of SA gaming and animation firms nevertheless demonstrates the challenges for improving diversity in a developing country context.

Keywords Creative industries · Innovation · Intellectual property · Diversity

JEL codes Z11 · L22

✉ Jen Snowball
j.snowball@ru.ac.za

Delon Tarentaal
d.tarentaal@ru.ac.za

Jonathan Sapsed
jonathan.sapsed@newcastle.ac.uk

1 Department of Economics and Economic History, Rhodes University; South African Cultural Observatory, Makhanda (Grahamstown), South Africa

2 Department of Economics and Economic History, Rhodes University, South African Cultural Observatory, Nelson Mandela Bay, Makhanda (Grahamstown), South Africa

3 Newcastle University Business School, Tyne, UK

1 Introduction

The digital environment has dramatically affected creative industries in all kinds of ways, requiring dramatic changes in all parts of the value chain, including business models, stakeholder relationships and intellectual property management (Brown & Waelde, 2018; Peukert, 2019; Weinberg et al., 2020; Schauerte et al., 2020). These effects are felt intensely in African countries, where new digital technologies provide both unprecedented opportunities for innovation and growth, as well as threats related to the insufficient protection of intellectual property (Nwauche, 2018).

An important part of adapting to the new digital environment is the ability of firms to innovate, to successfully exploit the affordances of the new technologies to generate and capture value. The expanded Oslo definition of innovation (OECD, 2018), which includes services and marketing innovation to add to familiar product and process innovation, has enabled a much broader understanding of what innovation means, and how it takes place within smaller firms.

This research examines the relationship between digital technologies, innovation, and diversity in the cultural and creative industries (CCIs) in a developing country context. Although the CCIs in South Africa are increasingly being acknowledged as an industry that can contribute to growth and job creation, innovation management and policy is still mostly STEM-focused (science, technology, engineering and mathematics). To date, there is thus little research on firms at the interface between technology and culture, and on how they innovate.

To begin to fill this gap, a study of CCIs operating in the Cape Town metropolitan area was conducted. The research design follows a study of the Brighton (UK) cluster (Sapsed et al., 2013), and some comparisons with this study are made as part of the discussion. The second part of the research focused on a sector-specific case study of gaming and animation firms in South Africa. An in-depth survey of 18 of the firms focused on the challenges and opportunities they face as producers at the cultural/digital frontier.

The article begins with a review of the theory of digital technology and innovation in the CCIs (defined, for the purposes of this research, using the 2009 UNESCO Framework for Cultural Statistics). Section 3 discusses the CCIs in a South African context. Sections 4 and 5 present the research methods and results.

2 The creative economy, digitisation and innovation

2.1 Digitisation, business models and innovation

In most national systems of innovation and related innovation policies, STEM disciplines are dominant (Jaaniste, 2009), a bias also evident in South Africa, as discussed below. The STEM bias places the cultural and creative sector outside of the innovation cycle, mostly connected with providing the cultural backdrop in which innovation occurs and/or as a component of a broad education which enables innovation in the STEM sector. However, a broader, multidisciplinary understanding of innovation has emerged to better appreciate 'artistic innovations' (Castañer & Campos, 2002) and advances in design producing 'stylistic innovation' (Cappetta et al., 2006), the 'soft innovation' found in creative industries (Stoneman, 2010) contrasting with hard STEM functionality. Innovation in creative industries has different drivers to those in science and engineering, partly depending on semiotics and symbols for value creation (Jones et al., 2015). This greater understanding of innovation derived from arts and design has occurred alongside the widening horizons of innovation research and policy. (Perren & Sapsed, 2013; OECD, 2018). However, it is not that innovations from STEM and Arts and Design are insulated channels but rather that CCIs can contribute directly in a number of ways, sometimes forming complementary assets to technology (Teece, 1986). For example: taking STEM applications to markets through marketing, design and digital content; contributing to experimental research in creative sector production; producing and distributing innovation throughout creative firms for commercialisation; and contributing to social innovation and utilisation through helping to solve environmental and social policy issues (Jaaniste, 2009).

The impacts of digitisation on the CCIs are an important testing ground for its impact in other industries: "Previously thought of as frivolous and an expensive luxury, the creative industries are now considered an industrial priority and a 'laboratory' for studying the transformation of modern economies and societies" (Mangematin et al., 2014:1). There are many ways in which the digital environment can drive entrepreneurship, resulting in "digital dividends" for both firms and societies that embrace the online environment (Table 1).

Galindo-Martín et al. (2019) tested their theories on a sample of 29 European countries and found that entrepreneurial innovations in the digital environment resulted in higher value added and stimulated competition, leading to further (ongoing) innovation, and faster economic growth – what they describe as "a virtuous economic circle". However, they acknowledge the risks associated with digital innovation and entrepreneurship, such as the development of monopolistic or oligopolistic structures that could stifle the gains from competition.

Table 1 The benefits of digital entrepreneurship for firms and societies. *Source* Adapted from Galindo-Martín et al. 2019

Digital dividends for firms	Digital dividends for societies
– Access to new markets	– Job creation and improved social climate
– Facilitation of labour market information and new jobs	– Better quality goods and services at lower prices
– Increased worker productivity and lower production costs	– Better access to public services
– Economies of scale	– Governments achieve economic growth and employment improvements, leading to improved well-being

The impact of digital entrepreneurship has both "creative" and "destructive", or disruptive, elements which fundamentally reconfigure value chains in the industry. For example, digital technologies affect the creative process in that they offer the opportunity for "users" or "consumers" to be much more active participants in the production process. Digital technologies also offer a multitude of ways to distribute and sell creative content that can be differentiated depending on the market segment, or even the individual. New technologies provide an opportunity for such arrangements to be reconfigured but may be constrained by the "dominant business logic" of the sector (Mangematin et al., 2014; Weinberg et al., 2020; Schauerte et al., 2020).

Li (2020) compared two groups of firms in the creative industries: those who were identified as using innovative business practices related to digital technologies, and those selected randomly from different CCI sectors. Carefully selected global case studies were analysed, but with a focus on global north (UK and European) markets. Li identifies three ways in which technology can change business models: through *automation* of existing activities and processes, *extension* of current ways of conducting business, and *transformation* of current business practices that replace traditional ones.

Findings showed that 90% of CCI innovators used digital technologies to transform their relationships with customers through, for example, offering personalised products and services, and different prices for different levels of exclusivity, which changed revenue models. Many were also able to provide specific services to target markets through market segmentation. 87% increased revenue through association with other firms (for example, groups of artists) and brand extension, which enabled them to increase their customer base and to enhance their credibility through such associations. The general sample of CCIs was more likely to use digital technologies to automate (rather than transform) their business models. Li (2020) concludes that digital technologies can lead to a variety of new business models, and that a new way of doing things may not completely replace a traditional model but leads to the adoption of a "portfolio of business models".

There are many examples of how cultural institutions can make use of digital technologies to enhance their traditional business models. Bakhshi and Throsby (2012) consider the experiences of UK audiences at live theatre productions (using the National Theatre as the example) and art exhibitions (using the Tate Gallery as the example) compared to audiences experiencing the same works either live-streamed to cinemas, in the case of the theatre production, or via an online virtual tour, for the art exhibition. A comparison of audience demographics showed that the in-cinema live-stream and online art tours attracted audiences from a greater proportion of people from lower income groups, thus potentially enabling audience diversification and greater access.

At the firm level of the creative process, Sapsed and Tschang (2014: pp. 134) argue that digital technologies affect not only business models, but also the way in which creative work is produced. Taking the example of the development of online games from both UK and US studios involved in digital art production, they demonstrate how software tools change the production process by allowing artists to experiment and include multiple iterations at any stage of the process, rather than these activities being confined to developmental stages. The sequencing of the production process becomes much more fluid, "enabling ideas to be [constantly] realized, tested and revised" (Sapsed & Tschang, 2014: pp. 139).

2.2 Diversity and innovation

2.2.1 Disciplinary diversity: creative-digital skills and 'fusion'

The bringing together of separate resources as a fundamental driver of innovation has long featured in innovation studies since Schumpeter's (1942) writing on 'new combinations', meaning the introduction of fresh resources or technologies to established products or equipment, or the importing of resources to be applied to one field from another. Innovation often arises from the synthesis of phenomena that were previously separate. This extends to knowledge bases and skills sets, such as bioinformatics or mechatronics. The benefits of combining skills have been shown to enhance creativity and innovation (Leonard & Sensiper, 1998) to the extent that most New Product Development activity uses the cross-functional form (Griffin, 1997). Cross-functional team working provides not only the immediate knowledge of the team assembled, but also direct channels to each member's personal network of contacts. A pool of the team's accumulated social capital is made available to the team (Sapsed et al., 2002) so performance is enhanced in teams with external communications (Keller, 2001). However, there are downsides of added stress through miscommunications and 'creative abrasion' (Leonard & Sensiper, 1998). Diverse teams tend to have lower group cohesiveness and job satisfaction, higher turnover, and stress (Keller, 2001) in spite of their innovative benefits.

UK researchers have pursued a research agenda on cross-functional diversity in the CCIs over the last decade, investigating the effects of the 'fusion' of digital technology with creative skill sets in urban clusters. The 'Brighton Fuse'(Sapsed et al., 2013) study showed that firms that combined creative design and technology to a high degree (4–5 on a 5 point Likert scale, termed 'superfused') had on average three-times the revenues growth of those that specialised (1–2, 'unfused') and higher rates of innovation. A follow-up study on self-employed individuals also showed greater income for the more fused, although interestingly lower growth rates for the 'superfused', probably for capacity or lifestyle reasons (Sapsed et al., 2015). Similar results were found in a study in the North East England region (Butt et al., 2017; Adamson et al., 2019). The 'fusion' found in these localised creative clusters was tested in a UK-wide sample of 5350, which confirmed the combination of creative and design skills with STEM knowledge enhanced small firms' growth performance (Siepel et al., 2019). This strand of research increasingly shows a powerful effect of skills combination in the UK creative economy, although these studies have not yet explored this effect in interaction with other forms of diversity, nor whether the effect applies in Developing Country contexts.

2.2.2 Social diversity

Inclusion and diversity in the CCIs in South Africa are a matter of social justice and transformation, but as we have seen above, research also suggests that firms that can draw on Heterogeneous Sources of Knowledge (HSK) are better innovators and, as a result, more competitive. Some research has shown that firms with higher levels of HSK benefit more from formal and informal collaborations around innovations, since they have a higher absorptive capacity for new ideas (Santoro et al., 2020).

There was an initial expectation that those working in cultural occupations would be more diverse than those in other occupations, since success in the sector was assumed to be based on talent or merit, rather than formal qualifications. However, studies done in the UK and US have shown that workers in the CCIs have tended to be from middle class, affluent backgrounds, and are mostly dominated by white people (Oakley, 2006; Eikhof & Warhurst, 2013; Siebert & Wilson, 2013; O'Brien et al., 2016).

One of the reasons put forward for the lack of diversity in the creative industries is that much of the work is short-term contract in nature. This makes social networks a very important success factor, and middle-class people, who tend to have more social capital, have a better chance of success. Short-term, project-based work also results in unpredictable employment patterns and incomes and limits on-the-job training (Eikhof & Warhurst, 2013; Siebert & Wilson, 2013). Freelance, short-term, and temporary employment all make for a precarious work environment, where workers, especially those starting out in the industry, will experience periods of unemployment. Especially for people from working class backgrounds, who may not be able to afford being unemployed, and women (who are often the primary family caregivers), long hours, travel and erratic working conditions are difficult to accommodate. There are also the typical entry conditions of the CCIs of internships and unpaid assistance, what has been termed 'hope labour' (Mackenzie & McKinlay, 2020) which is likely to be more feasible for the more economically privileged than the lower classes.

A study of CCI employment in Australia, Canada and the Netherlands found that employment challenges that lead to a lack of diversity in the CCIs were remarkably similar across countries (Hannekam & Bennett, 2017). The authors suggest that policy initiatives (such as extending access to benefits and protection, such as pensions and health insurance) would go a long way towards improving working conditions, and thus diversity, in the CCIs.

Many studies have found that there is an underrepresentation of "…women in key cultural sectors such as film, TV, radio, photography, IT and architecture" (Creative Skillset, 2014, in Oakley et al., 2017). Other studies (Conor et al., 2015) have found that inequalities in terms of race, gender, age, disabilities and class, are in fact becoming worse in some fields. The authors conclude that, without intervention, employment in the CCIs has not resulted in less inequality, particularly in terms of gender-based employment. The lack of a diverse and inclusive CCI workforce may have several negative consequences related not only to a lack of social justice, but also to the kinds of products and services that are produced.

3 The CCIs in South Africa and the South African policy context

3.1 The CCIs in South Africa

In 2018, the South African Cultural Observatory (SACO) produced a baseline mapping study of the CCIs (SACO, 2018). Findings showed that in 2016, the GDP contribution of the CCIs was just over R62 billion (US$4.2 billion), which represents approximately 1.7% of the total GDP in South Africa. However, the CCI growth rate of 4.9% (2011–2016) was considerably higher than the average growth rate for the whole economy (growth rate of 1.6% in the same period). Interestingly, the fastest growth rates (as well as the largest GDP contributions) were found in Domains E (Audio-Visual and Interactive Media) and F (Design and Creative Services). These are also domains that are more likely to be using digital technologies, and hence are relevant to this study.

Using data from the Labour Market Dynamics household survey conducted by Statistics South Africa, Hadisi and Snowball (2019) showed that the creative economy in South Africa (including both cultural and non-cultural support jobs in the CCIs) provided employment for 6.94% of the working population in 2016.

While not yet representative of the population demographics, there is some evidence that people working in cultural occupations in South Africa are becoming more diverse. A report (Hadisi & Snowball, 2019) based on national labour market data found that 86% of those in cultural occupations are black (made up of 73.2% Africans, 9.3% "coloured[1]" people; and 3.3% people of Indian/Asian origin). White people make up 14% of workers in cultural occupations, although they represent less than 10% of the population. Some domains are more representative, such as the Visual Arts and Crafts domain, where 94% of workers are black; while others, like Design and Creative Services still have an over-representation of white people (33.4%). Young people (under 35 years old) make up 35% of cultural employment, but are more likely to be employed informally (47.2%) than youth working in non-cultural jobs (33.6%). A concerning finding is that there is a far lower percentage of young women in cultural occupations (29.2%) than young men (38.4%). However, the reasons for these patterns (causality) in the South African context are not well established (Table 2).

There is limited data on ownership patterns in the CCIs in South Africa, but survey findings indicate that it is still biased towards white people and men in most parts of the industry. Analysis of a survey of 2400 CCI firms across all domains conducted in 2014 found that the most demographically representative domain was performance and celebration, where 65% of firms had a least on black owner, and the least diverse was Books and Press, where only 44% had at least one black owner. In terms of gender, firms with at least one woman owner were found in only two domains (58% in Visual Arts and Crafts, and 50% in Design and Creative services),

[1] The authors are aware that the use of the term "coloured" may be regarded as insulting in some contexts. In South Africa, it is used to refer to a population group with a specific cultural heritage (Afrikaans-speaking, with Cape Malay and sometimes Khoi-San heritage). In such a context, the use of terms like "mixed race" would not be appropriate.

Table 2 Cultural group and gender of those in cultural versus non-cultural occupations. *Source* Hadisi & Snowball, 2019; based on data from statistics South Africa, labour market dynamics survey

Cultural group/Gender	Cultural occupations (%)	Non-cultural occupations (%)
African	71.8	75.1
Coloured	10.1	10.4
Indian/Asian	1.8	3.1
White	16.4	11.4
Male	58.7	57.0
Female	41.3	43.0
Male: youth	37.8	39.5
Female: youth	30.3	36.6

and were lower in domains like Audio-Visual and Interactive Media (31% female ownership) and Books and Press (41% female ownership) (Snowball et al., 2017).

The Audio-Visual and Interactive Media Domain (which includes, film and video, podcasting and "video games (also online)") accounted for only 2.3% of cultural occupations in South Africa in 2016. However, it made up 16.3% of the impact of the CCIs on GDP and had a growth rate of 6.7% per year between 2011 and 2016, compared to 4.8% growth rate for the CCIs overall (SACO Mapping Study, 2018).

Although the South African gaming industry is currently small, it is growing at an exponential rate. A recent PWC (2018) report identifies the digital video games sector as one of "the biggest success stories" in the South African entertainment and media industries. The rise of mobile gaming via smartphones means that many more South Africans are able to afford to play online games. *e*Sports, competitive online games watched by spectators, are driving the popularity of online gaming, and are already offered at some South African schools and higher education institutions. Yet, other than industry reports, there has been little research on how the sector operates.

3.2 Cultural policy and innovation in South Africa

Twenty-five years after the advent of democracy in South Africa, several important policy documents are undergoing revision. At the same time, national interest in the CCIs and their role in the fourth industrial revolution are increasing. The South African Revised White Paper on Arts, Culture and Heritage (DSAC, 2017) recognises the importance of the link between the CCIs and digital innovation, both in terms of potential spillovers to other sectors of the economy, as well as for increasing productivity and innovation within the sector itself.

The White Paper proposes the establishment of a National Cultural Skills Academy to promote enterprise development and technological innovation for the sector (DSAC, 2017). Technology and innovation are also recognised as having an important role to play in the transformation agenda of the policy, where transformation can be broadly defined as the inclusion and empowerment of more diverse and demographically representative people in the industry:

> "The township and village economy entails the transformation of cultural knowledge into goods and services. In this respect, creating links between cultural knowledge – which includes science, technology and innovation – and cultural enterprises development is one of the most important challenges facing the township and village economy.... Digital technologies enable great advantages to the cultural industries such as opening up of new markets, easier and more efficient distribution and direct communication with the consumers of goods and services" (DSAC, 2018:49,52).

However, the White Paper acknowledges the challenges for the sector that new digital technologies pose, in terms of leaving some parts of the sector behind, and also in terms of intellectual property and copyright protection. To support innovation and digital transformation in the sector, the White Paper (2017:52–3) proposes that the DSAC should, for example, provide grants for digitisation and innovation in sectors much affected by the changes, support digital entrepreneurship in the CCIs, and incentivise network and cluster developments that facilitate spillovers between creative firms, and the rest of society. The Revised White Paper on Arts, Culture and Heritage was adopted in 2020, at a time of great economic hardship, even before the COVID-19 crisis, with government department budget allocations expected to fall as a consequence. It remains to be seen how implementation of these ideas will take place.

The South African Draft White Paper on Science, Technology and Innovation (STI) was released in 2018 (DST, 2018) and is still under discussion. The main aims of the new policy are to promote the use of science, technology and innovation in accelerating inclusive economic growth and development. Some of the proposed interventions around innovation include providing sector-specific innovation funding, and up-scaling support to smaller firms so that they can access equipment and support in commercialisation of new products and technologies. In general, the Draft White Paper on STI aims to broaden the understanding of innovation in line with the Oslo definition (OECD, 2018), to include not only formal research and development (R&D), but also incremental innovations occurring in smaller firms and even in the informal economy. Nevertheless, the STI White Paper still has a significant STEM bias and does not directly refer to the cultural sector or the CCIs.

In addition to aims related to the development of the county's national system of innovation, an important aim of the STI White Paper is to "Promote inclusivity and transformation", especially regarding race and gender representation. In monitoring the performance of the policy interventions proposed, indicators of inclusivity and diversity will be used. Specific support, for example, around the use of intellectual property for publicly funded research and development, will also be offered to under-represented groups (DST, 2018: p. 24).

4 Research methods and context: the Cape Town fuse and the gaming and animation surveys

The research methods used included a quantitative survey of CCIs in the Cape Town creative cluster in South Africa, and a qualitative analysis of diversity and transformation in the gaming and animation sector in South Africa. We choose these mixed methods to investigate both the breadth of the phenomenon across the range of CCI sectors with a larger sample of firms and practitioners, in tandem with deep insights into typical digital sectors known for their 'fused' creative work.

The City of Cape Town Metropolitan Municipality is South Africa's second largest metro (after Johannesburg) with a population of 3.7 million (Statistics South Africa, Census, 2011). In terms of population groups, 84% of the population are black (including 39% black African, 42% "coloured"; and 1.4% Indian/Asian). 16% of the population are white, a greater proportion than in South Africa as a whole (9%). Compared to many other parts of South Africa, living conditions are good, with 78% of the population living in formal housing, and 94% having access to electricity for lighting.

In 2014, Cape Town was designated the World Design Capital by the International Council of Societies of Industrial Design, and it is generally recognised as a city with a vibrant cultural and creative industry sector, especially in the film sector. A report on cultural occupations in South Africa (Hadisi & Snowball, 2019) found that the Western Cape province (where Cape Town is located) has 12.1% of all cultural occupations in South Africa, the third highest proportion after Gauteng (34.6%) and KwaZulu-Natal (17.6%).

The first research method was a quantitative survey of small, medium and micro CCI enterprises based in the Cape Town metropolitan area. Since no comprehensive business directory exists, a database of 349 CCI firms located in Cape Town was developed from publicly available sources (including data from the SA Cultural Observatory database, online telephone directories and web scraping of other social media platforms). All the firms in the database were invited to participate in the survey (Fig. 1).

The survey instrument was based on the Brighton Fuse project in the UK, which demonstrated how firms "connecting the arts, humanities and design with digital and ICT" could enhance their innovation levels and business performance (Sapsed et al., 2013). It included sections on activities, clients and business models; talent and skills; innovation; and barriers and enablers. A section on the demographics of owners and employees was included in order to explore issues of transformation, diversity and inclusion in a South African context.

Data were collected via telephone interviews and an online survey (using the same questionnaire). Only the director, manager or owner/operator of each firm was requested to participate. A challenge was that, although firms were carefully targeted, some declined to participate on the basis that they did not regard themselves as part of CCIs. Even some of those who clearly did qualify seemed not to be aware that they were part of a distinct economic sector. This speaks to the relatively low profile of the CCIs as a sector in South Africa, which, unlike mining, manufacturing and even tourism, has not received much policy or press attention. In total, 74 usable responses were

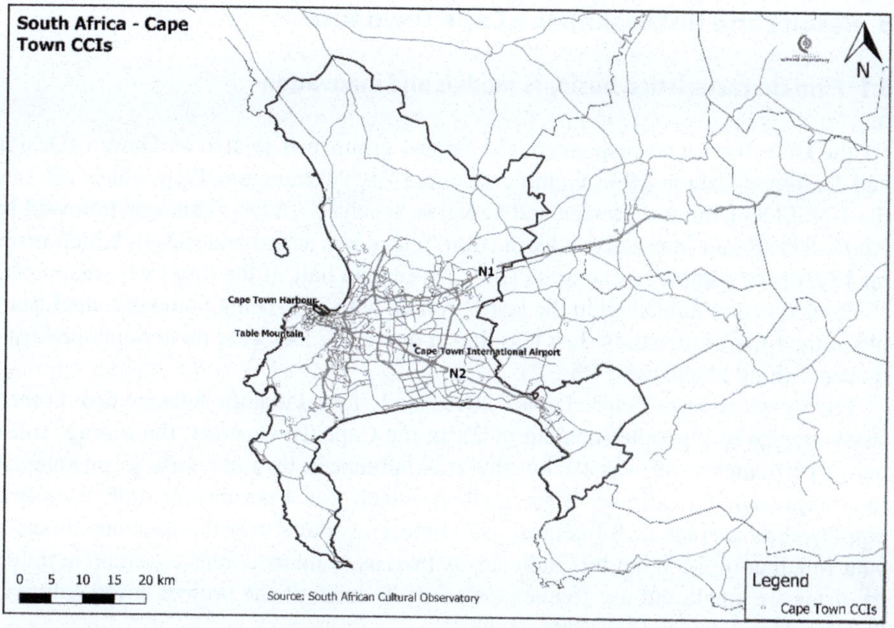

Fig. 1 The location of CCIs in Cape Town

received. Given the lack of a business registry, it is not possible to say to what extent the surveyed firms are representative of the overall CCI population in the study area, which limits the generalisability of the results. Methods of analysis included the production of descriptive statistics and an econometric model.

In 2018, the global gaming industry consisted of 2.3 billion unique consumers who had a combined spending of US$137.9 billion on games. This is a remarkable figure and can compete with the film and music industries. Games are also increasingly a substitute, or complement, to other entertainment formats, such as the special effects used in many large-budget films, and even education. Although the South African gaming industry is currently small, there has been extremely fast growth in terms of revenue generated by the sector (Interactive Entertainment South Africa, 2016), and the number of people who participate in online gaming in South Africa (Hall et al., 2017). However, there is currently little research into this potentially promising, and fast-growing, sector in developing country contexts.

Following a similar method, a database for the gaming and animation industry was constructed using extensive online searches for both gaming and animation companies, and via requests for participation at the Africa Gaming Summit (2019). One hundred and nineteen companies involved in gaming and/or animation in South Africa were identified. Qualitative data on the challenges and opportunities faced by the industry were collected via an online questionnaire, to which there were 18 responses. Thematic analysis was used to identify dominant themes within categories.

5 Results and discussion: the Cape Town fuse

5.1 Firm characteristics, business models and innovation

Of the CCI firms who responded, the largest group was related to Design (Design and Designer fashion 19%; Graphic design 14%, Architecture 1%), which fall into the UNESCO Domain "Design and Creative Services" (34%). This was followed by Audio-Visual and Interactive Media (film, television, video and radio), which made up 12% of the sample, and crafts (12%). More than half of the firms who responded (57%) had been established in the last 10 years, with 36% being younger than 5 years old at the time of the study. Just less than a quarter (23%) were owner operated (one owner with no employees) (Fig. 2).

The Brighton Fuse (Sapsed et al., 2013) study found that the average firm in their study employed 7 people (median of 2). In the Cape Town study, the average number of permanent staff was 19, but this was influenced by a few large companies. A more representative number is the median, which was 4 permanent staff. Each firm employed an average of 8 freelance (or contact) workers over the previous financial year (median of 5). What this indicates is that, as in many countries, creative industry firms are small, but use freelance workers to manage the project-based nature of their work and demand volatility (Table 3).

An important question in both studies was the responses to the statement about the extent to which businesses combined "ideas from creative arts" and "technology". Responses were recorded on a 1–5 scale, where 1 indicated "not important at all" and 5 indicated "very important".

33% of firms in the Brighton study were classified as "fused", that is, they combine creative design and technology in their work, and a further 33% were classified as "super fused", that is, they regard the combination of creativity and technology as "very important" for their work (Table 4).

The Cape Town study had similar results, with 62% of firms regarding the fusion of creative arts and technology as either important (rating of 4, 22%) or very important (rating of 5, 40%) for their business. A quarter of firms were "unfused", with

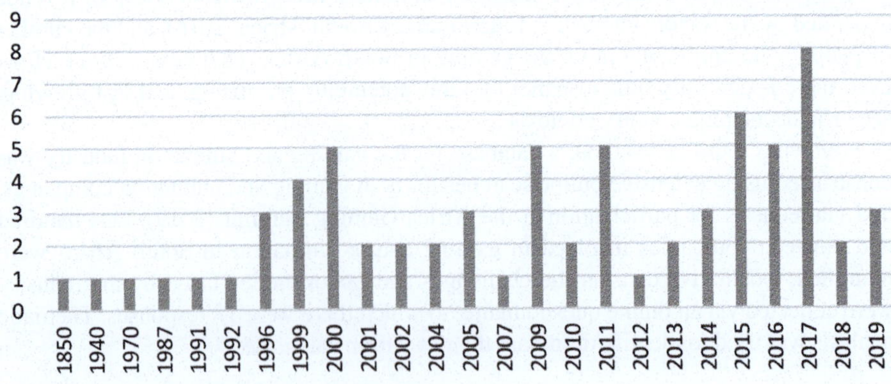

Fig. 2 Firms in the Cape Town sample by founding year

Table 3 Permanent and freelance employment in Cape Town CCI firms

	Permanent	Freelancers	Total
Number of firms with employment data	68	50	71
Full-time employees	1273	405	1678
Average	18.7	8.1	23.6
Minimum	1	1	1
Maximum	360	50	360
Range	359	49	359
Median	4	5	4

Table 4 A comparison of firm attributes in the Brighton and Cape Town study

	Brighton	Cape town
Mean (median) number of permanent employees per firm	7 (2)	19 (4)
Percentage of firms owner-operated	33%	23%
Percentage of firms in operation in the 10 years prior to the survey	50%	57%
Percentage of firms in operation in the 5 years prior to the survey	25%	36%
Fused (combining digital technology with creative arts important or very important)	66%	62%
Percentage of firms that engaged in innovative activity in 3 years prior to the survey	99%	82%

15% regarding it as "not important at all" and a further 10% giving it an importance rating of 2 out of 5.

The Brighton study also found that firms that were fused or super fused grew almost twice as fast as firms that were unfused. Fused firms were also more likely to be recent start-ups. Sapsed et al. (2013:20) suggest that "Old firms that remain unfused may face decline that could be offset if they were to open up to diverse knowledge bases".

In the Cape Town study, there was also some evidence that fused firms were slightly more likely to have experienced growth in the last financial year. Unfused firms had a slightly higher proportion of firms that became smaller or contracted in the last financial year (20%) compared to fused firms (16%).[2] However, the differences are not large, suggesting that fusion has, in general, not yet paid off for firms in Cape Town CCI firms (Table 5).

In terms of innovation, fused firms were significantly more likely to have engaged in some form of innovation in the last financial year (89%) than unfused firms (67%). Innovation was broadly defined in terms of innovation in products and services, processes, organisational innovation, marketing innovations, and formal R&D. In this

[2] Note that, because of the small sample size, caution should be exercised when interpreting the findings of the "neutral" group (importance rating of 3 out of 5), which consisted of only 9 observations.

Table 5 Levels of fusion, innovation and growth in Cape Town CCI firms

Level of Fusion	N=72	Proportion of firms in fusion category (%)	Proportion of firms that engage in innovation (%)	Proportion of firms that contracted in size (%)	Proportion of firms who reported constant earnings (%)	Proportion of firms who reported moderate or substantial growth (%)
Unfused (1 or 2)	18	25	67	20	20	60
Neutral (3)	9	13	78	44	33	22
Fused (4 or 5)	45	62	89	16	30	54

expanded definition of innovation, only 1% of Brighton firms did not participate in any innovative activity. The most common form of innovation was process innovation (the way of running the business), which was undertaken by 71% of firms. 61% introduced new services, and more than half produced materials eligible for copyright protection. However, IP rights (such as patents, trademarks and registered designs) were used by a tiny minority of firms in the cluster.

In Cape Town CCI firms, 82% of firms reported being involved in some form of innovation over the last three years. As in the Brighton study, the most common type was process innovation (82%). Within this category, digitisation (82%), big data usage (21%), and artificial intelligence (18%) were the most frequently mentioned. The next two most frequently chosen categories of innovation were the development of new products or services (72%) and/or the significant improvement of existing products or services (72%). Marketing innovations (50%) and organisational innovation (41%) were less frequently chosen. 45% of firms engaged in R&D, defined as "creative work undertaken to increase knowledge for the development of new and improved products, services and processes". Cape Town CCI firms thus show high levels of innovation (in the expanded definition), which provides further support to the argument that innovation policy should include the creative economy and that arts and cultural policy should include innovation (Fig. 3).

In the Brighton Fuse, 60% of firms identified direct service provision as an important revenue source, while only 8% identified royalties and licencing of other kinds of IP as important for revenue. Cape Town CCI firms had similar results, with by far the most frequently chosen source of income as the sale of services (both online and face-to-face), closely followed by sale of products. As in the Brighton survey, only a minority of firms listed IP (13%) or royalties (13%) as sources of revenue.

In terms of business models, Brighton cluster firms were largely business-to-business service providers. Sapsed et al., (2013) note that a challenge from small firms in the creative sector is often how to progress from being a service provider to bigger firms to being able to develop intellectual property and products in their own right. However, such progressions may be part of a pre-digital creative economy model in the modern era, a wide variety of business models were identified, such as the Retainer Model, Project Model, and Online Business Models.

Cape Town CCI firms also showed a mix of business models (Fig. 4). Respondents were asked to rate the importance of various ways of generating

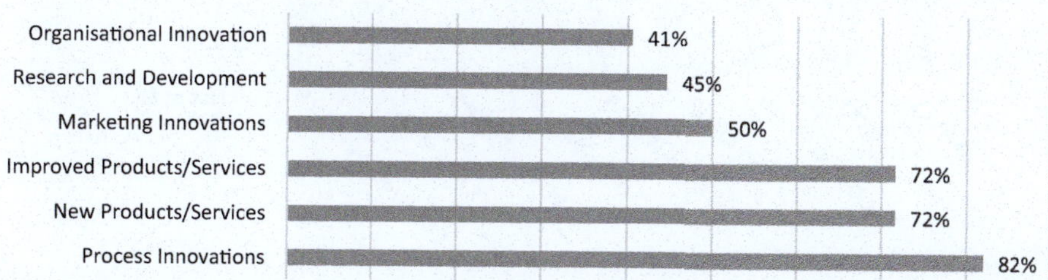

Fig. 3 Types of innovative activity undertaken in Cape Town CCI firms

revenue on a one to five scale, where one meant "not important at all" and five meant "very important". As shown in Fig. 4, the most important revenue source was direct sales of products and services (rated as very important by 56% of the sample and important by another 14%). This was followed by being commissioned, defined as "you deliver work for a client over a period with a clear end date and you keep the IP", which was very important for 39% of firms, and important for another 22%. Next most important was work for hire ("you deliver work for a client over a period with a clear end date and the client keeps the IP") which was very important or important for 54% of the sample. For just over a third (36%) of firms, the retainer model ("a client pays you to work for an extended period, often with an indefinite end date or intention of continuity") was an important or very important revenue source. For only a small proportion of CCI firms in Cape Town were online sources of revenue, such as freemium ("you provide free access to online services or content with extras chargeable for fee") or online micro-transactions, important sources of revenue.

To investigate Li's (2020) argument that firms adopting new technologies use a "portfolio of business models", the proportion of firms using multiple business models was analysed. Findings show that 57% of firms in Cape Town CCI firms rated three business models as "important" or "very important" for their sources of revenue, and that 32% were using four business models. This seems to support the idea that, rather than replacing the "dominant business logic" (Mangematin et al., 2014) (sales of products and services in this case), firms in the cluster are experimenting by adding additional models.

5.2 Ownership, talent and diversity

The Brighton study found that most firm owners were quite experienced, which could be a contributing factor to their success. The average age of firm owners was

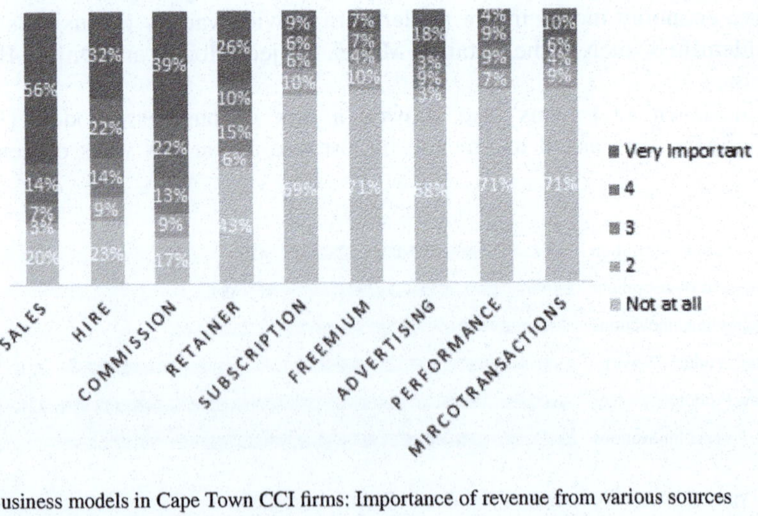

Fig. 4 Business models in Cape Town CCI firms: Importance of revenue from various sources

nearly 42 (with a range of 21–73). Two-thirds of owners were in their 30 s or 40 s. They were also highly educated – 85% had at least one degree, and 27% had post-graduate qualifications.

As found in a previous study (Snowball et al., 2017), most CCI owners (86.5%) were South Africans, but white South Africans are still over-represented. Like the Brighton cluster, Cape Town CCI firms are quite "grown up", with 64% of owners being older than 35. However, it does still provide important opportunities for young people – 30% of owners are in the 26 to 35-year-old age group and 6% are 18 to 25 years old. Gender distribution of owners was relatively equal: 42% of owners were women (7.5% indicated that they preferred to not answer the question, and the remaining 50.5% were men).

Employee demographics were somewhat less diverse that cultural occupations overall in South Africa. Of those firms who reported employee demographics (some firms in the sample were owner-operated), they employed on average 48% women, and 54% black people. No owners reported identifying as having a disability, but 8% of firms reported employing people with a disability (an average of 1.4% of their workforce).

The Brighton cluster study found that it was an "interdisciplinary cluster", with 31.4% having studied an Arts or Humanities subject at university, followed by nearly 25% who studied a STEM discipline. This is also the case in Cape Town CCI firms, which has a good mix of employee human capital (Fig. 5). An average of 51% of employees had a university degree in design (including graphic and product design); 42% had an arts or humanities degree; 32% had studied commerce (economics, business, management); and 20% had a STEM (science, technology, engineering, mathematics, also including computer science) degree. This finding suggests that the exclusion of the cultural and creative sector from South Africa's Draft White Paper on Science, Technology and Innovation (2018) may be a mistake, since there is clearly some overlap between the sectors, and given the high levels of innovation found in such multi-disciplinary firms.

In addition to the skills of internal employees, Cape Town CCI firms also made use of a wide variety of freelance (external) skills. The most commonly used skills overall were multimedia or web design skills (including audio, graphics, text still pictures, animation, video etc.), which were used by 80%

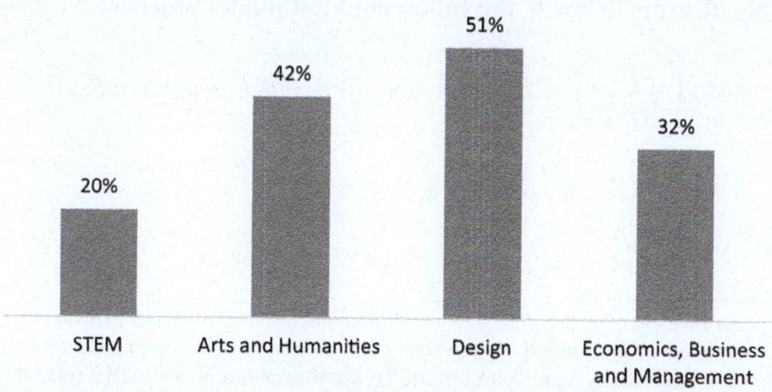

Fig. 5 Educational qualifications of Cape Town cluster employees

of CCI firms in Cape Town. Design (of objects or services) was the next most used skill (41% in-house, 23% external, and 9% both), followed by graphic arts (including layout and advertising), used by 70% of firms. In fourth place was market research, used by 54% of firms, followed by software development and/or database management, used by 53% of firms (30% external). Minorities used skills such as mathematics and statistics (31%), engineering (24%) and performing arts (27%) (Table 6).

Following the method from Snowball et al. (2017), a "transformation score" was constructed for each firm to give a composite measure of their level of diversity and inclusion. The transformation score has two components: employees and owners. The employee transformation score (ETS) was calculated by adding the proportions of female, black (including black, coloured and Indian/Asian people) and disabled employees for each firm at a particular level of fusion. The owner transformation score (OTS) was calculated by adding the proportions of female, black, and disabled owners for each firm at a particular level of fusion. Weightings were based on the relative importance of the variable in the South African context, as discussed earlier. The final transformation score (FTS) is calculated by doubling the OTS (since ownership is arguably a more important, and currently less diverse, dimension of inclusion) and adding it to ETS, the sum is then divided by 3. All scores are out of three (Table 7).

What the results clearly show is that fused firms have higher levels of diversity and inclusion at both the levels of employees and owners, than unfused firms. Cultural diversity, more equal gender representation, and a range of age groups could provide Heterogeneous Sources of Knowledge for firms, as discussed by Santoro et al. (2020). For innovative firms combining digital technologies and creative arts, demographic diversity could be an important part of developing their competitive advantage. From a social justice point of view, it is also encouraging that firms in these new areas are more inclusive than those (generally older) organisations that are unfused.

5.3 An econometric analysis of the determinants of growth

Econometric analysis was limited by the sample size,[3] but to further investigate the determinants of firms' growth, the following logit model was run:

$$\ln\left(\frac{p}{1-p}\right) = \beta_0 + \beta_1\mathrm{FA} + \beta_2\mathrm{FS} + \beta_3 F + \beta_4\mathrm{IA} + \beta_5\mathrm{FP}$$

[3] Several models investigating the determinants and characteristics of fused firms were run. However, these were constrained by the limited sample size, often exacerbated by missing data for some variables, and resulted in few statistically significant results. To avoid over-fitting, we used a relatively simple logit model, which produced the most statistically significant results, but we acknowledge the limitations of the analysis.

Table 6 Employee skills utilised by Cape Town CCI firms

	Graphic arts	Design	Multimedia web design	Software develop	Engineer	Maths stats	Market research	Performing arts
Internal	41%	41%	34%	22%	7%	18%	31%	14%
External	22%	23%	36%	30%	16%	14%	19%	11%
Both	8%	9%	9%	1%	1%	0%	4%	3%
Used	70%	73%	80%	53%	24%	31%	54%	27%
Not Used	30%	27%	20%	47%	76%	69%	46%	73%
Total	74	74	74	74	74	74	74	74

Table 7 Levels of diversity by fusion

Level of fusion	Number of companies	ETS	OTS	FTS
Unfused	18	0.944	0.556	0.685
Neutral	9	0.763	0.667	0.699
Fused	45	1.117	0.689	0.832

ETS - Employee Transformation Score

OTS - Ownership Transformation Score

FTS - Final Transformation Score = (ETS + 2 × OTS) ÷ 3

$$\ln\left(\frac{p}{1-p}\right) = -0,726756 - 0,051117\text{FA} + 0,033860\text{FS} - 0,210103F + 0,411939\text{IA}^{*} + 2,093088\text{FP}^{*}$$

where:

$$\ln\ln\left(\frac{p}{1-p}\right) = \log - \text{odds of Growth } \in (-\infty;\infty) \cap R$$

FA = firm age $\in (0;170] \cap Z$
FS = firm size $\in (0;360] \cap Z$
F = level of fusion $\in [1;5] \cap Z$
IA = number of innovation activities $\in [0;5] \cap Z$
FP = freelance proportion $\in [0;1] \cap R$

The estimated logistic regression reveals the impact of the listed independent variables on the log-odds of a firm experiencing growth (Table 8). Out of the five independent variables, only the number of innovation activities and the freelance proportion has a significant impact of the log odds of a firm experiencing growth. Both of these, in addition to the size of a firm, indicate that the log odds of a firm experiencing growth increases as the number of innovative activities, proportion of freelancers used, and the size of the firm increases. This is to be expected because as the number of employees increases (up to a certain point due to diminishing marginal returns of labour), the production of a company can increase due to a larger workforce coupled with an increase in innovation, and this can reduce

Table 8 Variables used in logit model

Variable	Measurement
Growth	1 = Firms who reported moderate or substantial growth 0 = Firms who reported constant or declining growth
Fused	1 = fused (4 or 5) 0 = unfused/neutral (1, 2, or 3)
Firm age	Years since firm was founded
Firm size	Number of permanent employees
Freelance employees	Proportion of freelance versus permanent employees
Innovation	Number of innovation types that the firm engages in

the time and cost of production (by making the production process more efficient) and/or increase the quality of the product, which in turn can lead to increased probability of growth.

To examine the logistic regression, inter-programming was deployed to determine the optimal values of the independent variables such that the probability of growth is maximised or minimised. $\ln\left(\frac{p}{1-p}\right)$ will be denoted as y^* to assist in the conversion of log-odds to probabilities:

$$y^* = \ln\left(\frac{p}{1-p}\right) = \beta_0 + \beta_1\text{FA} + \beta_2\text{FS} + \beta_3 F + \beta_4\text{IA} + \beta_5\text{FP}$$

$$p = \frac{e^{\beta_0+\beta_1 FA+\beta_2 FS+\beta_3 F+\beta_4 IA+\beta_5 FP}}{e^{\beta_0+\beta_1 FA+\beta_2 FS+\beta_3 F+\beta_4 IA+\beta_5 FP} + 1}$$

$$\therefore p = \frac{e^{y^*}}{e^{y^*} + 1}$$

To maximise the probability of growth, which will be referred to as the objective function, constraints need to be introduced such that the optimal values for the independent variables remain as integers (such as firm size which is calculated as the sum of employees which cannot be a fraction) and variables have to be in a certain range (firm age cannot be negative or exceed a certain level) as follows:

$p = \frac{e^{y^*}}{e^{y^*}+1}$ subject to:

$$1 \le \text{FA} \le 50$$

(Only 3 out of the 74 firms have ages greater than 50 which is why it is considered the maximum age for the estimation)

$$\text{FS} \ge 1$$

(Firm size must at least be equal to 1 and not zero to capture the owner-operated firms)

$$1 \le F \le 5$$

(Minimum fusion level is 1 and maximum fusion level is 5)

$$0 \le \text{IA} \le 5$$

(Minimum number of innovation activities can be 0 and the maximum is 5)

$$0 \le \text{FP} \le 1$$

(Minimum proportion of freelancers is 0, whereas the maximum proportion is 1). FA; FS; F; IA are integers.

The optimisation results are captured in Table 9 and compared to the results of the average firm:

Table 9 Optimisation results

Variables	Minimum	Maximum	Average
C	1	1	1
FA	50	1	15
FS	1	1	19
F	5	1	4
IA	0	5	3
FP	0	1	0,32
y^*	−4,3	3,2	0,2
p	1,34%	96,08%	55,35%

The maximisation of the growth probability indicates that higher growth rates are positively associated with firms that maximise hiring freelancers and the number of innovative activities while minimising the longevity of a firm, the number of permanent employees and level of fusion. The minimisation indicates that firms older than 50 years that are owner-operated with no freelancers or innovation activities and high levels of fusion only have a 1,34% chance of experiencing growth. The average firm analysis indicates that half of the firms in this study are more likely to be associated with achieving growth.

In interpreting the results, a few limitations should be noted: (i) the small sample size reduces the validity and reliability of the results; (ii) "survivor bias" is commonly noted in studies of entrepreneurship (that is, that more successful firms survive longer and are thus likely to be over-represented in the sample) and may be affecting the results here; and (iii) that cross-sectional data, while showing how variables are related, do not imply causality. Causality may indeed run in both directions, in that more successful firms have greater mean to invest in innovation and diversity their revenue streams, which in turn leads to better growth. There are several virtuous circles that could be set in motion in creative clusters, regarding resource availability, the attraction of talent, the demand-readiness and ability to quickly configure and reconfigure projects and arrangements, and many of these conditions are mutually reinforcing.

6 Diversity and inclusion in South African gaming and animation firms

6.1 Firm characteristics and the size of the sector

As an in-depth case study into firms using creative and digital inputs in South Africa, a database of gaming and animation companies was constructed, and a qualitative online survey sent to all companies who could be reached. The focus was on industry transformation (that is, the increased inclusion of black South Africans and women).

Using the methods described in Sect. 4, 59 gaming, or gaming and animation companies were found in South Africa, the largest group (48%) of which are in the Western Cape. Most of the gaming and animation companies in the database were founded in the last 10 years (65% have been founded since 2008). This is an indication of the growth of the sector over this period, as well as evidence of growing capacity to drive growth in the future. There was considerable overlap between gaming and animation: 46% of companies producing games also did animation work. 57% of gaming companies were classified as "very small", with annual turnover of less than R2 million (US$150,314) (Table 10). It is estimated that the turnover for the gaming and animation industry in the 2017/8 financial year was R476 million (US$35.8 million), of which R198 million (US$14.9 million) was attributed to gaming companies (including hybrid companies). This is a considerable increase from the R100 million (US$7.8 million) revenue for the gaming industry in 2015 found in a previous study (IESA, 2016).

Excluding one large outlier in the animation sector, companies were relatively small, employing at average of between 6.9 (animation) and 7.4 people (gaming). Overall, it is estimated that South African gaming companies currently create 310 jobs, an increase from 255 direct jobs found in previous research (IESA, 2016). Including hybrid companies increases this number to 460.

6.2 Challenges and opportunities

A challenge identified by the gaming and animation sector participants themselves is transformation – most people working in the sector are white men. Only 19% of gaming company employees and 30% of animation company employees were black, coloured or Indian/Asian people. This can be compared to employment in cultural occupations in South Africa in general, where 86% of people are black, coloured or Indian/Asian people (Hadisi & Snowball, 2019). Part of the reason given for the lack of diversity is that the dominant business model in online games is "free-to-play",

Table 10 Characteristics of companies who responded to qualitative survey

	Gaming*	Animation
Number of companies	7	11
Number of games	51	0
Average number of games	7.29	n/a
Number of employees	52	179
Average number of employees per company	7.43	6.9**
Percentage of black, coloured, and Indian/Asian employees	19.23%	30.17%
Percentage of permanent employees	90.38%	55.87%

*For the purposes of this analysis, only companies who had developed at least one game were classified as "Gaming"

**Including one very large company, the average number of employees for animation companies was 16.27

which means that users do not have to pay anything in order to try out the game, at least initially. Once the game is more developed, and the market is established, users have to pay to access further levels, or virtual goods. From a production perspective, the model aids game development, but it also means that, in the early stages of developing the game, there is no significant income. As is the case with other parts of the CCIs, where unpaid internships are common, the consequence is that only those from middle-class backgrounds (who do not need to immediately earn an income) can work in the sector. The sector is also prone to inconsistent demand, which was also identified as a challenge – what one respondent referred to as "feast or famine cycles" – associated with seasonal work.

There was general agreement amongst respondents that the sector is male dominated, and currently driven by "privileged white South Africans" who (i) could afford to attain the high levels of education and training needed; (ii) could afford to be in a risky industry with inconsistent demand and uncertain income; and (iii) were exposed to gaming and animation when they were young, and so recognise it as "a viable career path". In terms of how to improve transformation, respondents most often flagged access to education and technical skills training, but also to industry experience, as key. As one respondent put it:

> From my experience, game development in South Africa is a luxury niche sector that only a few can afford. To put it frankly, being a person of colour, coming from a financially struggling or even a financially comfortable background, whoever is funding your education is not going to want you to further your studies in an industry that is expensive and almost unheard of. As a result, you see people furthering their studies in the more popular "tried and tested" industries. Gaming is one of the biggest industries in the world and South Africa is missing out on a lot of opportunity by not tapping into it enough (Survey Respondent, 2019).

The most frequently mentioned challenge faced by companies in the sector was the lack of skills and experience, especially at the intermediate and senior levels. Only three of the respondents reported that it was easy or fairly easy to find skills needed by their company. Most others noted that, while there was an abundance of some kinds of graduates (artists), more technical skills (programmers) were difficult to find. One respondent emphasised that, to be successful in the sector, a person had to be both "highly talented in a creative sense" and "confident in the areas of technical proficiency", such as being able to learn new software quickly. Another respondent also noted that, for people with programming skills, competing industries (corporate and financial) offered larger starting salaries. There was also a wide consensus that the specific skills and expertise needed by the industry were not taught at educational institutions, with one respondent stating that it took "at least a year" of additional training and upskilling for graduates to become useful to the business.

However, many respondents confidently expected things to improve at the time of the survey (2019), or said that they were already improving, as the industry expanded and became better known. One respondent described how their company had gone from employing "all white males" five years ago to now having half their staff being women and black people. Another respondent emphasised that, "There is a chronic skills shortage so everyone who studies animation should find a job, if they are capable". Others discussed ways in which they could develop a "talent pipeline" in the industry (linked to the need to develop sustainable career paths), and maintaining and developing "skilled teams".

Respondents also identified several advantages associated with being in the gaming and animation sectors in South Africa. These included: the high quality of work being produced by South African companies; "unique African stories" and the cultural diversity of the country; lower production costs than competitors when bidding for international service work; talent already available in the industry; and access to world class technology and infrastructure. One respondent mentioned the potential benefit of creating their own IP (as compared to servicing international productions) as a potential area of growth. The young, growing population was also identified as an opportunity because "this is a youth business".

The gaming and animation sector case study demonstrates the potential of these, mostly small, newly established, CCI firms to contribute to growth and job creation in South Africa. While a highly entrepreneurial sector, they face the dual challenges of skills shortages (particularly with regard to the mix of creative and technical skills) and the need for transformation.

7 Concluding remarks

New digital technologies provide both unprecedented opportunities for innovation and growth in the CCIs. This research is the first, to our knowledge, to examine the nexus between digital technologies, innovation and diversity in the CCIs in a South African context.

The results of the Cape Town survey identified a group or cluster of CCI firms that are "fused", that is, they regard both digital technology and creative inputs as an important or very important parts of their production process. These firms employ people with interdisciplinary skills, and engage in much innovation, defined broadly as innovation in business processes, goods and services. Thirty-five percent of firms were founded in the past 5 years, pointing to a relatively new cluster.

While most firms are small, they supplemented the expertise and capacity of existing employees by drawing on freelancers – a medium of 5 freelancers were employed per firm in the previous financial year. Similar to what was found in the Brighton study, this business model allows them to be agile and productive in the volatile, project-based world of CCIs.

The logit model showed that firms that employed a higher proportion of freelance (versus permanent) employees were statistically significantly more likely to have experienced growth in the year prior to the survey. It may be that there is a short-term trade-off between workforce diversity and growth, as the results suggest that operating firms based on freelance contracts generate better growth prospects. It may well be more efficient for a small firm to contract freelancers as project needs occur, rather than retaining them as employees with all the continuous and incidental costs. However, it may not enhance growth prospects in all cases, since capacity is often limited, and practitioners in the animation and games sector study report that it is typically difficult to source talent when it is required.

There seems to be two groups of CCI firms in the sample: older, larger firms, that are currently unfused; and smaller, newer firms with higher levels of fusion. Although there is currently no statistically significant difference between their growth (turnover) rates, the Brighton study suggests that, as the cluster develops, these may occur. The implication is that firms in the first group may need to consider combining digital technologies with creative inputs in the future to keep up with the newer firms already doing so.

On a national level, firms in the Audio-Visual and Interactive Media, and Design and Creative Services domains contribute the most to cultural sector GDP, and are growing more quickly than the rest of the economy. Cape Town firms in these sectors are thus likely to grow in the future as they become more established. At present, they are more of a "developing fuse", being hindered to some extent by factors such as access to finance and infrastructure (internet speeds and bandwidth). It may also be that demand for digital marketing and other creative digital services that have driven the UK growth is not yet articulated in Developing Countries like South Africa.

More fused firms showed higher levels of innovation (defined broadly as innovation in products, processes and organisation). The logit model showed that firms that had engaged in more innovation activities were statistically significantly more likely to have experienced growth in the year prior to the survey.

An important finding in the South African context unexplored in the prior UK studies is that although they are not yet representative of the country's full demographic profile, fused firms were more likely to have demographically diverse employees and owners. This suggests that the skills diversity already known to support innovation is also enhanced by social diversity. Support for these kinds of firms would thus also feed into the public social justice and transformation agenda. The qualitative analysis of the gaming and animation sector highlighted the difficulty of transformation in the South African context, where population group (race) is still at least partly divided along income and education lines. Highly qualified black South Africans may not be able or willing to enter a sector where earnings are uncertain, and employment precarious. This is especially the case for the CCI sector, which is not generally recognised in South Africa as an important economic sector that offers viable career options.

In terms of policy implications, the findings suggest that the South African Draft Science, Technology and Innovation policy, which is currently under discussion, should also include the CCIs. The draft policy focuses almost exclusively on the innovation of STEM sector firms, leaving out sectors such as Design and Creative Services and Audio-Visual and Interactive Media. Firms in these domains contribute to South Africa's GDP and are also engaging in innovative activities at the interface between technology and creative inputs. In the same way, the South African White Paper on Arts and Culture currently does not pay much attention to ways in which the CCIs could contribute to innovation. Bringing these policies into alignment could help both the CCIs and promote industrial innovation.

Several research limitations are noted: Without a comprehensive national register or database of CCI firms, it is not possible to determine to what extent the findings are generalisable to the whole population. The small sample size also limits the reliability and validity of econometric analysis. Future studies could be improved by developing an indicator of fusion based on revealed preference, rather than self-classification (attitudinal) data used in this research.

Funding This article is based on two reports funded by the South African Cultural Observatory, which is a research institution funded by the South African Department of Sport, Arts and Culture. The reports are:

Tarentaal, D. and Snowball, J. (2019). Unlocking the growth potential of the online gaming industry in South Africa: Challenges and Opportunities. Report commissioned by the South African Cultural Observatory http://southafricanculturalobservatory.org.za/

Snowball, J., Tarentaal, D. Van der Linde, JC., Waelde, C., Nwauche, E. and Sapsed, J. (2019). The Overlaps between the digital and creative sectors: Innovation and Technology in the Creative Economy. Report commissioned by the South African Cultural Observatory http://southafricanculturalobservatory.org.za/

Funding for the Cape Town survey was provided as part of an international collaboration entitled *The roles of IP and diversity in the creative industries: Networking South Africa and the UK* that was funded by the Arts and Humanities Research Council (UK). Principal investigator: Prof Charlotte Waelde, Coventry University, UK.

Declarations

Conflicts of interest The author declares that they have no competing of interest.

References

Adamson, M, Brown, A, Clay, R, Cockshut, L, Cross, E, Hall, L, Lampitt Adey, K, Murray, S, Paterson, S, Sapsed, J, Stewart, P, Wood, L (2018) Creative Fuse North East Project Report. Available [Online] http://www.creativefusene.org.uk/wp-content/uploads/2019/02/Creative-Fuse-Project-Report-2019-final.pdf

Bakhshi, H., & Throsby, D. (2012). New technologies in cultural institutions: theory, evidence and policy implications. *International Journal of Cultural Policy, 18*(2), 206–222

Brown, A., & Waelde, C. (2018). Introduction. In A. Brown & C. Waelde (Eds.), *Research handbook on intellectual property and creative industries.*Cheltenham: Edward Elgar Publishing.

Butt, M., Cross, E., Holliman, N., Kempton, L., Legget, J., Mackenzie, E., Ross, H., Sapsed J., Swords, J., Vallance, P., Whitehurst, F. (2017) Creative Fuse North East Initial Report. http://www.creativefusene.org.uk/wp-content/uploads/2017/06/Creative-Fuse-North-East-Initial-Report-22062017.pdf

Cappetta, R., Cillo, P., & Ponti, A. (2006). Convergent designs in fine fashion: An evolutionary model for stylistic innovation. *Research Policy., 35*(9), 1273–1290

Castañer, X., & Campos, L. (2002). The determinants of artistic innovation: Bringing in the Role of organizations. *Journal of Cultural Economics., 26*(1), 29–52

Conor, B., Gill, R., & Taylor, S. (2015). Gender and creative labour. *The Sociological Review, 63*(S1), 1–22

De Beukelaer, C., & Fredriksson, M. (2019). The political economy of intellectual property rights: The paradox of Article 27 exemplified in Ghana. *Review of African Political Economy, 46*(161), 459–479

Department of Science and Technology (DST). (2018). The draft White Paper on Science, Technology and Innovation (STI White Paper). [Online] Available: https://www.gov.za/sites/default/files/gcis_document/201809/41909gon954.pdf

Department of Sport, Arts and Culture (DSAC). (2017). Revised White Paper on Arts, Culture and Heritage (4th draft). [Online] Available: http://www.dac.gov.za/content/revised-white-paper-arts-culture-and-heritage-fourth-draft-0

Eikhof, D., & Warhurst, C. (2013). The promised land? Why social inequalities are systemic in the creative industries. *Employee Relations, 35*(5), 495–508

Galindo-Martín, M., Castaño-Martínez, M., & Méndez-Picazo, M. (2019). Digital transformation, digital dividends and entrepreneurship: A quantitative analysis. *Journal of Business Research, 101*, 522–527

Gong, H., & Hassink, R. (2017). Exploring the clustering of creative industries. *European Planning Studies, 24*(4), 583–600

Griffin, A. (1997). PDMA research on New Product Development Practices: Updating Trends and Benchmarking Best Practices. *Journal of Product Innovation Management., 14*, 429–458

Hadisi, S., & Snowball, J. (2018). Employment in the cultural and creative industries in South Africa: An analysis using the national Labour Force Survey. South African Cultural Observatory CCI Mapping Study 2018. [Online] Available: http://southafricanculturalobservatory.org.za/

Hadisi, S., & Snowball, J. (2019). The employment of youth and women in cultural occupations in South Africa. South African Cultural Observatory. [Online] Available: http://southafricanculturalobservatory.org.za/

Hall, N., Watson, M. & Kitching, A. (2017). Serious about Games: Research Report. [Online] Available: http://seriousaboutgames.co.za/#

Hennekam, S., & Bennett, D. (2017). Creative industries work across multiple contexts: Common themes and challenges. *Personnel Review, 46*(1), 68–85

Interactive Entertainment South Africa (IESA) (2016). South African Game Industry Survey. [Online] Available: http://www.iesa.org.za/wp-content/uploads/2016/12/IESA-2016-Industry-Survey-Results.pdf

Jaaniste, L. (2009). Placing the creative sector within innovation: The full gamut. Innovation: Management Policy and Practice, 11(2), 215–229.

Jones, C., Lorenzen, M. & Sapsed, J. (2015). Creative Industries: A Typology of Change in Oxford Handbook of Creative Industries. In C. Jones., M. Lorenzen. & J. Sapsed (Eds). Oxford University Press, Oxford, United Kingdom. https://doi.org/10.1093/oxfordhb/9780199603510.013.030.

Keller, R. T. (2001). Cross-functional project groups in research and new product development: Diversity, communications, job stress, and Outcomes. *Academy of Management Journal., 44*(3), 547–555

Leonard, D., & Sensiper, S. (1998). The role of tacit knowledge in group innovation. *California Management Review., 40*(3), 112–132

Li, F. (2020). The digital transformation of business models in the creative industries: A holistic framework and emerging trends. Technovation, 92–93, 102012.

Mackenzie, E., and McKinlay, A. (2020) Hope Labour and the Psychic Life of cultural work. Human Relations. Online. [Available] https://doi.org/https://doi.org/10.1177/0018726720940777

Mangematin, V., Sapsed, J., & Schuessler, E. (2014). Disassembly and reassembly: An introduction to the special issue on digital technology and creative industries. *Technological Forecasting & Social Change, 83*, 1–9

Nwauche, E. (2018). Intellectual property and creative industries policy in Africa. In A. Brown & C. Waelde (Eds.), *Research handbook on intellectual property and creative industries (Chapter 7).*Cheltenham: Edward Elgar Publishing.

O'Brien, D., Laurison, D., Miles, A., & Friedman, S. (2016). Are the creative industries meritocratic? An analysis of the 2014 British Labour Force Survey. *Cultural Trends, 25*(2), 116–131

Oakley, K. (2006). Include us out—economic development and social policy in the creative industries *Cultural Trends, 15*(4), 255–273.

Oakley, K., Laurison, D., O'Brien, D., & Friedman, S. (2017). Cultural capital: Arts graduates, spatial inequality, and London's impact on cultural labour markets. *American Behavioral Scientist, 61*(12), 1510–1531

OECD (2018). The Measurement of Scientific, Technological and Innovation Activities: Oslo Manual 2018. Guidelines for Collecting, Reporting and Using Data on Innovation (4th Edition). [Online] Available: https://www.oecd.org/science/oslo-manual-2018-9789264304604-en.htm

Perren, L., & Sapsed, J. (2013). Innovation as politics: The rise and reshaping of innovation in UK parliamentary discourse 1960–2005. *Research Policy, 42*(10), 1815–1828. https://doi.org/10.1016/j.respol.2013.08.012

Peukert, C. (2019). The next wave of digital technological change and the cultural industries. *Journal of Cultural Economics., 43*, 189–210

PWC Entertainment and Media Outlook (2018). Entertainment and Media Outlook: An African Perspective 2018–2022. [Online] Available: pwc.co.za/outlook

SACO (2018). The mapping of the South African creative economy: A baseline. South African Cultural Observatory. [Online] Available: http://southafricanculturalobservatory.org.za/

Santoro, G., Bresciani, S., Papa, A. (2020). Collaborative modes with cultural and creative industries and innovation performance: The moderating role of heterogeneous sources of knowledge and absorptive capacity. Technovation, 92–93, 102040.

Sapsed, J., & Tschang, F. (2014). Art is long, innovation is short: Lessons from the Renaissance and the digital age. *Technological Forecasting and Social Change, 83*, 127–141

Sapsed, J., Bessant, J., Partington, D., Tranfield, D., & Young, M. (2002). Teamworking and knowledge management: A review of converging themes. *International Journal of Management Reviews., 4*(1), 71–85

Sapsed, J., Nightingale, P., Camerani, R., Mateos-Garcia, J., Voss, G., Coad, A., & Byford, J. (2013). The Brighton Fuse. Brighton. [Online] Available: http://www.brightonfuse.com/

Sapsed, J., Camerani, R., Masucci, M., Petermann, M., Rajguru, M. (2015) Brighton Fuse 2: Freelancers in the Creative Digital IT Economy. [Online] http://www.brightonfuse.com/wp-content/uploads/2015/01/brighton_fuse2_online.pdf

Schauerte, R., Feiereisen, S. & Malter, A. (2020). What does it take to survive in a digital world? Resource-based theory and strategic change in the TV Industry. Journal of Cultural Economics https://doi.org/https://doi.org/10.1007/s10824-020-09389-x

Schlesinger, P., & Waelde, C. (2012). Copyright and cultural work: an exploration. Innovation: The European Journal of Social Science Research, 25(1), 11–28.

Schumpeter, J.A. (1942). *Capitalism, Socialism and Democracy*. Harper, New York. https://www.cambridge.org/core/journals/american-political-sciencereview/article/abs/capitalism-socialism-and-democracy-by-joseph-a-schumpeter-new-york-harper-andbrothers-1942-pp-x-381-350/13A4BF9E884069B0C4144E266443B82F.

Siebert, S., & Wilson, F. (2013). All work and no pay: Consequences of unpaid work in the creative industries. *Work, Employment and Society, 27*(4), 711–721

Siepel, J., R Camerani, M Masucci (2019) Skills combinations and firm performance. Small Business Economics, 1–21.

Creative Skillset (2016). The Creative Media Workforce survey. London, England: Department of Culture, Media and Sport (DCMS). Creative Industries economic estimates. London, England.

Snowball, J., Collins, A., & Tarentaal, D. (2017). Transformation and job creation in the cultural and creative industries in South Africa. *Cultural Trends, 26*(4), 295–309

Statistics South Africa (2011). Census 2011. [Online] Available: http://www.statssa.gov.za/?page_id=1021&id=city-of-cape-town-municipality

Stoneman, P. (2010). *Soft Innovation: Economics, Product Aesthetics, and the Creative Industries*. Oxford University Press.

Teece, D. J. (1986). Profiting from technological innovation: Implications for integration, collaboration, licensing and public policy. *Research Policy, 15*, 285–305

Towse, R. (2014). *An Advanced Introduction to Cultural Economics*. Edward Elgar Publishing.

UNESCO FCS. (2009). *Framework for cultural statistics*. United Nations [Online] Available http://www.uis.unesco.org/culture/Pages/framework-cultural-statistics.aspx

Weinberg, C. B., Otten, C., Orbach, B., McKenzie, J., Gil, R., Chisholm, D. C., & Basuroy, S. (2020). Technological change and managerial challenges in the movie theater industry. *Journal of Cultural Economics*. https://doi.org/10.1007/s10824-019-09374-z.

Journal of Cultural Economics (2021) 45:735–738
https://doi.org/10.1007/s10824-021-09427-2

BOOK REVIEW

Diana S. Greenwald: Painting by numbers—data-driven histories of nineteenth-century art, Princeton University Press, 2021

Laura Pagani[1]

Published online: 8 August 2021

A new quantitative approach to art history is rapidly spreading. The traditional qualitative method of analysis of specific artists and artworks is increasingly complemented by many scholars with an empirical approach, based on statistical analysis, which is typical of social sciences including economics and economic history. The main contribution of Greenwald's book is to show how these two apparently distant approaches can be fruitfully joined to address important research questions in art history. To this aim, the author presents novel evidence on the artistic production of the nineteenth-century in France, the USA, and England and focusses on crucial topics in the art history of that period, namely, industrialization, gender, and the history of empire, providing new points of view. More generally, the book represents a concrete application of the benefits of an interdisciplinary approach in humanities and social sciences.

Greenwald opens with a description of the advantages of a quantitative approach to art history, including the possibility to analyze data about larger samples of the entire population of artists and artworks compared to those generally studied, which are typically artists and artworks selected for their quality and that, therefore, are not representative of the original population. Reducing the sample bias allows a better assessment of the reciprocal influence between social and economic changes and art production. In addition, large data collection allows statistical testing, a powerful complementary tool to explore the behavior of subjects active in the historical art world and to understand broader trends in society.

The book is based on the idea that social factors are crucial determinants of artistic production. While this was a leitmotif of the social history of art, cultural economics has endorsed such an idea for a long time. Since the 1980s, work by cultural economists and art historians, led by the late John Montias, has collected and in some cases discovered data on historical art markets from various regions and

✉ Laura Pagani
laura.pagani@unimib.it

1 Università di Milano Bicocca, Milan, Italy

periods, starting to examine the economics of artistic production and to explore relations between art price, profits of workshops, productivity of artists and more. De Marchi and van Miegroet (2006) have provided what is still an unsurpassed review of these early investigations. Art history was not indifferent to this approach, starting to collect and analyze other datasets on artistic production, for instance with the work of O'Malley (2005) on paintings commissioned in Renaissance Italy and the volume edited by Spear and Sohm (2010) extending the same kind of project to Baroque Italy. On these efforts were based early econometric investigations of these primary art markets (Etro & Pagani, 2012, 2013), which have stressed the high level of competition between painters, the impact of contractual restrictions and institutional factors on artistic production, as well as a variety of labor economic issues (Etro et al., 2015). In the last decade, further quantitative investigations have been extended to various primary as well as secondary markets of Western art. Meanwhile, new datasets keep emerging from different sources, ready to be explored by scholars of different disciplines. Greenwald builds on this tradition with a more specific focus on art historical problems, which is a crucial step for the development of a full-fledged quantitative approach to art history.

The book provides an accurate description of the three datasets used for the main investigations and made available for future research. For each of them, Greenwald describes the sources, the purpose for which they have been created, the sample size and their content. In doing so, the author introduces the reader to the institutional context within which nineteenth-century art developed in the three countries explored, including the influence of politics and of the academies of arts, the main exhibition venues and rules. It also provides evidence on broad topics like the trends in the number of artworks shown in specific locations, the geographical distribution of art exhibitions, the rejection rates of submissions and the average number of artworks per artist shown at given venues. Overall, a particularly valuable contribution of this part of the book is to let the reader know more about hundreds of thousands of artworks that have long been neglected in art history. Still, comparing Jean-Francois Millet's *The Gleaners* (1857) to Jules Breton's *Calling in the Gleaners* (1859), both tagged as "Gleaning" in one of the presented dataset, but deeply dissimilar from each other on view, Greenwald provides an illuminating example that very effectively underlines the importance of the complementarity between the two methodological approaches.

The first in-depth investigation regards the exhibitions at the Paris Salon. The key part is a quantitative analysis trying to identify the influence of the socioeconomic changes during the middle of the nineteenth-century on the amount of the landscape and rural genre paintings shown at the Salon. The main research question is whether the increase in the exhibition of these subjects, lower than what traditionally thought due to sample bias, represents a reaction to the ills of industrialization and urbanizations or, instead, stems from the settlement of artistic communities in the countryside favored by structural and more affordable links to Paris. Greenwald uses regression analysis and concludes that the easiness to access the countryside, as proxied by the train cost of travel to Paris, and the presence of artists' colonies influenced the amount of artworks with a nature-related content. The impact of the diffusion of railroads has a long tradition in quantitative studies (Donaldson, 2018), and this is a first application to art historical issues. However, while the econometric analysis can help to develop new prospects on underlying causes for the development of a specific artistic genre, it seems that Greenwald demands too much to the data, and the results are not entirely convincing. The main limitation is the small number of artworks in the sample in most French departments, which implies a very low variability in outcome variables, especially for rural paintings whose maximum number per French department is five. The sample includes around five hundred rural paintings, which means just 0.1 painting per exhibition and department on average. The maximum number of artistic colonies in a department is three, and once department fixed effects are controlled for, a very low variation is left in this variable, also considering that 95 percent of departments had no artist colony (or equivalently, only around four departments had at least one artist colony). With these observations, it is hard to conclude that artist colonies affected the number of depictions of the countryside, and the department fixed effect is undistinguishable from the presence of colonies. From a more technical point of view, one relevant concern is that once both time and department fixed effects are included in the full specification, there is no variation left to allow coefficients' estimation. Most importantly, multivariate analysis is not a sufficient tool for identifying causal relationships. The correlations cannot have a causal interpretation due to the sorting of artists who painted specific genres within colonies or in certain locations in France, with different distance from Paris. Another issue that plagues estimates is simultaneity, namely, the presence of unobserved factors affecting the probability of painting a given subject and specific regressors at the same time, for instance the formation of a colony. In view of this, the econometric analysis cannot be regarded as conclusive. It is nevertheless an important step in trying to address art historical questions with econometric tools.

The next topic explored is the experience of female artists in nineteenth-century American art. The author uses exhibition data from the National Academy of Design (NAD) and collection data from the Metropolitan Museum of Arts to perform her quantitative analysis that here is less ambitious—mainly descriptive—but nevertheless convincing. The main objective is to provide evidence on the amount of artworks created by women artists and on the share of these artworks that belong to museum collections. Greenwald starts documenting the low women's participation at the NAD, which increased from less than five percent at the beginning of the sample period (1830) to a maximum of 20 percent at the end of the century. Then, the author shows that works by female artists represented just six percent of artworks included in the Metropolitan Museum of Art's American Wing, only half as many as the share of artworks shown on average at the NAD. The proposed interpretation of this discrepancy is related to women overrepresentation in still life paintings, a less prestigious genre less frequently included in collections. A labor market interpretation of this evidence (in the spirit of Goldin, 2014) is one of the most intriguing parts of the book. Greenwald relates it to the higher opportunity cost of painting other genres for women with family care and domestic responsibilities. Painting subjects like oil landscapes required months of travel and work and was time inflexible. Making portraits required to adapt to the client's timetable. In addition, women typically painted in a domestic space because the possession of a studio was considered improper for them and required being economically independent, which seldom women were. However, large paintings of more prestigious genres required the availability of space. Overall, due to greater time and space constraints, women specialized in genres requiring less time, whose execution could be interrupted and completed in subsequent sessions, and whose size could be better managed within the domestic space. I find Greenwald's interpretation interesting although it misses a solid empirical support. Also considering that female artists often belonged to privileged backgrounds, could buy family services on the market and had the availability of large spaces, I think that more weight should be given to a gender-norms and stereotype-based interpretation. Spending too much time out of the domestic space, painting ambitious large paintings to be shown to a large audience could have been perceived as inappropriate for women. Moreover, market demand might have driven price differentials that could have affected specialization by female artists. A more in-depth empirical analysis could shed light on the weight of the different potential explanations.

The last detailed study is aimed at exploring how often the London Royal Academy of Arts exhibited artworks depicting images of the British Empire in the period from its foundation in 1769 to 1914. Greenwald uses the works' title to identify their location and shows that, in a sample of over 184,000 artworks, the British Empire was far less depicted than England and other European countries like Italy and France as well. The author discusses potential reasons for such under-representation. Physical distance, lack of transport and the role of demand are the most obvious reasons, although Greenwald's preferred explanation seems to be related to the need, on the one hand, to exhibit the secure and inclusive institutions of the metropole and, on the other hand, not to celebrate the brutal and unequal colonial institutions, designed to transfer resources. Although this institutional interpretation is fascinating, sound empirical evidence in its support is lacking. Something left for future research.

References

De Marchi, N., & van Miegroet, H. J. (2006). The history of art markets. In V. Ginsburgh & D. Thorsby (Eds.), *Handbook of the Economics of Art and Culture* (pp. 69–122). Elsevier.

Donaldson, D. (2018). Railroads of the Raj: Estimating the impact of transportation infrastructure. *American Economic Review, 108*(4), 899–934.

Etro, F., Marchesi, S., & Pagani, L. (2015). The labor market in the art sector of Baroque Rome. *Economic Inquiry, 53*(1), 365–387.

Etro, F., & Pagani, L. (2012). The market for paintings in Italy during the seventeenth century. *Journal of Economic History, 72*(2), 423–447.

Etro, F., & Pagani, L. (2013). The market for paintings in the Venetian Republic from Renaissance to Rococo. *Journal of Cultural Economics, 37*(4), 391–415.

Goldin, C. (2014). A grand gender convergence: Its last chapter. *American Economic Review, 104*(4), 1091–1119.

O'Malley, M. (2005). *The Business of Art*. Yale University Press.

Spear, R., & Sohm, P. (2010). *Painting for Profit*. Yale University Press.

Journal of Cultural Economics (2021) 45:739–740
https://doi.org/10.1007/s10824-021-09429-0

ACKNOWLEDGEMENTS

List of Reviewers

Luis Aguiar
Ramadan Jose Aly-Tovar
Francesco Angelini
Victoria Ateca-Amestoy
Andrea Baldin
Fernando Benites
Bernardino Benito
Anna Bernard
Enrico Bertacchini
Diana Betzler
Trine Bille
Thomas Boren
Amir Borges Ferreira Neto
Karol Borowiecki
Daniel Brou
Tobias Buerger
Vincenzo Butticè
Sam Cameron
Maurizio Caserta
Roberto Cellini
Silvia Cerisola
Cedric Ceulemans
Bronwyn Coate
Alan Collins
Eva Coll-Martínez
Paul Crosby
Tiziana Cuccia
Chiara Dalle Nogare
Erwin Dekker
María José del Barrio-Tellado
Van Chung Dong
Gillian Doyle
Susan Dumais
Joris Ebbers
Robert Ekelund
Meg Elkins
Andrea Ellero
Federico Etro
Martin Falk
Donata Favaro
Silvia Fedeli
Tal Feder
Terry Flew
Tim Fry
Javier García
Javier Gardeazabal
Michael Getzner
Jonathan Daniel Gómez Zapata
Richard Gretz
Jose Maria Grisolia
Allègre Hadida
Jessica Hale
Chris Hand
Christian Handke
Hogni Kalso Hansen
Martin Hansen
Christiane Hellmanzik
Luis César Herrero
Monika Herzig
B. Heyndels
Douglas Hodgson
Javier Husillos
Niccolo Innocenti
Sofie Jacobs
Monika Kackovic
Tally Katz-Gerro
A. Klamer
Stephan Klingner
Brooke Krause
Luciana Lazzeretti
Boram Lee
Renaud Legoux
Daniele Leone
Ellen Loots
Kenan Lopcu
Juan Carlos Lopez
Domitilla Magni
Maria Marchenko
Marco Martorana
Jordi Mckenzie
Natalia Mehle
Juan Montoro
Valeria Morea
Trilce Navarrete
Milad Nozari
Martin Obschonka
Antoni Olive-Tomas
Are Oust
Luca Pareschi
Christian Peukert
Marek Prokupek
Anne-Sophie Radermecker
S. Abraham (Avri) Ravid
Imke Reimers
Ilde Rizzo
Plácido Rodríguez
Luciano Rossoni
Ronald Rozenbaum
Michael Rushton
Anders Rykkja
Pier Luigi Sacco

Donatella Saccone
Rachel Skaggs
Hendrik Sonnabend
Christophe Spaenjers
Andrej Srakar
Elena Stepanova
Maria Jose Suarez
Sara Suárez Fernández
Peter Tait
Ayumu Tanaka
Walter van Andel
Brian Vander Naald
Filip Vermeylen
Paul Watt
Sebastian Weingartner
Aleksandra Wiśniewska
David Wuepper
Terry Yip
Ivo Zander
Yang Zhou
Marta Zieba

The manufacturer's authorised representative in the EU is Springer Nature Customer Service Centre GmbH, Europaplatz 3, 69115 Heidelberg, Germany. If you have any concerns regarding our products, please contact ProductSafety@springernature.com

Printed and bound by CPI Group (UK) Ltd, Croydon, CR0 4YY
28/09/2026
02224080-0001